United States History 101

Early Colonization to 1877

Complete Review

2nd edition

Our guarantee – the highest quality preparation materials.

Our books are of the highest quality and error-free.

Be the first to report a typo or error and receive a
$10 reward for a content error or
$5 reward for a typo or grammatical mistake.

info@sterling–prep.com

We reply to all emails – ***check your spam folder***

2 1

ISBN-13: 978-1-9475567-6-8

Sterling Test Prep products are available at special quantity discounts for sales, promotions, academic counseling offices, and other educational purposes.

For more information contact our Sales Department at:

Sterling Test Prep
6 Liberty Square #11
Boston, MA 02109

info@sterling-prep.com

Published by Sterling Test Prep

 Printed in the U.S.A.

From the end of the early colonial days to the end of the Civil War, this clearly explained text is a perfect guide for anyone who wants to be knowledgeable about the history of America and its democracy. As it goes through the sequence of the events of the past, it provides readers with the analysis necessary to make them more engaged and appreciative participants in the American future.

This book was designed for those who want to develop a better understanding of America's economic and cultural growth, the political and social challenges it went through, as well as the relationships between different historical events. The content is focused on an essential review of all the crucial facts and events from early colonization to 1877.

You will learn about historical figures and important events that played an important role in the founding of American government, American revolution, the Civil War, as well as the meaning and significance of the various social movements, and how each important historical event shaped the country's cultural heritage and political development. For systematized learning, the content is divided into two historical periods. It is centered around five focus areas: political history, economic developments, social developments, cultural and intellectual events, and foreign relations. This context-based approach to studying American history is more engaging than a raw fact-based approach.

Created by highly qualified history teachers, scholars, and education specialists, this book educates and empowers readers, helping them develop and increase their understanding of American history.

We congratulate you on your desire to learn more about the history of the United States. The editors sincerely hope that this guide will be a valuable resource for your learning.

220321gdx

We want to hear from you

Your feedback is important to us because we strive to provide the highest quality education materials. Email us any questions, comments or suggestions.

Customer Satisfaction Guarantee

For issues about this book, including printing issues, contact us and we will resolve any issues to your satisfaction.

info@sterling-prep.com

*We reply to all emails – **check your spam folder***

Thank you for choosing our products to achieve your educational goals!

Table of Contents

PERIOD 1

1500 to 1789

Major historical events of the period:

1492 – Columbus lands in the Bahamas

1520 – Spanish explorers bring smallpox to the Mexican mainland

1521 – Hernàn Cortés conquers the Aztec capital, Tenochtitlán

1598 – New Mexico is founded by Juan de Oñate

1600 – East India Company is founded

1602 – Dutch East India Company is founded

1739 – Stono Rebellion

1676-1677 – the rebellion of Nathaniel Bacon

1744-1748 – King George's War

1686 – Dominion of New England

1730s-1740s – the Great Awakening

1732 – Hat Act and Debt Recovery Act

1754-1763 – French and Indian War

1754 – Albany Congress

1763 – Chief Pontiac's rebellion

1770 – Boston Massacre

1773 – Boston Tea Party

1775-1783 – American Revolutionary War

1776 – Colonies declare independence from Great Britain

1777 –Articles of Confederation

1785-1795 – Northwest Indian War (Little Turtle's War)

1787 – Constitutional Convention

1787 – The Northwest Ordinance is formed

POLITICAL INSTITUTIONS, DEVELOPMENTS, BEHAVIOR, and PUBLIC POLICY:

Early Colonization to 1789

European expansion into the Western Hemisphere caused intense social/religious, political, and economic competition in Europe and the promotion of empire building.

European exploration and conquest were fueled by a desire for new sources of wealth, increased power and status, and converts to Christianity.

From the 8th to the 15th centuries, the Christian kingdoms of the Iberian Peninsula sought to drive out the Moors, Muslims from North Africa who had conquered most of the peninsula in the early years of Islam. The gradual *Reconquista*, or Reconquest, was not complete until 1492. In 1479, two of the Spanish monarchs, King Ferdinand of Aragon (1452-1516) and Queen Isabella of Castile (1479-1555), had married and united their kingdoms. Thirteen years later, their armies expelled the Muslims from their last stronghold.

The *Reconquista* was not a mere political conflict, but a crusade driven by a devotion to the Christian religion and hatred of infidels. Whereas Iberian Muslim rulers offered Christians and Jews considerable religious freedom, the Christian rulers sought to use a somewhat intolerant Christianity to unite their subjects and vanquish a common enemy.

Reconquista fighters saw themselves as obviously superior to enemies who rejected Christ and developed rules of war reflective of this view. These rules made it legal to enslave any conquered people. As soon as the *Reconquista* was complete, Muslims and Jews faced a choice of conversion or expulsion from the Spanish lands.

The *Reconquista* nourished not only religious devotion but a markedly militaristic mindset and a romantic understanding of war. Spanish fighters, especially the Castilians who were to conquer the Americas, also had roots in an agricultural society where personal relationships, reputation, and honor were the critical elements in determining a man's worth. At the same time, materialistic motives were apparent as well.

As the Spanish kings frequently lacked the funds to finance military actions, military leaders would risk their own money, securing in turn rights to conquered land and a share of the spoils. These pre-existing notions of simultaneously seeking monetary reward, divine favor, and a glorious reputation in romantically inspired military adventures made the conquistadors a perfect fit for their demanding roles of conquerors of a New World across the enormous ocean and of people they saw as savages and heathens. They were prepared for an adventure, and Admiral Columbus (1451-1506) gave them one.

Thanksgiving before the image of the Virgin

The Crusades had brought Europeans into contact with eastern cultures again after centuries of relative isolation. Temporarily recapturing the Holy Land allowed them to gain once again familiarity with the abundance of spices, silk, jewels, gold, and other goods flowing from China, India, and other parts of Asia beyond the Middle East. Unfortunately, South and East Asia were thousands of miles away, across deserts, mountain ranges, and lands where both the climate and the inhabitants were inhospitable. The long and treacherous journey from the East made spices and other goods expensive by the time they reached the West.

Admiral Columbus (1451-1506) underestimated the distance to the Indies (Asia). He proposed to open up new sources of wealth and glory by sailing westward rather than following the route around Africa then being explored by the Portuguese. In 1492, Columbus's persistent lobbying finally resulted in funding for his expedition. Ferdinand and Isabella did not have complete faith in Columbus, but they realized that the potential benefits were great and the costs relatively low.

Upon arrival, Columbus was quite disappointed by the people he found. Although they were friendly and peaceful, they did not have any of the vast riches Marco Polo and other travelers had written about. Indeed, they did not know how to work metals, and they had no weapons other than simple spears. Profitability was the main problem Columbus faced, and it derived from his deficient understanding of unknown geography. To the very end, he thought of the islands as part of the Indies, thinking that Hispaniola was Japan and Cuba the Asian mainland.

The landing of Admiral Christopher Columbus, c. 1492

However, it was apparent that the abundant ports and cities he had heard about were nowhere to be found, and that none of the people he met had any contact with the Great Khan of the Mongols. Columbus had hoped to ally with the Khan against the Muslims, as part of a farfetched scheme to use profits from the new possessions to reconquer Jerusalem. It had been prophesized that the reconquest of Jerusalem would bring about the Second Coming of Christ.

The fortress and trading post system that the Portuguese had set up on the coast of Africa was not a realistic option for the Caribbean either. Trading posts would only be useful if there were sizeable trade going on already, and there was no indication of that. Thus, Columbus soon realized that the only way of making the new lands profitable was colonization by European settlers and the exploitation of Indians as slaves.

While the colonies served primarily as sources of wealth and power, they continued to be imbued with a religious purpose. In the Latin American colonies, the preaching orders of the Roman Catholic church—Franciscans, Dominicans, and Jesuits—played vital roles. Friars took part in most expeditions, and conquest and conversion often went hand in hand (though with a questionable degree of success).

Within ten years of Cortés landing in Mexico, one Franciscan friar claimed to have personally converted more than 200,000 Indians to Christianity.

Most prominent in these activities were the Jesuits, the order established as a kind of special operations force of the Counter-Reformation. In Brazil, the Jesuits pushed European settlement inland, as they pressed farther up the rivers to create new, tightly knit frontier settlements of Christian Indians isolated from the sinfulness of the conquistadors. In Paraguay, their settlements were so numerous and successful, that it almost appeared as a separate country. The territory had its army and about 100,000 Indians under Jesuit tutelage.

European overseas expansion and sustained contacts with Africans and American Indians dramatically altered European views of social, political, and economic relationships among and between white and nonwhite peoples. With little experience dealing with people who were different from themselves, Spanish and Portuguese explorers poorly understood the native peoples they encountered in the Americas, leading to debates over how American Indians should be treated and how "civilized" these groups were compared to European standards.

Establishing contact with the Indians was shocking to the minds of Christian Europeans. In essence, the indigenous people of the Americas did not appear in the Bible or the other primary source of authoritative knowledge, the writings of the ancient Greeks and Romans. At the outset, it was not even clear whether or not the Indians should be considered human.

From the perspective of Christian Europe, this would require the Indians to have the ability to reason and a soul that could be saved from eternal suffering through conversion to the true faith. Once the pope had declared that Indians were human, the Spanish began to recognize their humanity as well. They saw them as a part of the united community of God and recognized that they had certain rights.

Spanish explorers raising memorial cross

Europeans generally and the colonists especially had few qualms about subjecting American Indians and Africans to harsh discipline and hard work or taking away other peoples' lands or humanity. The only major exception before the second half of the 18th century was the dissent of some highly articulate Spanish friars and theologians. Dominican friars on Hispaniola had come to convert the heathen but witnessed death and destruction on an unprecedented scale.

Mostly because of diseases the Europeans brought, with the added effect of violence and forced labor, the population of Hispaniola dropped from maybe several million in 1492 to less than 30,000 twenty years later. One day in 1511, Antonio de Montesinos gave the first sermon on the treatment of the native peoples:

> "Tell me, by what right of justice do you keep these Indians in cruel and horrible servitude? On what authority have you waged a detestable war against these people, who dwelt quietly and peacefully on their own lands? . . . Are these not men? Have they not rational souls? Are you not bound to love them as you love yourselves?"

The colonists were outraged by this attack, but the Dominicans continued to question the legality and morality of the colonial enterprise and forced a protracted debate among lawyers and theologians in Spain. The Dominican theologian Francisco de Vitoria used the medieval conception of natural law to demonstrate that Indians were rational beings with rights to life, liberty, safety, and property, which could not be abridged either by the pope or by the king of Spain. His writings went far in the direction of creating a foundation for international law, as well as suggesting the fundamental equality and dignity of all human beings.

The most famous defender of Indian rights was Bartolomé de Las Casas, formerly a priest who owned former Indian lands worked by forced Indian labor. He experienced a crisis of conscience in 1514, became a Dominican friar, and spent most of his life working for better treatment of the Indians. He argued that the European purpose in the New World should be peaceful conversion.

In 1550–51, Las Casas argued the case of the Indians at a hearing in Valladolid, Spain, debating for several months about the legal and theological aspects of colonization and empire. His primary opponent was the scholar Juan Ginés de Sepúlveda, who argued the Aristotelian point that the civilized had every right to rule over barbarians.

Las Casas and his supporters had some influence on the development of Spanish colonial law. However, most of the time, the protections guaranteed to Indians and Africans existed only on paper. Because he tended to exaggerate, Las Casas was also used to propagate the so-called "Black Legend," the idea that Spanish rule was more cruel and unjust than that of the other colonial powers.

In reality, it would be difficult to argue that the other powers of the 16th and 17th centuries were significantly better.

The differences in imperial goals, cultures, and the North American environments that different empires confronted led the Europeans to develop diverse patterns of colonization.

The European colonial powers (e.g., England, Spain, France, and the Netherlands) had some shared goals for the colonizing process. However, the substantial differences in the home cultures of these countries, as well as the variety of environments encountered in the New World, led to a remarkable diversity in the patterns and outcomes of imperial ventures.

The divergent considerations and purposes of governments played a significant role in creating differences in how countries administered and ruled the distant lands they claimed.

For example, the Spanish government was far more actively involved in governing its colonies than England. The Spanish model of centralization and control led to different trajectories of development than the mostly hands-off approach of the English. The land and its natural resources also greatly affected trajectories of development; areas suitable for growing export commodities, like sugar and tobacco, imported large numbers of slaves, while areas characterized by more mixed agriculture evolved differently.

In some areas, the economy became significantly more diversified, allowing the development of crafts, commerce, and small-scale manufacturing. Other factors, including warfare, laws, religion, disease, racial sentiments, gender roles, and relations between colonists and Indians, also made a difference. They ensured that the American colonies—despite their commonalities—ended up as something of a mosaic of social, economic, and cultural patterns.

Cultivation of tobacco at Jamestown, VA, c. 1610

The seventeenth-century Spanish, French, Dutch, and British colonizers embraced different social and economic goals, cultural assumptions, and folkways, resulting in distinct models of colonization.

One of the most significant differences between the colonial powers was the difference in cultural perceptions of economic development, or, more simply, the meaning of making money. To the Spanish elite, made up of the monarchy, nobility, and the church which dominated society and stamped their cultural values on the process of colonization, it was ultimately titles, honor, luxury, and the glory of God that mattered.

There was no glory in working hard or accumulating capital; money was supposed to be spent on luxuries and leisure, or even more prudently, on conquests, wars, and the conversion of heathens. They sought wealth primarily through extracting mineral resources or demanding tribute and labor from native populations and placed little emphasis on economic development in the sense of modernization or progress.

The Spanish outlook was aristocratic and pre-capitalist, and despite the many manifestations of their greed, they valued money to an end rather than an end in itself. Even Columbus himself died an unhappy man despite the vast wealth he had accumulated, feeling that he had not been recognized as an administrator and a religious pioneer.

The Dutch, who were mostly trying to gain their independence from Spain between 1568 and 1648, had a very different culture and a different order of priorities. In the 17th century, the Netherlands became the world leader in shipping, commerce, and finance. The government was a federal republic where merchants were profoundly influential, and colonial ventures were directed by joint-stock companies rather than the Crown.

These companies had their armies and navies and utilized force whenever it was necessary to secure profits, but capital gains rather than glory or honor were usually the aim. Over time, their overwhelmingly commercial orientation and impressive financial savvy were not enough to protect their leading position in the world economy, as they were surpassed by other nations that were militarily stronger.

The British colonies were unusual in that the government exercised very little control in their development compared to other colonial powers. The colonies were created almost haphazardly and for a variety of economic, religious, and political reasons. There was little or no uniform administration, and the colonists in America grew accustomed to having rights and privileges relatively independent from the Crown.

The North American colonies were generally seen as unattractive because they did not bring immediate profits from high-value commodities like gold, silver, or sugar. Those who were already rich and powerful saw little reason to waste their time or energy on these projects.

Instead, they became opportunities for Europeans from middle- or lower-class backgrounds who wanted to improve their status, become rich, or create religious utopias.

The cultural development of these colonies was, in turn, heavily influenced by the beliefs and customs of the immigrants who arrived there. Puritans in England, Germans in Pennsylvania, and Scottish Highlanders in the North Carolina hinterland all brought a unique set of behaviors and lifestyles that remained influential despite the necessary adaptations to the New World environment and the colonial system.

Settlers in North Carolina, c.1653

With the decline of Spanish power in the 17th century, France emerged as the most significant power on the European continent. However, this power relied on the ability of the government to extract soldiers and taxes from a large population to fight large-scale and expensive wars. This led the French government to discourage mass emigration to the colonies, and a reluctance to use scarce resources and human resources to defend American settlements. Canada and Louisiana seemed to have few natural resources that could be easily exploited, and efforts to develop these areas tended to be halfhearted. The French were more concerned with Haiti, which promised to be a major supplier of highly demanded sugar.

Competition over resources between European rivals led to conflict within and between North American colonial possessions and American Indians.

As the power of Spain began to decline in the early 17th century, the Dutch, who were at that time fighting for their independence from Spain, began to challenge Spanish hegemony in the Americas. France and England followed suit. Due to the continuing decline of Spain and the eventual defeat of the Dutch in several wars with the English, the rivalry between France and Britain eventually became the central conflict in 18th-century North America. The colonial powers also had Indian allies who played essential roles. In many cases, the Indians favored the more accommodating and less land-hungry French and Spanish rather than the increasingly populous and aggressive English colonies.

Between 1688 and 1748, the colonial powers were embroiled in three major wars that could arguably be classified as world wars. The first of these was King William's War (1688–97), known as the Nine Years' War in Europe, which was fought to prevent France, the significant power on the continent, from becoming too dominant. In North America, the war was fought for different purposes, as the French were few and seemingly weak there, trying to hold on to vast territorial claims on the Hudson Bay region and the St. Lawrence and Mississippi Rivers with a minimal settler population.

The French were able to inflict numerous defeats on the English colonists, partially because of the effective combination of French, colonial and allied Indian troops. The French were also victorious in North America because the English government chose to prioritize the West Indian colonies, as the profits from the sugar islands made them more valuable.

The arrival of the Indian allies at the French camp

Queen Anne's War (1702–13) was also part of a more massive European conflict, the War of the Spanish Succession. The goal was to limit the power of France, as a member of the French monarchy had inherited the throne in Spain. This meant that the British had to battle both Spanish and French forces in the Americas.

The British clashed with the French and their allies to the north, but this time with greater success. By the end of the war, France was forced to cede Nova Scotia, Newfoundland, and the Hudson Bay region. Meanwhile, Spanish Florida had been completely devastated by the brutal raids of the British and their Indian allies, inflicting so much death and destruction that the Spanish colony never quite recovered.

A generation later, two other wars erupted in the Americas, and once again, they were intertwined with a European conflict, the War of the Austrian Succession. In the War of Jenkins' Ear (1739–48), the main issue was the British monopoly on the slave trade to the Spanish colonies. Much of this war played out in South and Central America and the Caribbean, but in 1742 Spanish forces invaded Georgia. After this attack was repelled, the North American theater was relatively calm for some time.

By 1744, King George's War had broken out with renewed fighting between the French and the British. The British forces were able to capture the Fortress of Louisbourg in Nova Scotia, but this did not prevent French forces and their Indian allies from raiding frontier areas. The British settlements north of Albany had to be abandoned entirely until the war ended in 1748. The colonists in New York, and especially those in Massachusetts, suffered massive casualties during this war and were incensed when the peace treaty traded Louisbourg for a town in India.

Conflicts in Europe spread to North America as French, Dutch, British, and Spanish colonies allied, traded with, and armed American Indian groups, leading to continuing political instability.

Early modern Europe was a dangerous and violent place with numerous long, brutal wars. The continual conflicts between the great powers did not only take place at home but spread to include lengthy, costly, and destructive colonial wars as well. For example, the Spanish settlements in Florida were often attacked by English and French forces and their respective Indian allies, and so much death, destruction, and enslavement ensured that by the early 18th century, the whole area was almost devoid of people. Other Spanish colonies faced fierce Indian uprisings, such as the Pueblo Rebellion of 1680 and the Pima Revolt of 1751.

The 17th-century Beaver Wars, also known as the Iroquois Wars, were a series of wars between the Iroquois tribes supported by the Dutch and English and the Algonquian tribes supported by the French. The imperialist Iroquois sought to extend their domains and control the fur trade in the Great Lakes region, expanding from their eastern strongholds into new, western lands. In wars increasingly marked by extreme brutality, the Iroquois enlarged their empire and destroyed or displaced many of the other Indian tribes.

As enemy groupings disintegrated and fled to the west and south, large swaths of land in the Great Lakes region and the Ohio Valley became virtually depopulated. This strengthened the hand of England in colonial North America and even facilitated the settlement of this area by white Americans in the early United States.

The 18th-century Chickasaw Wars, although ostensibly a conflict between Indian tribes, had similar beneficial effects for British interests. The Choctaws, acting as proxies of the French in Louisiana, sought to defeat the Chickasaws, who were allied with the English and threatened French communications and trade along the Mississippi River. Even French efforts to wage European-style campaigns with heavy artillery proved futile, as did the decades-long Choctaw harassment consisting of raids, ambush attacks, and failed sieges.

Britain's desire to maintain a viable North American empire in the face of growing internal challenges and external competition inspired efforts to strengthen its imperial control, stimulating increasing resistance from colonists who had grown accustomed to a considerable measure of autonomy.

As the British colonies grew in population and productivity, the home government began to take more of an interest in their development. Whereas the colonies had emerged out of a variety of commercial ventures, idealistic projects, and personal ambitions and had practiced considerable autonomy in the early years, the government now tried to impose its authority on the American subjects of the Crown. Many proprietary colonies became royal colonies with royal governors who wielded considerable power that tended to increase over time.

The colonies typically had two other organs of government: the council appointed by the Crown and the assembly elected by voters. Although the power of the assembly was limited in some ways, it had a paramount prerogative of controlling taxation.

Agents of the assemblies also cooperated with the British Board of Trade, which wielded much power in colonial matters. Through measured protests against overzealous governors, the colonists were usually able to maintain considerable autonomy without engaging in outright conflict with the British government.

One example of the government's efforts to standardize legislation and impose imperial control on colonial matters it had long neglected was the Debt Recovery Act of 1732. The Debt Recovery Act intended to introduce uniformity throughout the empire in the treatment of people who were unable to pay their debts.

It stipulated that houses and slaves should be treated as equivalent to land in the collection of debts, meaning that slaves, buildings and real estate could be sold at auction if debtors could not satisfy their creditors otherwise. In Virginia, the assembly, called the House of Burgesses, passed a new law in the 1740s to counteract this law, making it more difficult for British merchants to collect on the debts of the influential Virginia planters.

The Hat Act, also passed in 1732, was a more direct attempt to extend mercantilism through regulations aimed at limiting colonial manufacturing to avoid any undesirable competition for manufacturers back in Britain. The Hat Act not only limited the numbers of hats that could be made, sold or exported by American hatters; it even specified how many workers and apprentices hatmakers could employ. The point of this legislation was to force colonists to buy more expensive hats imported from Britain and consequently fostered much resentment of a seemingly arbitrary power play on the side of the Crown.

Late 17th-century efforts to integrate Britain's colonies into a coherent, hierarchical, imperial structure and pursue mercantilist economic aims met with limited success, due mainly to the forms of colonial resistance and conflicts with American Indian groups. These were followed by nearly a half-century of the British government's relative indifference to colonial governance.

The move from autonomy or neglect to stricter control by the royal government was mainly tied to trade policies. The British Empire was set up to follow a mercantilistic model of political economy, which in practice meant a desire to control or even monopolize both exports to and imports from the American colonies. The British Empire regulated and often limited, the colonies' trade with other countries. It also limited trade with other colonies within the empire.

Also, the Navigation Acts specified that shipping to and from Britain and the colonies could only be handled by English ships, an effort to deprive the Dutch of their maritime supremacy. Eventually, Americans were even barred from producing finished iron goods—everything was to be imported from Britain.

In 1686, the royal government attempted centralization by revoking the old charters of the northeastern colonies and introducing a new administrative structure, the Dominion of New England.

The government had become concerned that the northern colonies were beginning to deviate from mercantilism by developing their trade and manufacturing, in effect competing with the home country. The proposal was intended to impose a system more like the Spanish colonies in the Americas.

However, this structure collapsed only three years later in the wake of the so-called Glorious Revolution in England. More generally, mercantilist policies were not particularly successful in preventing the development of a mixed economy of agriculture, commerce, and manufacturing in the colonies, or in convincing the colonists that their role was simply to make the home country rich.

One of the main reasons why mercantilism remained less than capable was a lack of sincere efforts to enforce the laws on the books. Instead, Britain preferred to look the other way and continued to allow the colonies to develop following the wishes of local white men with property.

The government was so concerned with their rivalry with the French that they thought it would be imprudent to alienate the colonists, especially as the French were often more successful in recruiting Indian allies than the British.

During and after the colonial war for independence, tribes attempted to forge advantageous political alliances with one another and with European powers to protect their interests, limit migration of white settlers and maintain their tribal lands.

The Revolutionary War offered stark alternatives to the Indian tribes as they typically had to choose sides between land-hungry colonists eager to settle their lands or a distant British government with a mixed track record. The Iroquois Confederacy, long a powerful united force with strong ties to Britain, was torn apart as some of the constituent tribes supported the revolutionaries, and others remained loyal to Britain.

In general, the victory of the colonists did not bode well for the Indians as the British government gave up its claims to the Indian Reserve west of the Appalachian Mountains, permanently leaving it as spoils of victory for the Americans. Ferocious counteroffensives employing scorched earth tactics had already met Iroquois and Cherokee offensives against the patriots.

While the British had been decisively defeated at Yorktown, there had not been any similar event to end the war between the newly formed United States and the Indians of the Northwest. Since those tribes were not a party to the Treaty of Paris that officially ended the war, they refused to accept American rights to the region. The forts in the region were also occupied by the British. The British continued to provide the Indians with weapons and gunpowder in exchange for furs.

The new American government nevertheless made provisions for taking over the land and distributing it among white settlers. The Land Ordinance of 1785 and the Northwestern Ordinance of 1787 outlined the rules of this process, but both Indians and settlers often refused to follow these rules. Tensions mounted, and violence was common.

As early as 1785, the Western Confederacy was forming to unite the Indians in the region against white encroachment. Among the many tribes involved were the Huron, the Shawnee, and the Miami. Raids against white settlements became familiar and were sporadically met by military action.

In 1790–1791, allied Indian forces led by Little Turtle and other war chiefs inflicted devastating losses on American military expeditions, including the troops of Arthur St. Clair. St. Clair, the governor of the Northwest Territory, lost more than 600 men and 200 civilian followers in one battle.

After this setback, the American government had to change its thinking about military operations against the Indians. Instead of relying on local militias, General Anthony Wayne built a legion of well-prepared soldiers. Finally, he handed the United States a decisive victory over the Western Confederacy at the 1794 Battle of Fallen Timbers.

Shortly after that, the war ended with a treaty in which the Indians recognized American sovereignty in the Old Northwest and surrendered massive tracts of land in Ohio and Indiana.

During and after the imperial struggles of the mid-18th century, new pressures united the British colonies against perceived and real constraints on their economic activities and political rights, sparking a colonial independence movement and war with Britain.

Starting in the mid-1760s, some colonists began to express serious concerns about the rule of the British in America. They rejected Parliament's authority to tax the colonies since the colonies were not represented in Parliament. They also resisted British efforts to collect duties and impose new laws that they perceived as detrimental to their economic well-being and political autonomy.

Following the Boston Tea Party (December 16, 1773) and the British response, known collectively as the Coercive or Intolerable Acts, colonial subjects divided into Loyalists, who supported the Crown, and Patriots, who felt that loyalty to the Crown was no longer possible.

By 1775, fighting broke out between Patriots and British soldiers in Massachusetts, and the conflict between the colonies and the metropole (colonial power) escalated into a full-fledged war. Representatives of the thirteen colonies declared independence from Britain in 1776, claiming that King George III (1738-1820; 1760-1820) had become a tyrant and no longer had any right to rule in America. These Founding Fathers of the United States espoused ideologies of republicanism and classical liberalism and insisted on a new understanding of social relations based on equality.

Boston Tea Party, throwing tea overboard on December 16, 1773

Great Britain's massive debt from the Seven Years' War resulted in renewed efforts to consolidate imperial control over North American markets, taxes, and political institutions—actions that were supported by some colonists but resisted by others.

When the war with France ended in 1763, Britain was left with enormous debts incurred in the protection of the colonies and the conquest of Lower Canada. Part of the reason for the proclamation limiting white settlement on the continent was the cost of administration and war connected with further expansion. In addition to limiting costs, the government also wanted to increase revenue. The British sought to accomplish this by making the collection of existing duties more effective and by imposing new duties on the colonies. Part of the rationale was that Americans should pay for their defense. Many colonists argued that in the absence of any French threat, there was little need for a standing army of British soldiers in the colonies.

The 1764 Sugar Act imposed duties on molasses and other goods, but these were still indirect or external taxes. However, the 1765 Stamp Act was a direct or internal tax on many kinds of printed materials. Although the British argued that the level of taxation was quite low, the colonists protested because they were not represented in Parliament. They believed that as English subjects, they could not be taxed without representation and pointed out that they also paid local taxes, which had contributed significantly to the war effort.

Opponents of taxation without representation formed the Sons of Liberty and worked to make the new laws challenging to enforce. Parliament meanwhile argued that the colonies technically were mere corporations subject to British authority and that the government considered the interests of the American colonists in a kind of virtual representation. In 1766, Parliament repealed the Stamp Act while sticking to the principle that Britain had every right to legislate for the colonies.

Reading the Stamp Act, c. 1765

The next year a new set of laws, the Townshend Acts, were passed to impose duties on many goods and to add to the existing trade regulations. These laws were met with new protests and boycotts, and tensions escalated, especially in Boston, where riots ensued when the authorities seized a smuggler's vessel. In 1770, a mob confronted British soldiers, resulting in five deaths. Although the soldiers involved in the shooting were acquitted, the incident became known as the Boston Massacre and added to the outrage of many colonial dissidents. Later that year, all the taxes were withdrawn except for a tax on tea.

Despite the concessions of the government, tensions continued to mount. Between 1772 and 1774, disgruntled community leaders in the thirteen colonies formed the Committees of Correspondence to coordinate action and provide information against what they considered to be the outrages of the government in Britain. The Tea Act, passed by British Parliament in 1773, was intended to ensure that the East India Company would be able to sell its tea in the American colonies at a lower price than colonial merchants and smugglers with access to Dutch tea. Since the act harmed the interests of many American merchants and smugglers while also violating the principle of no taxation without representation, the opposition was widespread. The Boston Tea Party (December 16, 1773) was a result of this opposition to the new legislation.

The response to the Boston Tea Party was four new laws: The Coercive Acts. Known among Patriots as the Intolerable Acts, they altered the Massachusetts charter, changed rules regarding the trials and quartering of British soldiers serving in the colonies, and shut down the port of Boston until the vast sums destroyed by the Tea Party had been compensated. Another new law extended the territory of Quebec to include the land beyond the Appalachians, thus limiting the thirteen colonies' opportunities for westward expansion.

The government saw these acts as a way of making an example out of Massachusetts, but many Patriots saw them as arbitrary and tyrannical. Corresponding committees began to function as shadow governments, and Patriots in Massachusetts formed the Massachusetts Provincial Congress and started training military recruits for battle against the British authorities. Eventually, the Continental Congress was formed and called for a general boycott of all British imports.

The independence movement was fueled by established colonial elites, as well as by grassroots movements that included newly mobilized laborers, artisans, and women, and rested on arguments over the rights of British subjects, the rights of the individual and the ideas of the Enlightenment.

The leaders among both Patriots and Loyalists were typically educated men who owned property. Many of the leaders of the Revolution were prominent planters from the South, especially Virginia. In general, Loyalists were more often well-connected, with close ties to British trade, finance, and official life.

Wealthy merchants, fur traders, government officials, and people associated with these groups were often Loyalists. Although a fair number of colonial elite men were

Patriots, the primary support for colonial protests came from backcountry farmers, artisans, and shopkeepers. Even common laborers were able to make their support for the revolution known, sometimes in rowdy mob actions.

Women also contributed to the resistance against Britain. They did their share by boycotting British imports and by supporting Patriot soldiers and spying on the enemy. Mercy Otis Warren (1728-1814) used literature to attack the Loyalists and organized meetings in her home. At the same time, many women were Loyalists and worked to secure British victory.

On either side, everyday activities became infused with political meaning. To avoid buying British textiles, Patriot women were forced to relearn the skills of spinning and weaving. The thinking behind the Revolution was heavily influenced by certain strains in English thought, especially that of liberals like John Locke and Republicans like James Harrington.

Portrait of Mercy Otis Warren, c. 1800

John Locke (1632-1704) believed that all men were born free and equal and that the origin of the legitimate government could only be a social contract where citizens retained some God-given rights such as life, liberty, and property. Thus, the government should be limited in its activities and rely on the consent of the governed while protecting their natural rights.

The American Patriots also believed that governments, whether at a state or federal level, should rely on checks and balances to ensure that no branch of government got the upper hand, a way of thinking influenced by the French Enlightenment thinker Montesquieu (1689-1755).

Even though Montesquieu had used the English system of government as an example of a suitably mixed constitution with an appropriate balance of powers, the American Founding Fathers were skeptical of monarchy and aristocracy in the British tradition. In the tradition of Harrington and other Republicans, they viewed the British government with high suspicion, focusing on the corruption of the royal court and the dangers of standing armies and public debts.

One of the most prominent prerevolutionary writers was John Dickinson (1732-1808), who authored the *Letters from a Pennsylvania Farmer* (1767-1768) in response to the Townshend Acts. Dickinson exemplifies another strain of thinking about colonial politics and governance little influenced by liberalism, republicanism, or the Enlightenment. Instead, Dickinson was a constitutionalist with a legal background.

As a lawyer and property owner, Dickinson argued that there could be no legitimate taxation without representation and that there could not be such a thing as "virtual representation." Dickinson acknowledged the British's right to control and regulate trade, to impose import and export duties, and even to rig the system in favor of British merchants. However, the principle that property owners had to be involved in the political process before paying taxes was, in Dickinson's view, inviolable.

Despite considerable loyalist opposition, as well as Great Britain's overwhelming military and financial advantages, the patriot cause succeeded because of the colonists' greater familiarity with the land, their resilient military and political leadership, their ideological commitment, and their support from European allies.

The victory of the United States in the Revolutionary War was by no means a foregone conclusion, given the considerable human and financial resources available to the vast British Empire. At the high point, the royal army was made up of almost 80,000 troops, whereas Washington only had 20,000 under his command.

However, taking the colonies against the will of many of the inhabitants was very difficult. The areas involved were vast, and it was difficult for the British to control rural areas or even protect Loyalists from the wrath of Patriots. Even though the Loyalists formed a significant minority among the colonists, they were rarely utilized by the British generals and often treated with mistrust.

This mistrust contributed to the failure to win the hearts and minds of the considerable part of the population that did not take a clear standpoint at the outset of the conflict. The British promise of freedom to slaves who would fight for the Crown helped recruit soldiers seeking emancipation but alienated the influential planters in the South.

The Americans had the advantage of being more familiar with the land than British regulars and German mercenaries. They had also learned tactics from the Indian wars that made it possible to keep an insurgency going, disappearing into the woods after quick ambush-style attacks. Washington mostly avoided big battles, which made it impossible for the British to inflict a decisive defeat on his army.

General George Washington, 1732-1799

Most importantly, France, Spain, and the Netherlands intervened in the war on the side of the rebels. The French especially spent enormous sums of money supplying the war effort and contributed soldiers and naval support as well.

The involvement of other maritime powers also forced Britain to shift its focus to the defense of other colonies, including the lucrative sugar islands in the Caribbean.

Another critical factor was the support of many, if not most, colonists for the revolution. Thousands of ordinary people were committed to the cause and the ideology and were willing to risk their lives or otherwise sacrifice for the cause. They were motivated and engaged by the many high-profile conflicts in the years preceding the American War of Independence and participated in town meetings, Sons of Liberty protests, and violent forms of agitation.

During the Revolutionary War, as many as 400,000 Americans took arms against what they considered to be a tyrannical government.

ECONOMIC DEVELOPMENTS:

Early Colonization to 1789

Before the arrival of the Europeans, native populations in North America developed a wide variety of social, political, and economic structures based in part on interactions with the environment and each other.

The spread of maize cultivation from present-day Mexico northward into the American Southwest and beyond supported economic development and social diversification among societies in these areas. A mix of foraging and hunting did the same for societies in the Northwest and areas of California.

Indians in the Southwest (present-day Arizona, New Mexico, and surrounding areas) made a living from agriculture for thousands of years before the Europeans arrived. They mainly grew maize (corn), introduced from Mesoamerica around 2,100 B.C. A variety of sedentary cultures developed in this arid region, relying on irrigation and other techniques to collect and conserve the water needed for agriculture.

Maize cultivation spread reasonably quickly across the drylands of the Southwest, possibly carried along by migrant agriculturalists heading north from Mexico. Despite the rapid rate of diffusion, maize did not become the primary source of nutrition right away for the hunter-gatherers who already lived there.

Instead, they incorporated maize farming into their wide selection of food sources, trying, as foragers usually do, to limit the risk that the failure of one food source might have catastrophic consequences. At first, maize was only a minor component of their diet and way of life.

Before the dawn of agriculture, bands of hunters and gatherers tended to be small. Except for exceptional circumstances, such as an essential ritual or a task that required extensive collaboration, their groups typically consisted of only ten to fifty people. It was only over time that the role of maize expanded, allowing for more extensive and more sedentary settlements.

Hunting and gathering remained important, but the productivity of agriculture allowed populations of 2,000 or more to congregate in one community. Other Indians lived in smaller settlements of a few hundred people or continued to live in tiny groups dispersed across the region.

Pueblo girl winnowing beans

Among the Ancestral Puebloans (the best-known farming society of the prehistoric Southwest), the size of settlements eventually became so large that the actual fields could be some distance from the tillers' dwellings. Even though this could be a disadvantage, the ability to join to pool food and other resources and to protect and defend the community was highly advantageous.

The forces of centralization and dispersal never reached a stable equilibrium. Instead, farming conditions and environmental changes caused communities to enter cycles of abandonment and regeneration. The intensive agriculture of the Pueblos ultimately proved to be unsustainable when sustained droughts began to occur in the 12th century.

Droughts resulted in widespread famine, and many significant settlements were left behind as the Pueblos sought new lands and new ways to survive. The traditional centers of population and civilization experienced an irreversible decline.

In the Pacific Northwest, an abundance of fish in the rivers and along the coastline allowed for an unusual phenomenon: the development of complex, settled communities among peoples who remained hunters and gatherers. Upon their arrival, the European explorers witnessed complex coastal societies unfamiliar with agriculture but still home to large villages and elaborate social hierarchies.

Pueblo cart

The North-western Indians had large, durable houses and economies that were specialized enough to participate in wide-ranging networks of trade. In the interior, some of the diverse Indian tribes retained the mobility and egalitarianism typical of hunter-gatherer groups. However, other communities, especially along the Columbia and Fraser Rivers, lived sedentary lifestyles and exhibited wealth and social inequality.

Among the latter peoples were the Chinook, who lived by the Columbia River (in present-day Washington and Oregon). They excelled at hunting elk and fishing salmon, and mainly depended on the abundance of fish in the river. Their society was very stratified, with a minority of shamans, warriors, and traders who limited their contact with less privileged commoners who made up most of the population. They even prevented their children from playing with peers from less prestigious backgrounds.

To mark their status, the Chinook would flatten the heads of infants to distinguish them and maintain their superiority over round-headed people. Since those without deliberately deformed heads could be used as slaves, having a round head implied not only inferiority but servility as well. The Chinook picked up the practice of slavery from other tribes farther north.

In California, the Indians were not precisely farmers but engaged in horticultural practices to increase their access to food and medicinal plants. They employed these gardening practices in a variety of environments, including forests, grasslands, and wetlands. They also used fire to facilitate the growth of crops (fertilizing the soil by ashes) and to reduce the risk of more massive, disastrous fires. Burning also prepared new areas for cultivation or allowed new, wild growth that would attract game. Even old, cultivated areas could be put to the torch to enable continued use, leading toward a more sedentary lifestyle.

Societies responded to the lack of natural resources in the Great Basin and the western Great Plains by developing mostly mobile lifestyles.

The high desert region between the Rocky Mountains and the Sierra Nevada is known as the Great Basin. It is an arid region, most of it poor in flora and fauna, but in some small areas, water is plentiful, affording some plants and animals opportunities to thrive. Overall, the land is not suitable for farming, nor is there much game for hunting. Seemingly inhospitable, the land has nevertheless been a site of human habitation for thousands of years.

In the Great Basin, Indians had to be extremely mobile and knowledgeable to exploit the few ecological niches successfully, often spread dozens of miles apart, which allowed them to eke out a living. Their familiarity with local microenvironments was crucial to survival, as was the ability to utilize a wide range of wild plants as food and fiber—the Southern Paiute gathered seeds from more than forty species of grass.

In this unyielding environment, bands remained small, with no more than thirty people in the desert and maybe up to one hundred in slightly more forgiving areas. They were almost always on the move but knew of places near water sources that could be used to set up camp. Leadership was not authoritarian, but a matter of leading by example, advising juniors in the band and working towards consensus decisions that everyone could accept. At any rate, those who did not agree were free to leave. Membership in these small bands was quite fluid, even though members were often closely related.

On the Great Plains east of the Rockies, some Indians farmed and lived a semi-sedentary lifestyle in small villages along the rivers. The main challenge to plains agriculture was that rainfall could be insufficient for raising maize. In the northern areas, the growing season was shorter as well.

Consequently, the progress—or rather fluctuations—of agriculture on the plains followed trends in precipitation, conquering drier lands to the west in wetter periods and falling back toward the east when the threshold was not met. Some Indians lived in fortified villages of up to several hundred people along the Missouri River, raising corn, beans, and squash.

For most of those who lived on the plains, much depended on the bison. Even men engaged in farming would typically leave the village to follow the great buffalo between planting and harvest. The Indians used fire to engineer the grasslands where the bison thrived, and also tried to regulate the bison.

Before the Europeans brought horses and guns to the Americas, bison had to be hunted on foot, herded or instead chased and trapped into corridors and corrals where they could be killed or stampeded across high cliffs called buffalo jumps. This elaborate system of hunting large numbers of bison often provided a considerable surplus that encouraged not only feasting but significant trade as well. This enabled some groups to maintain a nomadic hunter-gatherer lifestyle, exchanging meat and hides for corn from the farming villages.

In the Northeast and along the Atlantic Seaboard, some societies developed a mixed agricultural and hunter-gatherer economy that favored permanent villages.

The Eastern Woodland culture consisted of Indian tribes inhabiting the eastern United States and Canada. These woodlands stretched from the Atlantic Ocean to the Mississippi River and the Great Lakes and were favored with relatively moderate climates and ample precipitation. Across such a vast area, there was, of course, some variation concerning both climate and specific natural resource endowments. In general, conditions were suitable for hunting in the vast forests and farming along the numerous lakes and rivers.

There were, of course, differences in ways of life, including diet, housing, clothing, and modes of transportation. Nevertheless, the Indians of the woodlands lived in similar ways. Their societies were stratified and distinguished between chiefs, noblemen, and commoners. Intertribal disputes over land, the audacity of young men, and quests for revenge made brutal warfare a staple of everyday life. Fortified villages were a necessity.

Mostly, these Indians were farmers and deer hunters. They made bows and arrows, stone knives, and clubs for hunting and war, and they made pottery and vessels made from wood and bark for cooking. The Iroquois, a confederation of northeastern Indian tribes in the Great Lakes region and the Northeast, were mainly farmers but combined agriculture with gardening, hunting, fishing, and foraging.

Algonquin Indian

The Iroquois cultivated many plants, including pumpkin and tobacco, but their main crops—the "three sisters," a special providence from the Creator—were corn, beans, and squash. They knew how to combine these organisms in single plots where bean plants climbed the corn stalks, with the big leaves of the squash underneath keeping the soil moist and shaded, thus preventing the growth of weeds. This technique could keep the soil fertile for decades. When the land eventually lost that fertility, the whole community would have to uproot and move. The Iroquois also knew how to conserve meat, fish, vegetables, and berries for the winter.

Iroquois dwellings

The success of the Iroquois adaptation to their productive environment enabled strong population growth. Large numbers of warriors provided the foundation for a culture of imperialist expansion, with frequent wars against the less sedentary Algonquian tribes in the surrounding areas. Over time, Iroquois expansion was only halted by the Algonquian move toward farming, which raised their populations sufficiently to withstand the Iroquois onslaught.

In southern New England, Algonquian tribes relied predominantly on slash-and-burn agriculture. They cleared fields by burning, farmed for a year or two, and then moved the village to a different location to repeat the process. Many Algonquians continued to depend mainly on hunting, fishing, and gathering, especially in the Far North.

The Algonquian economy continued to revolve around the seasonality of food resources. They lived in villages of a few hundred people belonging to the same clan. These villages often dissolved into smaller groups of people roaming around to sites where food was plentiful at a time of year. Later, these groups could join again in a new village or join with others in new ways. It was a flexible system adapted both to the availability of foodstuffs and the threat of war.

Spanish and Portuguese traders reached West Africa and partnered with some African groups to exploit local resources and recruit slave labor for the Americas.

The Atlantic slave trade took place across the Atlantic Ocean from the 16th to the 19th centuries. Most of those who came to the Americas by way of the brutal Middle Passage were from Central or West Africa, sold by other Africans to European traders who arrived at the many forts and trading posts established primarily for this purpose. The number of slaves was so high that more blacks than whites came to the Americas before the late 18th century.

Only about 5 percent of the slaves were taken to North America; the rest were brought mainly to South America (especially Brazil) and the islands of the Caribbean to work on plantations. They laboured to produce coffee, tobacco, cocoa, and sugar for European consumers who held these new commodities in high esteem and were able to create new, pleasant lifestyles for themselves. The slaves also grew cotton and rice, toiled in gold and silver mines, built houses, and cut timber. Some were skilled laborers, craftsmen, or domestic servants.

The first African slaves in the New World came from Europe rather than directly from Africa. In the early 16th century, they arrived on ships carrying a variety of goods for sale rather than on dedicated slave ships. This was an extension of the already existing Portuguese traffic in slaves, which existed for decades before Columbus' first voyage. Portuguese mariners had grown accustomed to buying African slaves on the West African coast and taking them to the Atlantic islands or even to mainland Portugal, where black slaves had become common in Lisbon and on some of the great estates.

The arrival of the first slave ship directly from Africa may not have come until 1526. By 1550, many transatlantic slave ships were headed for the Spanish colonies in the Caribbean, and the first slave vessels had also begun to arrive on the Spanish Main. In this early period, many were sent to work in the mines, especially the gold mines on Hispaniola.

Colonial slave market in the 17th century

Since the Spanish did away with some of the more unsavory parts of the slave trade business, the Portuguese remained dominant. They also served their own needs for manpower, with the traffic to Brazil, eventually accounting for almost half of the Atlantic slave trade. Starting around 1560, it was the demand for sugar in Europe and the corresponding demand for labor on Brazilian sugar plantations that drove this trade.

By 1630, Africans had replaced the original Indian labor force operating Brazilian sugar mills, and these mills were producing almost all the sugar consumed in Europe. Later, sugarcane planting spread to islands in the Eastern Caribbean, rendering the sugar complex the central fact of life in many colonial societies, including possessions of the Spanish, Dutch, English, and French. The success of sugar encouraged the significant westward expansion of the slave systems across Latin America and the present-day United States.

While the demand for plantation commodities, the environment of the tropics, and European ideas about race and identity were significant determinants of how the slave trade developed, African agency was also a key factor. Both Europeans and Africans had long traditions of slavery, but unlike the Europeans, Africans did not use skin color to determine someone's eligibility for slavery. Instead, they often chose to make criminals, debtors, and prisoners of war into slaves. As the transatlantic slave trade expanded, some African wars began with the specific purpose of taking slaves.

The merchants who sold slaves to the Europeans and the chiefs who supplied those merchants usually had strict criteria for who could become a slave. As a consequence, the supply of slaves depended not only on whom plantation owners wanted to purchase, but also on whom influential Africans wanted to sell. The victims of the slave trade were also able to exert agency at times. Slave rebellions occurred frequently, and the risk of such events probably increased costs to the point that it somewhat reduced the scope of the overall traffic.

The introduction of new crops and livestock by the Spanish had far-reaching effects on native settlement patterns as well as on the economic, social, and political development in the Western Hemisphere.

When the Europeans arrived in the New World, wheat, barley, and rice did not grow there, nor were corn, potatoes, and sweet potatoes found in Europe and Asia. The Americas had very few domesticated animals: llamas and alpacas, dogs, guinea pigs, and some species of fowl. There were no horses, cattle, sheep, or goats. The Columbian Exchange would change all this and transform the environment on each of the continents.

The exchange of crops affected both hemispheres. When corn made its way to China, or potatoes to Ireland, the supply of food increased and supported higher population levels. Similarly, wheat and cattle shaped the post-Columbian future of the Great Plains and the Texas grasslands, the Argentinian Pampas, and the Brazilian interior.

The introduction of horses proved a great opportunity and advantage to many Indians. Especially in the case of the Plains Indians, horseback riding created an entirely new way of life. It changed how people lived, how they interacted with their environments, and how they felt about themselves. With time, horses aided the Europeans in their ultimate quest to "pacify" or subdue the Indians.

Typical Cayuse and his mount

The Spanish had a famous equestrian tradition, one of the most successful horse cultures Eurasia had ever seen. After 1492, they used their skill as mounted combatants to conquer vast swaths of lands in the Americas. From Mexico, conquistadors also struck north into the American Southwest, continuing onto the Great Plains.

Even with the presence of Spanish horsemen, it took a long time before the use of horses spread to the indigenous population in North America. The Spanish in New Mexico were well aware that their monopoly on horses was key to maintaining control in a vast and sparsely populated region. The Indians began to help themselves to horses, starting with the Pueblo uprising in 1680.

After that, horse culture spread at breakneck speed. Trading and stealing horses from other tribes became a prominent activity among the Indians in the Southwest, the Great Plains, and the Great Basin. Fifty years after the Pueblo rebellion, horses had become integrated into Indian culture as far away as the northern Rocky Mountains, and another fifty years later, horse culture had become predominant throughout the Trans-Mississippi West.

Having horses allowed for a new way of life, partially by promoting more efficient hunting expeditions. Assaulting the bison was a much less daunting task from horseback than on foot. The horse facilitated long-distance trade and travel in ways that opened the indigenous groups to new goods, impulses, and ideas. At the same time, horses once again proved to have tremendous military consequences.

Adopting horses early on gave some tribes the advantage they needed to punish their enemies and expand their hunting lands, which in turn forced the other tribes to exploit the reach and power of the horse to survive rapidly changing conditions. For some, the world simply seemed to have enormous potential when seen from horseback—endless possibilities on the horizon filled mounted warriors and huntsmen with a spirit of freedom, pride, and confidence.

The first cattle were brought by Christopher Columbus on his second voyage across the Atlantic to Hispaniola. The imported cattle reproduced rapidly, and soon imports were no longer needed. A generation later, Caribbean cattle were brought to Mexico and, within a few decades, had reached north into what is now Texas and south into Colombia and Venezuela.

The cattle adapted to this new ecological setting and roamed the verdant grasslands in vast herds. Wild cattle sometimes constituted a nuisance for Indian farmers, but the Indians also soon found the cow to be very beneficial for them. Cattle provided meat, milk, tallow, hides, transportation, and a source of labor.

Admiral Christopher Columbus, 1451-1506

Even as the Indian population declined due to the smallpox scourge and other epidemics, there was a rapid increase in European livestock as cattle, sheep, and horses flourished on new farms or formerly unclaimed lands. In a way, the Indian population of Mexico, for example, was replaced by European livestock.

In the economies of the Spanish colonies, Indian labor, used in the *encomienda* system to support plantation-based agriculture and extract precious metals and other resources, was gradually replaced by African slavery.

Since the Spanish needed the Indians as workers and payers of tax or tribute, they strove to uphold some aspects of Indian life to the extent that it served their own goals and did not contradict Spanish domination or the tenets of Christianity. Even in Mexico and Peru, where indigenous religion and clergy virtually disappeared, the traditional aristocracy remained, with the backing of Spanish colonial authorities. These noblemen served as middlemen, imposing tax and labor demands on the population at large.

By the middle of the 16th century, taking Indians (other than prisoners of war) as slaves had become illegal in Spanish America. New forms of imposing labor and taxes had been introduced. So-called *encomiendas* were granted to conquistadors and other members of the Spanish elite. These grants meant that Indians were "commended" to an authority figure who was supposed to offer protection in return for service and taxes.

Although the Inca and Aztec Empires also had demanded labor and tribute from their subjects, the new demands of the *encomenderos* who held Spanish grants were often excessive. At the same time, the responsibility for protection was too frequently neglected.

Thus, the sense of reciprocity usually encountered in traditional Indian culture was often lost somewhere along the way. *Encomiendas* covered the region from New Mexico in the North to Chile in the South, usually proving destructive to indigenous communities. Even the holders of grants were often troubled and disappointed by the performance of the *encomiendas*, especially as the Indian populations continued to decline.

The government in Spain also had concerns about the system, as they feared the establishment of a powerful aristocracy so far from their seat of authority. The institution was dismantled by limiting the ability of children to inherit *encomiendas*, and by prohibiting certain kinds of labor demands.

Encomiendas remained in some areas of the empire, but mostly in marginal areas. Instead of grants of people, grants of land would form the new basis of wealth.

Meanwhile, the colonial government used royal officials to demand Indian labor and tax more directly. Indian communities were required to offer laborers to work on state projects, such as building churches and roads, or in labor gangs working in mines and on plantations. Thousands of Indians were recruited for this forced labor. Although they were paid a wage, they often encountered systemic abuse and work requirements that could have grave consequences both for individuals and the community at large.

Some Indians decided to leave their communities to avoid taxes and forced labor, going to work for Spanish landowners or city dwellers instead. Uprooted Indians thus became mobile wage laborers for mines, farms, and urban enterprises.

At the same time, the decline in Indian populations also encouraged a corresponding increase in the use of African slaves to meet labor requirements in the colonies. African slaves were with the Spanish from the very beginning, even among Cortés's army, as he went to conquer the Aztecs and occupy Tenochtitlán.

Later, slaves were put to work farming sugar and rice in Mexican fields. The numbers were quite a bit smaller than in Brazil and Haiti, but the black population nevertheless outnumbered the Spanish settlers in the colony.

Introduction of slavery

The Spanish colonies, which valued sugar plantations and gold and silver mines, often made widespread use of slave labor. This was the case in Cuba, Venezuela, Colombia, Peru, and Ecuador. In parts of Spanish America where plantation agriculture and giant mines were not so dominant, Africans were instead few and far between, although some slaves were engaged as craftsmen or house servants.

Portuguese Brazil, rather than the Spanish colonies, was the world's leading sugar producer. Unlike most agricultural produce, sugarcane had to be processed with the use of expensive and sophisticated machinery on the spot. It was cut and pressed in a sugar mill, and the juice was then heated to make the sugar crystallize. In other words, sugar production was a combination of farming and manufacturing, requiring unusual amounts of both capital and labor. The labor was also unusual in that it was exceptionally strenuous and intense in the harvest season, and the mortality rates on the plantations were correspondingly high. Some free workers participated in this process as skilled laborers or artisans, but slaves did most of the work. In Brazil, African slaves soon constituted half of the total population.

Based on a single crop produced by slave labor, Brazil became the first great plantation colony and a model that would later be followed by other European nations in their Caribbean colonies. Ever since, despite the diversification of the economy, Brazilian society has continued to reflect its origins in plantation hierarchies and slavery. The white planter families emerged as a powerful and wealthy aristocracy taking control of local communities. They established connections to merchants and government officials to maintain their control of the flow of money and the use of force.

At the bottom of the social hierarchy were the slaves who were treated merely as property. This harsh, unmerciful version of slavery was quite different from African circumstances where slaves, despite their lowly social status, were treated as human beings with individual dignity, and in many cases, included as part of the extended family.

However, American slaves were subject to a new form of trade, where they were virtually interchangeable commodities. Most slaves only survived for a few years in the New World, but others replaced them from the ships plying the triangular trade between the Americas, Europe, and Africa.

New crops from the Americas stimulated European population growth, while new sources of mineral wealth facilitated the European shift from feudalism to capitalism.

Corn was not known in the Old World before the voyages of Columbus, but it quickly became a staple crop in the earliest stages of the Columbian Exchange. By 1630, Spain was heavily invested in the commercial production of corn, far surpassing the traditional subsistence farming in Mesoamerica.

Similarly, potatoes and sweet potatoes were unknown in Europe before the exploration of the Americas. The white potato came from the Andes Mountains in South America, where the indigenous people had developed a multitude of varieties adapted to varying microenvironments. It eventually became a staple crop in Europe and was brought to North America by Scotch-Irish immigrants in the 18th century.

The potato is a good source of many nutrients, and in many European locations, a plot of potatoes was much more productive in terms of calories than an equivalent plot of other food crops. The sweet potato also became an essential crop in Europe.

Peppers were grown in Central and South America. Spanish explorers took pepper seeds back to Spain as early as 1493, and the plants soon spread across Europe. Today, they are grown in tropical areas of Asia and Africa, as well as in the Americas. Tomatoes also originated in the New World, specifically in the highlands of South America. They were brought to Mesoamerica in an intercolonial exchange, but of course also to Spain, where their use in new sauces earned the label "Spanish" cuisine.

The explorers also took peanuts back to Spain, where they are still grown. From Spain, traders and explorers took peanuts to Africa and Asia. Peanuts were brought to the southern part of North America along with the Africans who were shipped there as slaves.

Some Indians used cacao beans as currency, and Columbus took some to Europe as an example of American money. Cortés watched the Aztec court drinking chocolate, and eventually, this drink also became familiar and appreciated by European colonists. By the early 17th century, the drink was becoming popular in Europe itself, and later in that century, the first chocolate house was opened in England.

New crops from the Americas made the European diet more varied and sophisticated but also contributed significantly to population growth. This is especially true of corn, and even more importantly, potatoes. Incorporating potatoes into the European diet allowed higher food production and a form of insurance against catastrophic grain harvest failures that could result in misery and famine.

The highly nutritious potatoes also strengthened the immune systems of Europeans suffering from debilitating diseases like dysentery, measles, and tuberculosis. The introduction of potatoes was accompanied by higher birth rates, lower mortality rates, and a rapid rise of the population in both Europe and the United States.

The abundance of gold and silver in the mountain ranges of the Americas revolutionized the European economy. In the 16th century alone, the supply of these precious metals multiplied by a factor of eight. This flood of the new currency was so overwhelming that it tended to destabilize rather than strengthen the old order of things in Europe. This had certainly not been the intention of the Spanish monarchs. The feudal system, where land ownership was paramount, was challenged as money, a new measure of wealth, came into play in a much more significant way.

The new money could be used to invest in new ventures in trading and manufacturing and was, of course, much more liquid and accessible than land. The feudal aristocracy in Spain, moored to the land by regulations that prevented them from participating in middle-class business activities, was left out as a new economic order emerged, where elites in other more dynamic and mercantilist countries came to the forefront.

Since the Habsburg monarch Charles was both King of Spain and Emperor of the Holy Roman Empire (Germany and the surrounding areas), money spread quickly across Austria, Germany, Italy, the Netherlands, and Switzerland.

Spaniards gambling

The wastefulness and warmongering of the Spanish kings meant that most of the bullion from America had to be devoted to paying off debts, and on several occasions the Crown was even forced to default on those debts, meaning that despite the enormous riches obtained in the Americas, Spain was virtually bankrupt.

Precious metals rather than land now became the foundation of power and status. A new class of merchants and capitalists emerged that would eventually dominate not only Europe but the whole world.

Even on the fringes of Europe, the Ottoman Empire, which controlled Turkey, the Balkans, and most of the Middle East and North Africa, were far from immune to the impact of American silver. The impact was suddenly felt in 1584 when the Ottoman currency fell precipitously amidst shocking price inflation. The currency fell to half of its former value and never regained its significance in world trade again.

Arguably, the influx of silver from the Americas did more to undermine the worldly power of the Islamic countries in the centuries that followed than any other factor. In fact, throughout the world, the new European wealth eroded the value of holdings in every other country in the Old World, while allowing Europe to expand and form a Eurocentric system of world trade.

The silver of America made possible a world economy for the first time, as much of it was traded not only to the Ottomans but to the Chinese and East Indians as well. All the great civilizations of Eurasia were thus brought under the influence of American silver and its destabilizing effects. Europe's prosperity boomed, and its people wanted all the teas, silks, cotton, coffees, and spices which the rest of the world could offer in the new global economy.

Improvements in technology and more organized methods for conducting international trade helped drive changes to economies in Europe and the Americas.

The exploration of the Americas was made possible in part by prior technological developments in Europe. The Spanish and Portuguese had pioneered a vessel called the caravel, which made oceangoing exploration possible. These were relatively small, narrow, but sturdy ships, often with two lateens (triangular) sails. Their larger counterpart, the carrack, usually had a full rig, that is to say, two square sails and one lateen sail. They were slower and harder to board but could carry more cargo. European navigators had acquired the magnetic compass from the Muslims.

Caravel with oars

It was probably the Portuguese who first used mariner's quadrants to accurately measure the angle from the North Star (or the Southern Cross, in the Southern Hemisphere) and thus determine latitude, which was crucial in the unknown waters.

Portuguese galleons and carracks

Longitude could not be determined accurately. Navigators would generally try to follow a certain latitude from east to west and then try to estimate the ship's speed by observing the hull's movement and the hourglass. Having guessed what the speed was, they could guess what their position was, although with limited accuracy.

The importance of oceangoing ships was such in the new world economy that Europeans continued to pursue new navigational technologies. By the 18th century, they had developed octants that made the measurement of latitude even simpler and more accurate. Around the same time, astronomers developed a method for predicting the angular distance between the moon and other celestial bodies.

Using this technique, the navigator at sea could use a new device, a sextant, to measure the angle between the moon and a planet or star, calculate the time at which the moon and the celestial body would be at that angle, and then compare local time with the standardized time of the national observatory. Knowing the time difference between the two points allowed a precise determination of longitude. After millennia of navigation, seafarers were finally able to determine the exact position of their vessel at any given time.

Spanish Armada

The expansion of European economic interests into new areas around the world also led to innovations in the field of business organization. This was not so much the case with the Spanish and Portuguese, whose ambitions of honor, glory, and aristocratic leisure were, in a sense, feudal and medieval.

The later Dutch and English colonial projects had much more of a mercantile and capitalist flavor. Among the innovations they pioneered in response to the quest for colonial riches were two of the most important financial innovations of all time, the joint-stock company and the stock exchange.

The earliest joint-stock company in England was the Company of Merchant Adventurers to New Lands, chartered in 1553. More significant and vastly more wealthy and influential was the East India Company, granted a royal charter by Queen Elizabeth I in 1600. This royal charter gave the Company, as it became known, enormous trade privileges in India, effectively a temporary monopoly on trade between England and Indian ports. The Company went far beyond mere trading ventures, supporting its mercantile clout with veritable armies and navies, and eventually expanding its political power until it was mainly the government of a colonized subcontinent.

Similarly, the Dutch East India Company was a tremendously powerful political, military, and economic force. Starting in 1602, the Dutch East India Company issued shares that could be traded on the Amsterdam Stock Exchange. This brilliant financial innovation made it easy for joint-stock companies to attract investor's capital since it became much easier to both buy and sell shares.

The Dutch East India Company was arguably the world's first modern corporation. It was allowed to operate with limited liability as investors could only lose what they had invested, and were not liable for any further debts incurred by the company.

Henry Hudson (1565-1611) sailed on the river which now bears his name on behalf of the Dutch East India Company, and his explorations led to the establishment of New Netherland (present-day New York). Eventually, Dutch interests in the Americas would come to be pursued by a separate Dutch West India Company. Before that time, the joint-stock Virginia Company established in England in 1606 had already established a settlement at Jamestown.

Henry Hudson, c. 1610

The abundance of land, a shortage of indentured servants, the lack of an effective means to enslave native peoples, and the growing European demand for colonial goods led to the emergence of the Atlantic slave trade.

One of the big problems confronting planters in the British colonies was that both white and Indian laborers had options and could be challenging to control. White indentured servants could run away and blend into the population, or even band together and demand government intervention on their behalf. Easy access to land ownership in the colonies also made the idea of doing backbreaking, poorly paid work for others unappealing to Europeans. Similarly, if Indians were forced to do plantation labor, they could use their local knowledge and connections to disappear.

At the same time, Indians were very vulnerable to Old World diseases, while Europeans succumbed to malaria more easily than Africans. Thus, if Africans could be subjected to the harsh slave codes of the Caribbean, mainland planters could have a more reliable source of labor. This facilitated the export of tobacco from the Chesapeake area and rice from South Carolina and enriched a planter aristocracy at a tremendous human cost.

Depiction of a tobacco wharf in colonial America

The slave trade expanded rapidly to absorb the demand for new slaves to work on the plantations and farms and in the households and shops of whites in British North America. About 500,000 Africans were brought from Africa and the Caribbean to what is now the United States before the end of the transatlantic trade in 1807. This was about 6 percent of the total number of slaves brought from Africa to the Americas. Slaves on the North American mainland reproduced at much higher rates than elsewhere, which in turn led to the development of a sizable internal trade in slaves.

Along with other factors, environmental and geographical variations, including climate and natural resources, contributed to regional differences in what would become the British colonies.

The climate and natural resources of the British colonies affected settlement patterns and differences in long-term trajectories of development. The climate made New England less vulnerable to infectious diseases, but winters could be severe, the growing season was relatively short, and the soil tended to be rocky.

Abundant timber resources were useful for the shipbuilding industry, which in turn supported the growth of fisheries and seaborne commerce. The Middle colonies farther south had a milder climate and good soil for farming, which lead to the development of prosperous agricultural communities.

Grain, corn, and meat were sold to other colonies, and functional ports and the central location of these colonies allowed for the rise of merchants and artisans in the two biggest cities of the colonial era, Philadelphia and New York.

Exploring northern Georgia

In the southern colonies, the warm climate allowed for a long growing season and the spread of plantations that grew export commodities. In Virginia, there was a mix of plantations and family farms and mixed agriculture of cash commodities, food crops, and livestock.

Planters dominated the tidewater areas, while the backcountry, as well as the less fertile land of North Carolina, was settled mainly by small farmers. Subtropical South Carolina and Georgia more closely resembled the Caribbean colonies, with a strong focus on growing rice—and later indigo and cotton—by using slave labor.

The demographically, religiously, and ethnically diverse middle colonies supported a flourishing export economy based on cereal crops. In contrast, the Chesapeake colonies and North Carolina relied on the cultivation of tobacco, a labor-intensive product based on white indentured servants and African chattel.

The middle colonies, including New York, New Jersey, Pennsylvania, and Delaware, were more diverse concerning religion and ethnicity than New England, which was dominated by Puritans from the English low country. Both the Netherlands and Sweden had tried to establish colonies in this region, and the vast tracts of fertile land soon attracted immigrants from Germany, France, Scotland, Ireland, and other places in Europe.

Some immigrants came as indentured servants but ended up as successful craftsmen or farmers. Pennsylvania, founded by Quakers, offered religious freedom to a wide variety of sects and denominations, and New York offered citizenship to anyone who embraced Christianity. Quakers, Baptists, Methodists, Episcopalians, Lutherans, Amish, and Mennonites flocked to the middle colonies from other colonies and Europe.

Quaker woman preaching in New Amsterdam (Manhattan)

The fertile soil allowed farmers in the middle colonies to grow a significant surplus of grains for export. Pennsylvania became the largest producer of food on the continent. The rivers of the area offered useful connections between port cities and a hinterland that supplied fur and lumber. These rivers also supplied energy for mills and other manufacturing enterprises.

The economy flourished, but not everyone benefited equally. In some areas, land ownership was controlled by the Dutch *patroons* and Englishmen favored by the Crown, and the riches of the cities tended to be concentrated among a few prosperous merchants. Although there was a sizable middle class of farmers, artisans, and shopkeepers, there was also a vast underclass of tenants, laborers, servants, and slaves.

While the economy of the middle colonies was diverse and encompassed hunting, trapping, fishing, farming, crafts, mining, metalworking, manufacturing, shipping and trade, the economy of the Chesapeake colonies, Virginia and Maryland, relied to a great extent on tobacco.

Large plantations were the centers of economic activity, to the detriment of urban development. Planters brought in indentured servants and slaves to work the land, secured the best farmland, and organized most of the shipping themselves. Population growth was slow, as there were limited opportunities for poor European immigrants, and the mortality rate was high due to widespread epidemics.

The rebellion of Nathaniel Bacon in 1676–77 appealed to disempowered whites by attacking both Indians and local authorities in Virginia but was soon struck down by the power of the Crown and the planter class. The rebellion was spurred by a decline in tobacco prices, which caused economic hardship. In the 18th century, Chesapeake farmers and planters chose to reduce their risk of failure by diversifying crops, and they began producing more grains, flax, and meat.

The colonies along the southernmost Atlantic coast and the British islands in the West Indies took advantage of long growing seasons by using slave labor to develop economies based on staple crops; in some cases, enslaved Africans constituted the majority of the population.

While the development of the British West Indies and the mainland colonies were intimately connected politically, culturally, and economically, the Caribbean islands had their unique characteristics. Their intense focus on producing sugar and their dependence on trade for virtually everything else gave them little of the semblance of self-sufficiency found in some mainland colonies. The vast estates, plantations worked by hundreds of slaves and often owned by wealthy men who did not even live on the islands, were another distinguishing characteristic.

Barbados, for example, had been founded as a colony for growing tobacco, but soon shifted to sugar as competition from the Chesapeake colonies intensified. Slaves—and, at first, convict laborers from Ireland—cut down tropical forests all over the island to grow sugarcane. Almost 400,000 slaves were brought to the island, but death rates were high, and many were resold in other American markets. Nevertheless, by the 18th century, blacks outnumbered whites by three to one. This was a relatively low ratio compared to many of the other colonies.

The colony of Carolina, split into North and South Carolina in 1729, had its twin origins in the cultures of Barbados and the Virginia backcountry. The northern part of the colony, settled by Virginians, lacked land suitable for plantations and natural ports facilitating international trade. The southern part became a colony in the Caribbean mold, featuring large plantations, a slave majority, and a monocultural focus after rice became the predominant crop early in the 18th century. South Carolina was also a center for trade in Indian slaves. Eventually, the colony began efforts to attract European immigrants to the backcountry, partially as a defense against potential slave rebellions.

Georgia was established much later than the Carolinas. It had a stunted development due to the original prohibition of slavery in the colony. Only a few Europeans settled there before slavery became legal in 1749.

Therefore, the early history of Georgia was like that of North Carolina. With the introduction of plantation slavery, Georgia was becoming like South Carolina and, by extension, the Caribbean possessions.

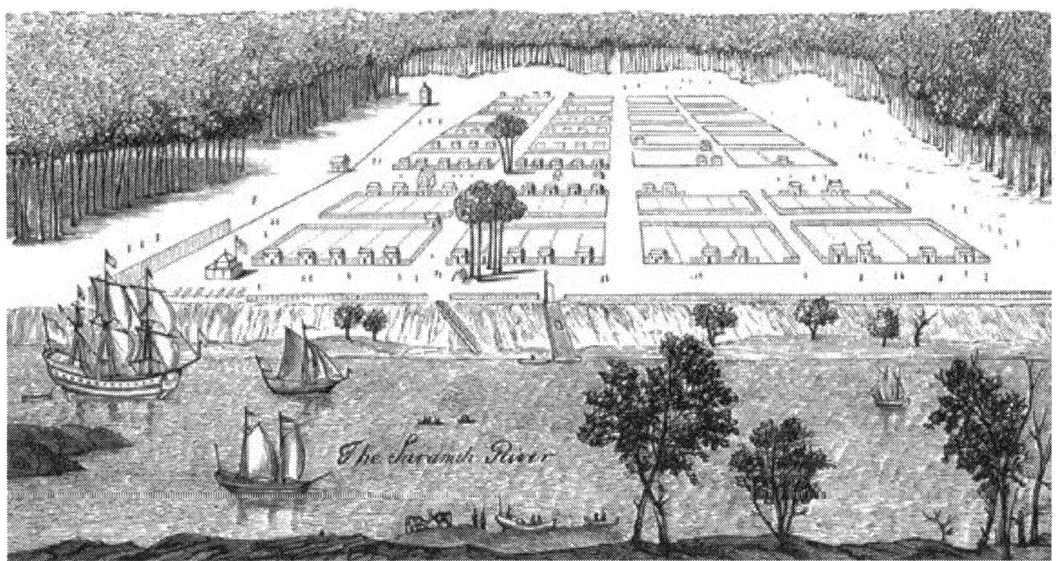

Savannah, from a print of 1741

As European nations competed in North America, their colonies focused on gaining new sources of labor and on producing and acquiring commodities valued in Europe.

Since the main aims of colonization were to take control of land and resources and sell exports to Europe, the colonists had a pressing need for a labor force. Many workers were needed on the vast "new" lands to raise crops and livestock, labor in mines, mills, docks, shops, and workshops, or to work as craftsmen or servants.

Because of this need, colonial elites worked tirelessly to find new labor sources, including both free and indentured immigrants, convicts, Indians, and Africans. Early labor forces were often a mix of African, Indian, and European workers. However, where large plantations dominated, there was a tendency to rely almost exclusively on slaves of African descent eventually.

Scene on a plantation

These massive plantations in the South produced many of the leading export commodities that North America had to offer, primarily tobacco, rice, and indigo. Also, the northern colonies exported wheat and wheat flour, corn, fish, livestock and horses, and some lumber and metal products. Foodstuffs were sold to the planters on the Caribbean islands, where sugar was by far the dominant export, integrating the mainland colonies into the sugar economy.

The French colonies on the mainland exported little of value except for large numbers of furs. New Spain (present-day Mexico and the southwestern United States) had an economy long focused on mining. By the 18th century, silver exports were supplemented by other colonial exports like sugar, tobacco, cocoa, cotton, and dyes. The failure to distribute water resources equitably was a disaster for agriculture, which in turn meant that the Indian population that provided most labor continued to decline.

Carolina rice field

By supplying American Indian allies with deadlier weapons and alcohol and by rewarding Indian military actions, the Europeans helped increase the intensity and destructiveness of American Indian warfare.

Trade was an essential aspect of relations between indigenous people and colonists in North America. The fur trade was especially crucial because furs were considered highly fashionable symbols of status in Europe. In return for furs, European traders offered iron knives and axes, textiles, blankets, utensils, cookware, and jewelry that Indians could use to improve their standard of living or display their social status.

Over time, the Indians became dependent on these items and often preferred them to traditional goods that could be made with local resources and indigenous knowledge. Also, the traders introduced strong alcoholic beverages like rum and whiskey. Perhaps because many of the Indian tribes saw spiritual potential in a trance- or dream-like states, alcohol quickly became incredibly popular. Social problems arose consequently, and some colonies made attempts to prohibit the sale of alcohol to Indians. However, high demand and correspondingly high profits made most of these laws ineffective.

The dependence on alcohol made several of the tribes dependent on furs, which in turn encouraged both ecological mismanagement and intermittent warfare with other tribes over hunting grounds. These wars were facilitated by and became bloodier as a result of another European trade good: firearms. The trade for weapons was on such a scale that the price of beaver pelts could be quoted in the number of pistols or guns.

The French and English also supplied their Indian allies with firearms as part of their efforts to limit each other's influence. Their encouragement of wars for territory and hunting grounds increased the prevalence and scale of conflicts in colonial North America.

Trading with Indians

"Atlantic World" commercial, religious, philosophical, and political interactions among Europeans, Africans, and American native peoples stimulated economic growth, expanded social networks, and reshaped labor systems.

European explorers, merchants, conquerors, and settlers initiated much of the activity that eventually linked the Atlantic World together. Other groups played essential roles as agents in this process as well. The creation of an Atlantic World contributed significantly to the creation of a world economy, promising great wealth for some, modest comforts for others and devastation, ruin and enslavement for many of the indigenous people of Africa and the Americas.

American precious metals allowed a more dynamic, freer economy in Europe, and colonial stimulants, like tobacco, sugar, and cocoa, promoted harder work and a culture of mass consumption, paving the way for the Industrial Revolution. Labor systems were transformed as Indians, and Africans were exploited as slave labor, while European colonists could rise from subordinate positions to become independent farmers, traders, and craftsmen.

The Atlantic exchanges were not merely economic. The crossings of people, books, habits, and customs spread new ideas and beliefs and forced both colonizers and colonized to adjust their views. Religious and political philosophies shaped how colonies were organized, especially in some of the English colonies purposely established as New World utopias.

At the same time, the European encounter with America led to a new understanding of the world, forcing intellectuals and scientists to reconsider the ancient writers and the Bible as infallible sources of authority. The discovery of new lands and peoples opened new intellectual worlds and brought old verities into question. The newly emboldened Europeans and Americans then set out to revolutionize the world through science, technology, and political transformation.

The growth of an Atlantic economy throughout the 18th century created a shared labor market and an extensive exchange of New World and European goods, as seen in the African slave trade and the shipment of products from the Americas.

The labor systems of the New World drew upon the availability of conquered Indians and Africans who could be bought in the West African ports. European workers were also essential; before 1700, most white immigrants came to the Americas as indentured servants rather than free men and women. Some of them were convicts, but most paid for the costly passage to the Americas with years of their lives.

Like slaves, they received no wages but were provided with room, board, and simple clothing. They were not allowed to marry or have children, and their working conditions were often miserable. At the end of their contract, they were free to leave and use whatever skills they had acquired to secure their financial independence.

However, this solution to the problem of securing labor was not particularly satisfactory to either the white elite or to the indentured servants themselves. Similarly, using Indians as slaves became controversial in the Spanish possessions, and their death rates and tendency to escape made African slaves a relatively favorable alternative, especially for plantation owners who needed a large labor force to grow sugar and other staples.

Slavery did not become equally widespread in areas without plantation agriculture, suggesting the role of practical considerations in developing new labor systems.

Sugar cane

The success of plantation products, especially sugar and tobacco, both increased the demand for workers and enabled the planters to invest in more land and more slaves. Thus, the success of sugar and tobacco in Europe and the success of slavery in the Americas were tightly entwined and dependent on each other.

At the same time, the flow of sugar and tobacco provided a stimulus to European workers, enabling them to work harder and encouraging them to enter labor markets to make the wages without which they could not procure colonial goods. While Africans and Indians became dependent on European wares, the Europeans grew equally dependent on colonial commodities. Entrepreneurs on both sides of the Atlantic consequently made significant profits.

SOCIAL DEVELOPMENTS:

Early Colonization to 1789

European overseas expansion resulted in the Columbian Exchange, a series of interactions and adaptations among societies across the Atlantic.

Millions of years ago, the supercontinent Pangaea was torn apart by continental drift, and North and South America were separated from Eurasia and Africa. The long journey of separation and divergence caused evolution to take different directions in the Old and the New World, leading to the emergence of new species that had no counterparts across the ocean.

After 1492, one species—human beings—began to reverse this process by establishing connections that transferred plants, animals, and microorganisms between Afro-Eurasia and the Americas. This transfer is called the Columbian Exchange and represented not only a spectacular ecological reversal but also a significant turning point in world history.

The arrival of Europeans in the Western Hemisphere in the 15th and 16th centuries triggered extensive demographic and social changes on both sides of the Atlantic. Spanish and Portuguese exploration and conquest of the Americas led to widespread deadly epidemics, the emergence of racially mixed populations, and a caste system defined by an intermixture among Spanish settlers, Africans, and Native Americans.

Spanish explorers: Cortés, Coligni, de Soto and Verazzani

Before the Columbian Exchange, the peoples of Eurasia and the Americas differed in ways that would have spectacular effects once regular communication between the two hemispheres was established. Eurasian civilizations had more centers of high population density, kept an extensive range of domesticated animals, and suffered from many infectious diseases unknown in the New World. Trade, migration, and war allowed these diseases to spread widely across Europe and Asia. As these diseases became endemic over time, Europeans also developed some level of resistance or immunity to smallpox and other epidemics.

The Indians of the Americas had not had the same opportunity to develop natural immunity to many of the diseases prevalent in Europe. Deadly epidemics followed in the wake of European explorers, and once established, they were able to spread from one Indian population to the next without direct contact with whites.

Microorganisms could, of course, travel in the other direction as well; it appears that the voyages of Columbus brought syphilis (i.e., a harrowing and deadly venereal disease), from the Americas to Europe. In general, the exchange of diseases was asymmetric and took a far higher toll in the New World.

The rapid spread of smallpox in the Americas was one of the most devastating events of world history. It cost far more lives than all the wars and conquests initiated by the conquistadors and other European colonists, and a much higher proportion of the population died than in the Black Death, the catastrophic epidemic which hit Europe in the 14th century.

Only about 10 percent of indigenous populations survived the spread of smallpox and other epidemic diseases between the late 15th and the early 17th centuries. In some cases, entire cultures disappeared, and lands were laid waste, forever altering the demographic composition of two continents and facilitating the rapid establishment of European dominance.

In 1520, a group of Spaniards from the smallpox-ravaged island of Hispaniola (today divided between Haiti and the Dominican Republic) landed on the Mexican mainland. Another Spanish force defeated them under the leadership of Hernán Cortés, who had arrived in the previous year. One of his men contracted smallpox, and when his party set off for the Aztec capital Tenochtitlán, they brought the deadly disease with them. The Spanish soldier eventually died, but smallpox had already spread to the Aztec population.

Having been forced to flee after an initial confrontation, Cortés returned in 1521 to find the large city completely devastated by disease and death. Large numbers had already perished, including most of the Aztec army. Unable to mount a proper defense of the capital, the Aztecs were easily defeated by Cortés and his Indian allies. The Spanish entered in triumph only to see streets covered in the dead and dying, as well as houses that had become tombs as all the inhabitants had passed away.

Meeting of Cortés and Montezuma

The Inca Empire was similarly overwhelmed and demoralized by the effects of smallpox. There, the disease had arrived and began to wipe out the population even before the Spanish conquerors appeared on the scene. The efficient road system that tied the empire together also had the effect of aiding the rapid spread of disease. Within months, both the old emperor and his immediate successor had died, along with most other persons of authority.

Warring factions emerged in this power vacuum, and a young leader, Atahualpa, eventually came to power. After this brutal civil war had already further destabilized and weakened the Inca, a small group of highly motivated Spaniards led by Francisco Pizarro was able to capture Atahualpa, take Cuzco (the capital) and swiftly establish Spanish authority over what had once been an impressive indigenous empire. Much of the Inca population succumbed to smallpox, and other European diseases led to further devastation.

Heroic defense of Cuzco

As the Europeans began to bring African slaves to the Americas, they also brought yellow fever along. This disease was endemic in Africa, so many Africans were immune. However, this was not the case with those of European descent, who suffered high mortality rates in American yellow fever epidemics into the 19th century.

Europeans were able to establish their hegemony in the Americas centuries before they achieved the same result in Africa partly because of the difference in the impact of the disease. The tropical diseases made Africa a "white man's grave," while in the Americas, the collapse of indigenous cultures in the face of shocking epidemics made conquest and control easy.

Early conquistadors and settlers were typically men. As they desired female companionship, intermarriage became common in Spanish America. This gave almost instantaneous rise to a mixed-race population, called *mestizos,* which quickly became the numerically superior part of the population in many of the Spanish colonies. Some indigenous women were forced to become wives or concubines. Over time, the amount of European, Indian, and African "blood" a person possessed became one of the central organizing principles of Spanish American society, and a kind of hereditary caste system evolved.

The racial hierarchy created by the Spanish elite assumed that people could be meaningfully classified according to racial and ethnic origins because these determined the differences between people. The caste system was more than a way of ascribing social status; it had economic implications as well. Those who belonged to the lower end of the system met proportionally higher demands for taxes and tribute payments. Socioeconomic status largely corresponded with skin color, appearance, and family background.

The Peninsulars (those born and raised in the Iberian Peninsula) occupied the most important government offices. They held much of the wealth, while darker skin and non-European ancestry entailed poverty, inferiority, and servitude. Being white allowed a person to claim status and respect, while people of color faced obstacles and prejudice. Even whites born in the colonies faced discrimination by the Peninsulars, which eventually led the former group, known as *criollos*, to seek independence for the Latin American countries in the early 19th century.

The term *Zambo* identified individuals of mixed African and Indian descent. Marriages and liaisons between Africans and Indians took place throughout the Spanish colonies and their borderlands. At times, groups of runaway slaves would mix with local Indian populations. In one unconquered region of present-day Ecuador, a group of shipwrecked slaves took control of an indigenous community.

Another group, who had revolted on a slave ship and wrecked it on the border between Honduras and Nicaragua, united with the local Miskito people. They eventually came to dominate society and engage in extensive slave raids.

Many Europeans developed a belief in white superiority to justify their subjugation of Africans and American Indians, using several different rationales.

Three early modern developments were responsible for the entry of racial stereotypes into the European view of the world: the emergence of the transatlantic slave trade, the formation of social structures in colonies settled by Europeans, and the *Limpieza de Sangre* (i.e., purity of blood) on the Iberian Peninsula. The latter had an indirect link to colonial development in the New World, while the first two were intimately connected with it.

Controversy exists regarding whether racial concepts already existed at the beginning of the slave trade. When Africans were sent to the New World as slaves, it may, in part, have been because they were already seen as inferior. However, the slave market system followed its own logic and led to the further development of concepts of race.

The rules of the new markets governed the establishment of the transatlantic slave trade. Besides, the Europeans usually did not take slaves themselves, but instead purchased the slaves from other Africans or Arab intermediaries. In other words, they needed to build business relationships with African merchants and chiefs based on equality or at least some element of mutual recognition and respect. Nevertheless, the trade increasingly contributed to the perception that Africans in the New World were inferior.

Dutch selling slaves to the Virginia planters

The widespread use of African slaves necessarily contributed to the racialized social structures of the New World. The structures usually preceded the explicit and eventually elaborate justifications for their creation and maintenance. The social system of the Spanish Colonial Empire appeared to be organized strictly according to racial origins with clear distinctions between whites, blacks, Indians, and intermediate categories.

This system was much more rigid in theory than in practice, and some people were able to transcend racial boundaries and improve their position in society. As this shows, the racial elements of the system of social stratification did not necessarily indicate ubiquitous racism. Unlike later developments in the British colonies, the Spanish and Portuguese Colonial Empires allowed the intermingling of peoples and the crossing of racial lines, rather than seeing the mixing of races as an abomination and a threat to society.

Unlike their European competitors, the English eventually sought to establish colonies based on agriculture, sending relatively large numbers of men and women to acquire land and populate their settlements, while having a relatively hostile relationship with American Indians.

Unlike the Spanish quest for precious metals and the Dutch and French involvement in the fur trade, English colonization of the North American mainland sought to reproduce a European way of life by focusing on family farms.

This was especially true of the northern colonies because the southern colonies featured slave-based plantation agriculture more closely resembling Caribbean models than anything seen in Europe.

Access to land, combined with a measure of political and religious autonomy, made these colonies attractive to immigrants, including couples, families, and single men and women. Heads of immigrant families could be rewarded with land grants. Others received grants directly from the Crown, bought or rented land, or simply chose to squat on land that had not yet been distributed to other white settlers.

The new landowners were often mobile and opportunistic, utilizing farmlands in an unsustainable way and then moving on to greener pastures when the soil was exhausted. The access to ample, fertile land nevertheless made farming by far the most important activity in the English colonies, engaging most of the population until the 19th century. Also, English settlers engaged in shipping, shipbuilding, fishing, and trade.

The British hunger for farmland and other natural resources combined with the lack of racial intermixing in these colonies led to a pattern of frequent and often enduring hostilities between the colonists and the indigenous people.

Although there were many examples of cooperation, peaceful trade, and even military alliances between whites and Indians, tensions were often persistent and resulted in raids, plunder, and retribution as well as outright wars leading to conquests and massacres.

Part of the problem stemmed from different conceptions of the rights to land; the Indians generally believed that such rights only extended to specific uses of the land and its resources at a given time or season, while the British equated landownership with absolute and unrestricted control of the land to the exclusion of others.

The introduction of crops and domestic animals from Europe also disturbed existing ecological systems and posed a further challenge to the Indian way of life.

The British–American system of slavery developed out of the economic, demographic, and geographic characteristics of the British-controlled regions of the New World.

The sale of slaves to the British colonies in North America accounted for a tiny proportion of the transatlantic slave trade. At first, most slaves did not even arrive directly from Africa, but rather from other colonies in the Caribbean.

Even though African captives arrived in Virginia as early as 1619, the British system of slavery in the Americas developed on the islands during the first half of the 17th century.

Following the Brazilian model, these Caribbean colonies thrived by focusing on the production of sugar on large plantations where almost all the workers were black slaves. Slaves became the majority on these islands; their rights were minimal, and their lives often short.

The treatment of slaves differed significantly from the African tradition, where slaves were more commonly treated as inferior members of the family with the ability to gain their freedom after some years of service.

Slavery on the North American mainland was initially of a more complex and human nature, with Africans sometimes treated more like indentured servants or at least as people who eventually might gain freedom for themselves or their children. The term "slave" was not even used, and for some time, there were no laws specifying the conditions of these workers.

As the availability of indentured servants from England declined and Africans became a more substantial proportion of the workforce, political leaders in the southern colonies took steps to ensure that the institution of slavery would ensure a constant supply of laborers.

They turned to the models of the Caribbean and sought to define slavery as a permanent situation where people would be treated as property for life.

Domestic slave trade, c. 1650

In the northern colonies, which were unsuitable for plantation agriculture, slavery was less common. Maintaining slaves over the long northern winters made less sense as there was little farm work to be done.

Still, there were substantial numbers of slaves, especially in the cities, where they more typically performed household chores or worked in shops and workshops. Some historians argue that northern whites tended to own slaves as a status symbol rather than primarily to make a profit.

However, the New England colonies were also heavily involved in slave trading, where there was much money to be made.

Unlike Spanish, French, and Dutch colonies, which accepted intermarriage and cross-racial sexual unions with native peoples (for Spain, with enslaved Africans), English colonies attracted both males and females who rarely intermarried with either native peoples or Africans. This led to the development of a rigid racial hierarchy.

In the Spanish colonies, intermixing of races had been taking place since the very beginning. It resulted in a complex but, to a certain extent, flexible status hierarchy based on skin color and birth. When the French and Dutch established colonies in the Americas, there were few Europeans involved, and especially few European women.

As for the Spanish, this led to widespread intermarriage, and mixed-race offspring could rise to prominent positions in colonial society. Louisiana law prohibited Catholics from marrying non-Catholics, but there were no restrictions based exclusively on race.

By contrast, some of the English colonies began to legislate against marriages between whites and slaves, and later between whites and any black or mulatto person. The Chesapeake planters were especially fearful of a coalition of white and black laborers and sought to ensure rigid separation of the races to discourage cooperation across color lines.

The rules against miscegenation extended to the northern colonies as well, especially since beliefs about race often were fused with religious sentiment. Massachusetts and Pennsylvania, with their strong religious foundations, also had stringent rules against interracial sex and marriage. Free blacks or mulattoes who were caught having sex with whites could be sold into slavery.

Although intermarriage was frowned upon and often prohibited, interracial sex was nevertheless reasonably common, occurring both as everyday transgressions of community norms and as one aspect of masters' abuse of slaves in a slave society. As many as one in three black Americans living today have a male ancestor of European descent, mostly because of such liaisons between slave women and their owners.

However, being of the mixed-race did not qualify an individual for an intermediate status in British colonial society. On the contrary, most offspring of black-and-white unions were, and remained, slaves throughout the colonial period.

Reinforced by a strong belief in British racial and cultural superiority, the British system enslaved black people in perpetuity, altered African gender, and kinship relationships in the colonies. It was one factor that led the British colonists into violent confrontations with native peoples.

While slavery and the slave trade expanded, Europeans elaborated on racial ideas, which served to legitimize the unprecedented use of fellow humans in new and more brutal forms of slavery. Blacks were typically portrayed as not only inferior and savage but often as subhuman or a different species of humans altogether. These notions justified the introduction of chattel slavery, in which slaves were treated entirely as property.

Although these ideas evolved partially in response to economic developments, the English had often associated blackness with wickedness and death even before interactions with the African continent became common.

Historically, the English had fewer connections with Africa than Mediterranean peoples such as the Spanish and the French, and their ideas about black people were often rooted in legends and outrageous tales about demons and monsters rather than personal interaction.

Power and ideology allowed slave masters control of slave families. Slave owners often preferred to purchase male slaves, but since these were also in demand in the Caribbean, the mainland colonies ended up with a greater balance of women and men than elsewhere. Sometimes slave women were brought in to provide companionship for male slaves, or more strategically, to ensure the reproduction of the slave population.

In slavery, Africans saw their accustomed gender roles and kinship structures challenged or fundamentally changed. Men were forced to hoe the fields, a task reserved for women in West Africa. Both men and women performed their work as part of the owner's commercial plan rather than to feed their families, to the extent they were even allowed to have families. Although masters often encouraged procreation, they viewed slaves as property, meaning their rights as spouses and parents were severely limited or even non-existent.

African women, who saw the role of mother as the most important of all, experienced tremendous physical and mental anguish from constant demands that they not only bear children at regular intervals but return to the fields quickly after that.

Furthermore, the pregnancies were often the result of rape by the master or someone in the household. Obligations toward children limited opportunities to resist or attempt to escape, and the breakup of families was a common form of disciplinary action against slaves who were considered unruly.

Slave auction

Notions of superiority and inferiority also affected the relationships between white settlers and indigenous people. The New England Puritans believed that the Indians had been lured into settling in the New World by Satan to lead them away from God.

When epidemics broke out among the Indians due to the introduction of European diseases, they took this as confirmation that God favored them and meant to punish the natives. Even brutal warfare and outright massacres were justified in the same way and seen as righteous actions in the name of the Lord.

Africans used overt, and covert means to resist the dehumanizing aspects of slavery.

Despite the fear of violent retribution, slaves sometimes managed to demonstrate their agency by resisting slavery in various ways. These included "passive" acts of resistance: avoiding work, pretending to be sick, and ignoring the commands of masters and overseers. More direct forms of resistance included destroying equipment, organizing slowdowns, and even severe attempts to confront the power of owners such as arson, large-scale sabotage, and murder.

Another way of resisting was simply running away. Typically, running away was a negotiation tactic. Slaves hoped that by disappearing and avoiding their work, if only briefly, they might convince their owners to improve the terms and conditions of their enslavement.

Although slave owners, in principle, had full control over their property, the humanity and agency of the slaves forced them to bargain about the pace and amount of work to be completed and many other aspects of slaves' lives.

Some slaves also attempted to run away for good. The slaves who ran away had often served in roles that allowed them to leave the plantation on occasion, providing them with more familiarity with the outside world.

In colonial times, they often headed to cities with a free black population or swamps, forests, and other inhospitable areas where they would be challenging to find. If there were numerous runaways in an area, they sometimes managed to form Maroon communities, which helped them elude capture or even violently confront search parties.

The most dramatic form of resistance, and one that was greatly feared by slaveholders, was rebellion or armed uprising. Such conspiracies and insurrections were more common on the Caribbean islands, where blacks often represented an overwhelming majority of the population and where large numbers of Africans with a common culture and language were sometimes brought in within a short period. However, they also occurred in both the northern and southern colonies on the North American mainland.

The most massive colonial uprising was the Stono Rebellion of 1739. On the mainland, rebellions were usually doomed from the outset, as reinforcements could always be brought in to subdue the slaves and execute anyone believed to have been involved.

Also, slaveholders did their best to divide and conquer slave populations by differentiating between light and dark skin, house slaves, field slaves, plantation slaves, or family farm slaves. This prevented slaves from building the kind of cohesion and unity required to carry out mass uprisings.

European colonization efforts in North America stimulated intercultural contact and intensified conflict between the groups of colonizers and native peoples.

Indian trade with the Europeans, and with it, access to European goods and technologies offered new lifestyles, new status symbols, and new ways of waging war. Better tools, weapons, and household goods were significant advantages that could tilt the balance of a preexisting rivalry between tribes in favor of those most closely connected to the white newcomers.

These opportunities also induced indigenous people in French, English, and Dutch territories to increase their trapping activities, as furs were highly sought after in Europe.

For these reasons, Indians often thought it beneficial to maintain a working relationship with European settlers, despite the disruptive effects of a disease, the introduction of new flora and fauna, and the outright expropriation of land. Thus, early colonial relations were often a mix of cooperation and intermittent conflict.

The rapid and continuous increase of the white population and the corresponding quest to control land and other natural resources inevitably created tensions that, at times, erupted into murder, massacre, skirmishes, and war.

In the long run, Indian resistance tended to be futile, as wars typically ended in defeat and the surrender of rights and land. As white settlement moved beyond the coastline, conflicts intensified and multiplied as both Indian refugees, and European colonists encountered and confronted the tribes of the interior.

Continuing contact with Europeans increased the flow of trade goods and diseases into and out of native communities, stimulating cultural and demographic changes.

There are many examples of the changes wrought by social contact. The Catawba people, once a formidable tribe in the Southeast, were so devastated by 18th-century smallpox epidemics that most of its members died, and the rest had to accept a settlement on a small reservation in South Carolina.

Similarly, the Huron tribes in present-day Ontario succumbed to epidemics in the 1630s and then in the 1640s came under attack by the Iroquois Confederacy, which was trying to secure control of new territories and replace members who had died from the European diseases.

The Hurons, initially farmers who had been drawn into the fur trade by their French allies, were dispersed, some joining the Iroquois and others making desperate attempts to resettle in new lands. By that time, however, most of the Huron population had died.

King Philip, or Metacomet, 1638-1676

Like the Hurons, who divided into traditional and pro-colonist factions at the time of their collapse, the Wampanoags ended up devastated by disease and war and failed to preserve much of their identity and culture, which had been challenged by contact with Massachusetts colonists. The Wampanoags, who eased the colonists' transition to America and are remembered in the celebration of Thanksgiving, initially forged peaceful relationships with the white settlers to access trade goods and win allies against their Indian enemies.

Eventually, the leader of the Wampanoags, King Philip (1638-1676), concluded that the influence of the colonists—especially the spread of Christianity and the hunger for land—was detrimental to traditional Indian culture. King Philip initiated a bloody conflict with the English colonists in 1675 that lasted till 1678. The consequences of the war mostly harmed the Wampanoags and allied tribes; despite heavy losses, the English successfully defended their settlements. Thousands of Indians were killed, died from disease, or were sold into slavery.

The increasing political, economic, and cultural exchanges within the "Atlantic World" had a profound impact on the colonial societies in North America.

The concept of an "Atlantic World" is used to describe the complex exchanges between Western Europe, West Africa, and the colonies in the Americas. In numerous areas, including not only the political, military, legal, and economic histories but also the demographic, social, cultural, and intellectual histories of this megaregion, national boundaries were transcended by international cross-cultural exchanges.

The many connections between different points in the Atlantic World developed in a complicated web of exchanges that often transcended the scope of any national or colonial government's authority. The development of chattel slavery, religious awakenings, trade expansion, epidemics, environmental change, and even colonialism itself should be seen in this light.

Thousands of ships carried millions of men and women, including explorers, soldiers, officials, traders, farmers, preachers, laborers, servants, and slaves from Europe and Africa to the Americas. They brought precious metals, agricultural commodities, furs, pioneers and colonists, who may or may not have been successful, across the Atlantic.

Every journey brought a new set of encounters and reshaped the cultures of both the Americas and the Old-World continents, connecting millions of lives in time and space.

The presence of slavery and the impact of colonial wars stimulated the growth of ideas on race in this Atlantic system, leading to the emergence of racial stereotyping and the development of strict racial categories among British colonists, which contrasted with Spanish and French acceptance of racial gradations.

In the 18th century, the difference in racial ideas between Spanish, French, and British colonizers persisted. The Spanish continued to rely on complex hierarchies of status and power where mixed-race individuals such as mulattoes and mestizos were viewed differently from blacks and Indians.

A caste system provided each person with a social status depending on their specific mix of European, African, and indigenous descent. Such subtleties did not exist in the British colonies, where mulattoes were mostly the same as blacks, and mestizos were rare and lacked the special status of intermediaries between colonists and natives.

In the French model, Indians and Métis could even be "natural" subjects of France and part of that community. This reflected the lack of French settlement in New France and the corresponding dependence on Indian or mixed-race intermediaries in building commercial ties and brokering alliances.

Race became extraordinarily central in the version of slavery that evolved in British North America. In other times and places, slaves and masters had often come from the same racial background. This meant that some slaves could be freed and become integrated into society on equal terms, but this was not possible in the colonies.

There, slavery became intimately tied to differences in racial characteristics, leading to lasting segregation and inequality. Since black slaves were "chattel," the law in practice defined white people as human beings and black people as things or property.

French Métis

As regional distinctiveness among the British colonies diminished over time, they developed broadly similar patterns of culture, laws, institutions, and governance within the context of the British imperial system.

Colonization involved adaptation to a new environment, a process of building new institutions, and creative transformations of cultural practices. The simple and in many ways different colonial societies of the 17th century became more complex and similar in the 18th century.

Subject to many of the same regulations, political institutions, and laws, the colonies found commonalities that they could eventually use to present a more united front against the British government. This happened despite the lack of any real movement away from British culture and political thought in the colonies. Instead, it was the collective experience within the imperial system that made understanding and cooperation possible.

One of the main reasons for cultural convergence was the spread of print culture. The printing presses in the colonies, along with materials imported from Britain, supplied both literary and more popular written works in vast numbers at very reasonable prices.

Poems, sheets of music, chapbooks, and stories about robbers and pirates were exceedingly popular. At the same time, the rapid spread of literacy meant that colonial Americans were also reading about politics, history, and religion, coming together as a kind of unified reading public.

The educational system that taught people how to read also created a sense of uniformity, even though there were significant differences between the colonies. In New England, education was especially valued, as the Puritans saw illiteracy and ignorance as to the work of the devil.

In the middle colonies, education involved more practical considerations, teaching boys work-related skills in addition to reading, math, and religious subjects. In the South, schooling was more rudimentary, except for the children of aristocrats who could afford to hire tutors and governesses.

Puritan, Massachusetts, c. 1640s

Education equipped most white males in the colonies with the tools needed to stay informed about outside events and develop a sense of identity transcending the family and the local community, thus facilitating communication with like-minded people elsewhere in the vast colonial empire.

CULTURAL AND INTELLECTUAL DEVELOPMENTS:

Early Colonization to 1789

Native peoples and Africans in the Americas strove to maintain their political and cultural autonomy in the face of European challenges to their independence and core beliefs. European attempts to change American Indian beliefs and worldviews on underlying social issues such as religion, gender roles within the family, and the relationship of people with the natural environment led to American Indian resistance and conflict.

A fundamental justification for the Spanish conquest of the New World was the Christianization of the Indian population and its adoption of Spanish values and ways of life. An excellent example of the challenges involved in this program in New Mexico, founded in 1598 when Juan de Oñate, the scion of a wealthy mining family, established a colony in the upper Rio Grande Valley. At the time, the Pueblo Indians in the area lived in villages called pueblos, and Franciscan missionaries built mission churches on the outskirts of these existing villages. By 1680, they had established thirty missions and a similar number of religious stations in the region.

The relationship between the Pueblo and the Spanish was always strained. As many as twenty thousand Pueblos converted to Christianity, they adopted Christian marriage and burials and participated in feast day processions and other rituals. While the Pueblos were baptized, attended church, and accepted communion. They also continued to perform traditional religious ceremonies considered anathema by the Spanish.

Spaniards destroying Mexican idols

The Franciscan missionaries were frequently outraged by such transgressions. They would seek to punish indigenous beliefs and behaviors by desecrating shrines, destroying religious objects, and imposing corporal punishment on traditional religious leaders. The Pueblos were forced to build new churches and to pay tribute to the *encomenderos* who were supposed to offer military protection from warlike tribes in the region.

By the 1630s, the Pueblos erupted in rebellion against the Spanish colonizers and their assault on the Indian way of life. In the following decades, tensions continued to mount as epidemics, drought, poor harvests, and raids by the Apache and the Navajo negated the anticipated march to progress.

In the 1670s, a missionary accused Indian villagers of witchcraft, and some Pueblos were executed or flogged. By the 1680s, the Pueblos' discontent was unleashed in a rebellion of unprecedented scale and ferocity.

Led by a victim of religious persecution, the Indians sought to remove every trace of the European way of life. They killed their livestock and cut down their trees, and took river baths to wash away the effects of baptism. Many missionaries were killed, and the city of Santa Fe laid to waste. Almost 400 people were killed in the uprising, and it took twelve years before the Spanish returned.

By that time, some of the Pueblos welcomed the Spanish. They wanted the Spaniards to protect them against enemy raiders and to regain the benefits of trading with the Europeans, who had access to goods otherwise not available. The Spanish also decided to reach a new understanding with the Pueblos.

The *encomienda* system was no more, and fewer labor demands were made. They granted land to the Pueblo villages, and appointed an advocate to protect their rights and argue their cases in court. Even the Franciscans became more tolerant, avoiding the subject of traditional Pueblo ceremonies as long as they were performed in secret. In general, the Spanish colonizers attempted to define norms and roles in the new colonial societies.

New notions of gender were constructed in the context of the Roman Catholic family and religious structure. Spanish women were seen as naturally more virtuous and valuable than others; their virginity was "protected," and a woman's adultery was punishable by death. The women of other races or mixed-blood were seen as having exotic bodies.

The women of other races or mixed-blood could also be portrayed as innocent mothers and wives in the mold of the Virgin Mary. However, they were more typically regarded as highly sexual beings, seductive, and available for Spanish men.

The Spanish sometimes married indigenous women, and even more frequently had sexual relationships with them, often resulting in mixed-race offspring. Thus many never became "proper" mothers and wives but rather mistresses raising illegitimate children. Latin American life had a strong flavor of patriarchy, a system women could only escape by joining a convent.

Despite slavery, Africans' cultural and linguistic adaptations to the Western Hemisphere resulted in varying degrees of cultural preservation and autonomy.

The Middle Passage, or the slave voyage to the Americas, was a traumatic experience for the slaves. After being captured, they could be branded, shackled, forced to walk long distances, and confined to dark dungeons for long periods even before they boarded ships where filth, disease, and abuse were the order of the day. Some chose to commit suicide either before or during the long journey to the Americas. Despite these traumas, Africans were also able to keep some of their culture, language, belief systems, traditions, and memories. Some even organized rebellions and took control of slave ships.

Differences between European cultures as well as the various origins of the slaves in Africa and the environmental settings of the Americas meant that slave societies differed considerably from each other, but there were many similarities as well. Every slave system differentiated between African-born slaves and American-born descendants. Status systems also evolved with hierarchies where free whites were at the top, slaves at the bottom and free people of color, often mixed-race, held an intermediate position.

Color and "race" played a role in American slavery; it had not played in Africa. Slaveholders gave American-born slaves more opportunities to acquire skills and perform domestic duties, especially if they were mixed race—often a consequence of abuse or sexual relationships between slave women and male members of the slaveholding family. They were less likely to do the excruciatingly mindnumbing and backbreaking work in the fields and mines, and more likely to be given their freedom by masters, a process of liberation called manumission.

Sugar plantation

This system, created by those who owned slaves, did not necessarily correspond with notions of status among the slaves themselves. Africans who had been nobles or fetish priests in their homelands sometimes continued to exercise authority, or at least influence, within the community of slaves. The differences in origin, birth, and color did tend to split slave communities along racial and ethnic lines, which slaveholders usually saw as an advantage. After all, they did not want the slaves to be capable of collective action on their terms.

In the Americas, Africans kept at least some features of their traditional cultures alive, whether language, art, or traditional practices and beliefs. The exact level of continuity was very variable, depending on the extent to which members of the same tribe were transported together in sufficient numbers to obtain a critical mass. Ongoing connections between the Old World and the New also enabled slaves to maintain their culture over time.

Yoruba culture, for example, virtually flourished in northeastern Brazil due to the frequent trade contacts with the Bight of Benin. Members of the various Akan groups were predominant in Jamaica, while Ewes were plentiful in Haiti. Slaveholders could make efforts to obtain a mix of slaves from different ethnic groups, but the regular patterns of the slave trade often undermined such efforts.

Despite Africans' hopes of retaining their identities, the brutal facts of reality indicated that they had to adapt and change. They also had to be open to developing new forms of culture based on the heterogeneity of cultures on diverse plantations. Also, they had to bow down to the culture and manners of the slaveowners, so that the new Afro-American cultures reflected adaptions of African cultures to American realities. In this sense, the new cultures were dynamic and creative, but their development was, of course, by no means free or unfettered.

Religion was one crucial aspect of a culture where both forced adaptation and creative syncretism occurred. The Spanish and Portuguese colonists and missionaries were eager to convert Africans to Catholicism, and some slaves also became very devout Christians. They even organized in new Catholic fraternities divided by African origins. Still, beliefs and practices carried from Africa remained important and raised the ire of the Inquisition, which investigated paganism, heresy, and demonic deeds. Africans were frequently accused of witchcraft.

In the English islands, Africans continued to perform religious rituals rooted in African tradition. These practices were called obeah, and those who served as ceremonial leaders had high status in the slave communities. Similarly, religions derived primarily from African sources, such as candomblé and Vodun, remain significant to this day in Brazil and Haiti, respectively. They have survived centuries of attempted suppression.

It was easier to bring beliefs and customs across the Atlantic than religious institutions. Without a class of clergy or religious specialists, most aspects of religion were subject to change in a new and extremely challenging setting. Slaves often held both Christian and traditional beliefs simultaneously or attempted a syncretic fusion of the two.

For Muslim Africans, this was far more difficult. As late as the 19th century, a significant slave rebellion among Muslim slaves of Hausa and Yoruba origins targeted both whites and infidel blacks.

While the drudgery, brutality, and isolation of plantation slavery certainly discouraged it, resistance and rebellion were nevertheless an import feature of black history in the Americas. Wherever there were slaves, there were people evading work, running away, or even directly confronting owners and overseers. From the outset in the early 16th century, slaves in Spanish America disrupted communications, plotted rebellions, and sought other ways to subvert or escape authority. Communities of runaways formed throughout the Americas, and such communities, especially flourished in Colombia, Venezuela, Brazil, and some of the islands in the Caribbean. Some of these communities became veritable towns or small kingdoms.

For example, 17th century Palmares (in Brazil) contained numerous villages and possibly as many as 10,000 inhabitants. This society of runaways was made up of both African and American-born slaves, organized and led by Angolans. They successfully fought back against Portuguese and Dutch aggression for a century. Similarly, the "Maroons" of Jamaica managed not only to break away from their chains but also to be recognized as a virtually independent community.

Slave rebellions organized by African ethnic groups were a regular feature of life in the Caribbean and Brazil. In North America, where slave survival and reproduction rates were higher, and the American-born contingent correspondingly larger, such rebellions based on ethnic unity were much more challenging to orchestrate. Nevertheless, other, more subtle forms of resistance were an essential part of slave existence in North America as well.

In Suriname, large numbers of runaways fought a protracted war against the authorities in the 18th century. Despite the brutal prosecution of the war by slaveowners and the government, the war eventually came to a standstill, and the Maroons were able to create a kind of separate society based on West African cultural forms fused with the ways of Europeans and Indians, a new and genuinely Afro-American culture. Today, many descendants of these runaways live in Suriname and French Guiana, still maintaining some of their traditions, customs, and beliefs.

The New England colonies, founded primarily by Puritans seeking to establish a community of like-minded religious believers, developed a close-knit, homogenous society and—aided by favorable environmental conditions—a thriving mixed economy of agriculture and commerce.

Both economic and religious factors motivated the founding of the New England colonies (Massachusetts, Connecticut, Rhode Island, and New Hampshire). Unlike the Spanish colonies—where missionaries set out to spread the official religion of the home country—the New England colonies were settled by religious dissenters.

The religious dissenters were mostly Puritans, who had sought to purify the church at home but decided instead that they would have to create a new society across the Atlantic. They took an "errand into the wilderness" to show the world a "city upon the hill," an ideal community for other Christians to observe and eventually emulate.

The Puritan settlement was remarkable in that a large number of people—20,000 in the 1630s alone—arrived there in a time when crossing the Atlantic was a significant endeavor in terms of both cost and safety and the conditions in the promised land very uncertain. Before long, they had founded numerous towns and set up churches on their favored Congregationalist model, which, in contrast to the Church of England, allowed each church substantial autonomy. Attending church was mandatory, but only a select few, the "saints," were church members.

As Calvinists, the Puritans believed that every individual was predestined for either salvation or damnation, and they developed elaborate tests and procedures to make sure that only the former group was recognized as members of the church. This was important because Massachusetts was a theocratic society in which only church members could vote in elections, individual morality was heavily regulated, and dissenting views could be punished by death or banishment from the colony.

One of those banished was Roger Williams, who considered religion a private matter and wanted to separate church and state and make church attendance voluntary. After being exiled, he founded Providence and was able to start a new colony in Rhode Island.

Unlike the other New England colonies, Rhode Island became known as a land of religious freedom. Among the Puritan colonies, Connecticut was somewhat more open to religious diversity than Massachusetts, as it did not limit voting rights to church members.

Roger Williams building his house in Rhode Island, c. 1636

Despite the hierarchical division of people based on religious factors, colonial New England was a relatively egalitarian society for its time. Most of the inhabitants lived on small farms where they produced much of what they needed for themselves.

Their religious beliefs indicated that God had called them to do hard work, and that material success was a sign of divine favor. For these reasons, the Puritans strove to improve their material lot and engaged in a variety of crafts and trades.

The colonial economy grew, and the average standard of living was quite high, even though New England crops such as barley, oats, and rye were also produced in Europe and not in high demand as exports.

Growth was supported by active provincial and local governments that worked to improve the infrastructure of the region and even subsidized the building of mills and other early manufacturing works. The legal system was adapted to capitalist development by securing the sanctity of contracts and property rights. New England became famous for its entrepreneurial spirit.

Clashes between European and American Indian social and economic values caused changes in both cultures.

Indian culture was forced to change by the advent of Europeans, at first merely by the force of disastrous epidemics and dramatic population decline. Later, the ways of the Europeans altered Indian practices at a deeper level. Indigenous people were encouraged to fight wars against each other to capture slaves for white buyers, and the goods they received in return, such as alcohol, caused not only cultural change but also dependence and social problems.

Indians were also encouraged to hunt animals such as deer for their pelts only, rather than focusing on food needs. This led to the overhunting of game. Similarly, European land use put vast tracts under monoculture, eliminating other uses for the area and exhausting the soil. Thus, European influence had a tremendous impact on the Indian way of life.

At the same time, Indian culture also influenced the European colonists. This is especially true of the Spanish colonies, where widespread intermixing of races led to a parallel mixing of cultural, social, and economic values. The British settlers also adopted aspects of Indian culture, most importantly, the system for raising corn.

Styles of artistic expression were also influenced both ways. Colonial officials expressed considerable concern about their subjects "going native" by adopting Indian lifestyles, especially in the case of whites who had been captured in raids or war.

In many cases, long-time captives refused to return to what the colonists thought of as civilized life instead of running away from settlements to rejoin their captors.

Spanish colonizing efforts in North America, particularly after the Pueblo Revolt, saw accommodation with some aspects of American Indian culture. By contrast, conflict with American Indians reinforced the English colonists' worldviews on land and gender roles.

After the Pueblo Revolt, Spanish colonial officials used heavy-handed tactics to squelch new insurgencies, but their overall strategy was higher accommodation of Indian culture. The activities of the Franciscan missionaries were restrained, and the Pueblo were able to worship according to their tradition and perform their rituals. They were also granted land, and a Spanish lawyer was sent to serve their interests in courts of law. Similarly, after a joint Spanish and Pueblo force were able to strike a decisive blow against nomadic Comanche raiders, finally, the colonial government in New Mexico sought peaceful coexistence rather than the destruction of the tribe.

In contrast, the English colonists often failed to accommodate native interests, primarily because the English were so numerous and so eager to secure new lands for farming and other activities. Their entrenched view of their superiority also made the English inclined to push their values and culture on neighboring peoples.

The "praying towns" instituted by the Puritans in New England were meant to convert Indians not only to Christianity but more broadly sought a full conversion to a European way of life. They insisted that Indians should be farmers rather than hunters and gatherers and should adjust their clothing, hairstyles, manners, and family relations to a European norm. Women lost much of the stature and influence they previously possessed in traditional settings. This wholesale conversion to a new way of life was very different from the methods of the French Jesuits in Canada, who tolerated syncretism—a mix of Christian and native rituals and practices—in their conversion efforts.

Several factors promoted Anglicization in the British colonies: the growth of autonomous political communities based on English models, the development of commercial ties and legal structures, the emergence of transatlantic print culture, Protestant evangelism, religious toleration, and the spread of European Enlightenment ideas.

Starting in the late 17th century, the diversity and novelty of the individual British colonies on the North American mainland began to disappear in some ways. Colonists had adjusted to the climate and health risks and found ways to sustain growing populations with food. Families became more European in structure, and even warfare became more European, increasingly focused on colonial rivals rather than Indians. The Crown began to take a greater interest in the far-off colonies and imposed a more coherent legal and political structure on them. The colonies became increasingly anglicized, meaning that they came to resemble England to a higher degree.

The colonies also became more cosmopolitan as more urbanization was taking place, and information from the Old and New Worlds could be gathered from pamphlets and newspapers due to the spread of print culture. However, this was less prevalent in the

South, home of the slave plantations, than in the North, home of colleges, seminaries, and law schools. The southern elite outwardly emulated the English elite, but their way of life was fundamentally different. At the same time, they were still dependent on their commercial ties with England.

Across the colonies, the dominant elites were beginning to depart from their original projects, utopian or not, and express admiration for the workings of the British system of government. Colonial intellectuals absorbed the discourse of leading British writers on politics, law, and religion. They saw themselves as British patriots and fought wars against the Spanish and French with remarkable enthusiasm and imperial fervor. European innovations in religious thought inspired even the religious revivals, and American thinkers familiarized themselves with the classical liberalism of John Locke as well as the great minds of the French and Scottish Enlightenment.

Even before the influence of Enlightenment freethinkers, some colonies began to expand religious toleration in a bid to welcome a variety of immigrants rather than trying to create a new society where everyone shared the same beliefs, as had been the case most prominently in Massachusetts.

Rhode Island was founded in explicit opposition to the Puritans' zeal for persecuting dissenters, and the foundation of Maryland also coincided with an articulation of principles of religious tolerance. However, the Maryland Toleration Act did not go as far as Rhode Island, as only Christians who believed in the Trinity were accepted. The primary purpose of religious toleration in Maryland was to secure a haven for English Catholics in the New World.

William Penn, 1644-1718

In Pennsylvania, founder William Penn allowed migrants of all faiths to settle. He and his fellow Quakers were convinced that people should find God in their way, and unlike the other colonies, no official church was established in Pennsylvania.

Penn believed that religious toleration would ensure peace and prosperity in the new colony and invited persecuted groups to leave Europe behind and find freedom in the New World. Religious freedom did not mean religious equality. Only Christians could participate in politics as voters or officeholders.

Resistance to imperial control in the British colonies drew on colonial experiences of self-government, evolving local ideas of liberty, the political thought of the Enlightenment, greater religious independence and diversity, and an ideology critical of perceived corruption in the imperial system.

In addition to the long history of salutary neglect on the part of the Crown, leading to a long-standing tradition of self-government and relative autonomy in the colonies, colonial thinkers also applied Enlightenment ideas to the question of colonists' rights against the king. They were suspicious of authority, and often embraced the notion of popular sovereignty—the people as the source of authority—proposed by John Locke.

Locke, writing in the late 17th century, believed that government was a result of a contract between the people and those in power, a social contract that created and maintained society. Unlike some previous writers, Locke held that such social contracts always had limits because some of the rights of the people, such as life and liberty, were "inalienable rights" and could not be given away.

John Locke, 1632-1704

The doctrine of the divine right of kings suggested that the monarch could not be subjected to any authority on Earth and answered only to God.

Power, according to this theory, came from God, and the people had no right to judge or depose the king, no matter how disappointed they might be with his decisions or how his representatives committed many travesties.

Any attempt to do so would be turning away from God since the king ruled by God's grace. In 18th-century America, the government was something created by man rather than ordained by God. The king had no divine right to rule, and his actual role was to serve the people and preserve their liberties—not only in the home country but in the colonies as well.

In addition to the influence of new political ideas came the complicated religious situation in America. The colonies represented a variety of religious projects and a spirit of denominational competition. This, too, drew on a long tradition of questioning the authority of established churches and dissent in matters of thought and belief. This contributed to the general anti-authoritarian mindset of the mid-18th century, especially after the tremendous success of the evangelical Great Awakening.

The Great Awakening was an outburst of emotionally charged revivals across many of the British colonies in North America in the 1730s and 1740s. It broke away from the theological boundaries, social hierarchies, and traditional rituals of Protestant Christianity by introducing a new brand of much more individualistic and personal faith.

This personal faith was based on stirring sermons, strongly felt belief, and a deep need for salvation and redemption, leading in turn to further quests for introspection, moral improvement, and compelling religious experiences. The Great Awakening had a lasting impact not only on religious affairs but stimulated new ways of thinking about politics and social issues as well.

Interior of Christ Church, Boston

Resistance to perceived excesses on the part of the British government also drew on the ideology of republicanism. Republican thought, originating in the ancient world and the Renaissance, came to America through English Republicans who saw the virtue of the citizenry rather than the judgment of the king as the best guarantee for a prosperous and free commonwealth.

Republicans saw power as essentially corruptible and feared the tendency of all governments to culminate in tyranny unless vigilant citizens watched them. While placing a new emphasis on freedom and civic virtue, this line of thinking also instilled Republicans with a certain paranoia and a tendency to develop conspiracy theories.

According to American Republicans of the 18th century, politics must be seen as a continuing struggle between freedom and power. Power must always be kept in check for the people to maintain their liberties because it would otherwise be prone to aggression and corruption. Therefore, any just and virtuous society is dependent on the civic engagement of engaged citizens.

In extreme cases, virtue would have to mean not only opposition and protest but also an armed revolution against the ruling government. Every man of substance, that is to say, every property owner should be able to carry arms if necessary, to stave off the abuses of ambitious kings. Republicans were especially concerned about the use of military force and taxes as instruments of imperial aggrandizement.

DIPLOMACY and INTERNATIONAL RELATIONS:

Early Colonization to 1789

Spain sought to establish control over the process of colonization in the Western Hemisphere and to convert or exploit the native population.

The voyages of Columbus soon turned into a diplomatic issue. The lands Columbus had found were south of the Canary Islands (outside the northwesternmost part of Africa) and thus conceivably reserved for the Portuguese under the 1479 Treaty of Alcáçovas. Ferdinand and Isabella hurried to secure their claim by seeking support from the pope, who proposed a western boundary for Portuguese claims.

This eventually led to the Treaty of Tordesillas, signed in 1494, which divided Castilian and Portuguese claims along a north-south line, 370 leagues, west of the Cape Verde Islands. This would eventually justify the Portuguese claim to Brazil and the Spanish claims elsewhere in the Americas, as the treaty formally divided the non-European world between Spain and Portugal.

Queen Isabella of Castile (left) and King Ferdinand V of Aragon (right)

As early as the peace treaty signed by France and Spain in 1559, the two parties agreed that attacks west of the Azores or south of the Tropic of Cancer should not be a reason for war in Europe.

In practice, this meant that all colonial areas were subject to continual warfare outside the customary rules of a declaration of war, Christian ideas of "just war." Spain reserved the right to attack anyone trading in the Caribbean, and the other nations reserved the right to attack and capture the Spanish treasure fleets. Outside Europe, anything was fair game. This principle became known as "no peace beyond the line."

The English started their American involvement as privateers and smugglers in the 16th century. After 1600, they set up several colonies on the mainland of North America and in the Caribbean, disregarding Spanish claims. In 1655, they even took Jamaica, a colony already set up by Spain. In 1670, the Spanish finally faced reality and recognized the English settlements as legitimate.

This ended the anarchic era of "no peace beyond the line," and it became possible to some extent to distinguish between pirates and lawful traders. This was not the end of piracy; on the contrary, the first half-century after 1670 is often considered the golden age of pirates and buccaneers.

An example of the sometimes-chaotic colonial rivalry between the European powers before 1670 was the early white settlement in Florida. The first colonial outpost there was established by the French in 1564, with the specific purpose of attacking Spanish treasure galleons sailing past. The following year, a Spanish expeditionary force was sent out to destroy the settlement, and the Spanish commander ordered summary executions of the surrendering Frenchmen.

A few years later, in 1573–74, the Spanish government changed its policies toward the Americas, deciding that the church, rather than the military, should be the chief representative of the Crown in the Americas. Part of the rationale behind this new policy was that the missionaries would be less ruthless and exploitative in their dealings with the indigenous people.

However, the Franciscan missions in 17th-century Florida turned out to have hugely disruptive effects on the Indians. They now had to live in mission villages and become full-time farmers, incorporating European crops and animals into a new way of life. They were very vulnerable to the diseases brought by the colonists, resulting in many deaths and a steady decline in population. Military assaults by English and French forces further destroyed the population.

French and Dutch colonial efforts involved relatively few Europeans and used trade alliances and intermarriage with American Indians to acquire furs and other products for export to Europe.

The French sent numerous explorers to North America and made pioneering discoveries around the Great Lakes and in the Mississippi Valley, founding settlements from Quebec and Montreal in the North to New Orleans and Baton Rouge in the South.

Peopling these settlements proved a tremendous challenge. The Company of New France (Canada) failed to bring the promised number of colonists across the Atlantic. The imposition of direct royal rule in 1660 did make a difference, but these areas were never able to compete with the English colonies in terms of population.

Instead, they became mostly dependent on friendly Indian tribes militarily, commercially, and regarding finding wives for French men. Indians who joined the settlements were legally accepted as French and, in principle, eligible to take up residence in France itself without any process of naturalization. Despite the French efforts to invite Indian partners and allies, the lack of actual colonists gave France a severe disadvantage in the colonial rivalry with England.

Indians at a Hudson Bay Company trading

After 1660, competition between French and English colonists over the lucrative fur trade escalated. The English challenged the monopoly of the French by chartering the Hudson Bay Company, while at the same time, French and mixed-race individual traders also sought to circumvent regulations. Eventually, a system emerged that wealthy merchants in Montreal were able to send out licensed traders far and wide to procure furs.

Most of the actual trapping continued to be done by the Indians, and the fur trade played a significant part in the many wars between the Great Lakes tribes throughout this period. Thus, the European competition over the furs of beavers and other animals, due in significant part to the popularity of beaver hats across the Atlantic, ended up severely destabilizing a vast region in the Americas.

The expansion of fur trading and exploration into the Mississippi Valley led to the foundation of the vast colony of Louisiana, stretching in parts the entire north-south length of the present-day United States and from the Rockies to the Appalachians.

The lack of easily accessible natural resources and the failure of the French government to provide the infrastructure, commercial facilities, and physical safety necessary to make the colony attractive for settlement meant that few Europeans chose to migrate there.

The Dutch in New Netherland (encompassing present-day New York and parts of the surrounding states) were also primarily interested in the fur trade. Like the French, they relied to a great extent on building alliances and trading with the local Algonquian and Iroquois tribes. The port of New Amsterdam, today's New York City, became a vital hub for exporting furs and other American commodities to Europe.

The Dutch West India Company tried to support colonization and population growth by granting vast tracts of land to so-called *patroons* who would, in turn, invite immigrants to become tenant farmers on their land, but this policy was only moderately successful. After the Anglo-Dutch wars of the 1660s–70s, New Netherland was ceded to the English.

The Dutch trading with the Indians

The goals and interests of European leaders at times diverged from those of colonial citizens, leading to growing mistrust on both sides of the Atlantic, as settlers, especially in the English colonies, expressed dissatisfaction over territorial settlements, frontier defense, and other issues.

Colonial subjects were often dissatisfied with their European rulers, who saw the colonies primarily as a source of resources and revenues for the mother country. They especially complained about the distribution of lands and occasional failures to protect vulnerable settlements against European rivals or hostile indigenous people.

Also, they often circumvented laws and taxation by smuggling goods from one colony to another, thereby weakening the grip of the European powers.

The fur trade is an essential example of this latter tendency because of its significance to Indians, colonists, and European governments. While governments tried to control the fur trade and introduce monopolies, widespread smuggling occurred in and between the English, French, and Dutch colonies.

The same thing happened with tobacco from the Chesapeake colonies; it is sometimes suggested that the amount of tobacco smuggled was at least equal to the amount of tobacco exported through approved channels. Some settlements in the Caribbean were created with smuggling as their primary purpose.

European governments sought to limit the colonial production of commodities that could be made in the home country. In England, the 1699 Wool Act prohibited American colonies from exporting wool or yarn and cloth made from wool to Britain, and it also restricted trade in wool between the colonies. At other times, governments could issue regulations that favored their colonies over those of their rivals, or some colonies at the expense of others.

The Molasses Act of 1733 favored planters in the British West Indies by taxing molasses imports from the colonies of other countries. This legislation favored sugar growers in the British colonies.

The Molasses Act of 1733 was very harmful to the interests of New England and the middle colonies since they had grown accustomed to buying less expensive molasses from French, Spanish, and Dutch possessions.

This favoritism demonstrated that many British leaders considered the West Indian colonies more critical to the imperial economy than the mainland colonies.

Britain's victory over France in the imperial struggle for North America led to new conflicts among the British government, the North American colonists and American Indians, culminating in the creation of a new nation, the United States.

The continuing conflicts between Britain and France finally ended in a decisive British victory in the French and Indian War, forcing France to give up virtually all its possessions in North America.

Disputes over who should bear the costs of the lengthy war, as well as other matters that divided colonists and the imperial government, brought new tensions into play.

Both Brits and colonial Americans increasingly feared conspiracies on the other side, and the Crown's efforts to reassert control over the colonies after a long period of salutary neglect eventually prompted an armed rebellion and the Declaration of Independence (July 4, 1776) for the thirteen colonies.

First shot in the French and Indian War, May 27, 1754

Throughout the second half of the 18th century, American Indian groups repeatedly evaluated and adjusted their alliances with Europeans, other tribes, and the new U.S. government.

The French and Indian War (1754–1763) was the fourth in a series of conflicts between the British and the French in North America, all with significant participation by indigenous tribes.

Before the war broke out, much of the territory claimed by the two European powers was in effect controlled by Indians: the Mi'kmaq and the Abenaki, in what are now the borderlands between Canada and the eastern parts of the United States; the Iroquois along the Great Lakes and the Ohio River; Creeks, Choctaws and Cherokees in the South; the Huron, Ojibwa and other tribes in the Northwest, and so on.

The French and Indian War got its name because many of these tribes sided with the French. French allies included most of the Algonquian peoples to the north as well as many other tribes in what the United States is now.

In contrast, the leading Indian ally of the British was the Iroquois Confederacy. The Indians tended to favor the French because the much smaller French population constituted less of a threat to Indian livelihoods and behaved less aggressively toward Indian neighbors.

Some of the tribes were eventually convinced to remain neutral, following the British promises that white settlement in the interior would be limited after the war. These promises would later lead to increased tension between the British government and ambitious colonists who wanted to make use of these lands for their purposes.

The English population growth and expansion into the interior, disrupted the existing French Indian fur trade networks and caused Indian nations to shift alliances among the competing European powers.

Britain had been trying to tap into the fur trade in the French territories in North America since the 17th century. In the 1740s, tension intensified as traders from the British colonies crossed into the interior to trade with Indians in the Ohio Country, land which was claimed by France.

During King George's War, Britain imposed a moderately successful blockade on French trade to and from North America. As French traders lacked manufactured goods with which to purchase furs, British traders soon became dominant in the Ohio Valley. An expedition into this area, led by Pierre-Joseph Céloron, failed to reassert French dominance.

In the early 1750s, new French military and diplomatic expeditions were sent into the area in response to Indian recalcitrance and the British decision to assign lands in the West to an Ohio company. The French and Indian War began when George Washington, leading colonial troops and Indian allies, attacked a small scouting party under the leadership of Joseph Coulon de Jumonville.

By that time, the long-standing relationship between the Iroquois and British had become increasingly strained because of British claims to Indian lands. The Mohawk, one of the Iroquois tribes, had declared the "Covenant Chain" broken, leading to the Albany Congress in 1754, where representatives from several of the colonies tried to establish some form of cooperation to improve relationships with the Indians.

It was only the 1758 Treaty of Easton that succeeded in satisfying the Iroquois and other tribes under their suzerainty by establishing the Allegheny Mountains as a boundary for white settlement.

Sir William Johnson in treaty with the Mohawks in 1768

The Cherokees, long-standing allies of the British, revolted against the governments of Virginia and the Carolinas in 1758, after a long series of disappointments and misunderstandings. The Cherokees were not allying with the French, but fought a war, lasting till 1761, drawing thousands of British soldiers away from the northern theater.

After the British defeat of the French, white–Indian conflicts continued to erupt as native groups sought both to continue trading with Europeans and to resist the encroachment of British colonists on traditional tribal lands.

At the end of the French and Indian War, the British took over the forts in the Great Lakes area, and the Ohio country surrendered and abandoned by the French. The Indians in the region, especially those who had allied with the French, were treated as conquered people who had no say in the future development of the region.

This was true of the Algonquian tribes around the Great Lakes and the Huron, Illinois country tribes, such as the Miami and Kickapoo, and even some of the Ohio country tribes which had signed the Treaty of Easton. Also, one of the Iroquois tribes, the Seneca, had become unhappy with their alliance with the British.

Jeffrey Amherst (namesake of Amherst College), the British commander-in-chief in North America at the time, felt that the Indians were unlikely to be able to resist the British without the support of the French.

Consequently, he treated them with contempt, cut back on gift-giving and gunpowder sales, and left only very small garrisons to defend the forts. At the same time, a religious awakening broke out among the Indians, with the prophet Neolin urging indigenous people to avoid the bad habits and corrupting influence of Europeans altogether.

In 1763, when these tribes learned that France was prepared to give up their territorial claims in the region, widespread uprisings broke out, starting with the attack on Detroit by the Ottawa Chief Pontiac. The Indians failed to capture Fort Detroit and Fort Pitt (Pittsburgh), but took control of eight other forts in the next several months.

Although the conflict only lasted until the next year and ended in diplomatic accommodation, the relationship between colonists and Indians reached a new low as massacres were perpetrated and hatred stoked on both sides.

Pontiac's attack on Fort Detroit, July 31, 1763

The Royal Proclamation of 1763, reiterating the British government's commitment to keeping white settlement east of the mountains, had already been underway before Pontiac's Rebellion. The massive uprising created a new sense of urgency as officials scrambled to appease the Indians.

The idea was to (at least temporarily) separate colonists in the East from Indians west of the Appalachians, establishing what was termed an Indian reserve. Colonists now faced prohibitions against making private purchases of land west of the mountains; all land had to be purchased by the Crown after negotiations with the indigenous leaders.

Both speculators and prospective settlers among the colonists were disappointed with the proclamation, and some whites were already living beyond the boundaries established by the Crown. There was pressure on the British government to enter new negotiations with the Indians.

In 1768, treaties with the Cherokee and Iroquois granted the colonists access to lands in what is now Kentucky and West Virginia.

In response to domestic and international tensions, the new United States debated and formulated foreign policy initiatives and asserted an international presence.

The significant breakthrough for American diplomacy was the alliance with France, entered upon in 1778. Alliances with Spain and the Netherlands soon followed and turned the Revolutionary War into a war of great international significance. The efforts of Founding Fathers Benjamin Franklin (1706-1790), Thomas Jefferson (1743 to July 4, 1826), and John Adams (1735 to July 4, 1826) as diplomats were crucial for international recognition of the United States and securing financial and military support for the war effort.

In 1789, Jefferson became the first secretary of state under the new constitution. The need for coordinated and effective foreign policy was one of the reasons for creating a new constitution to replace the more decentralized Articles of Confederation.

The outbreak of the French Revolution in 1789 caused both international tensions and extensive debate within the United States. Many Americans were hoping for France to turn into a republic like the United States, and thus a natural ally against the monarchy in Britain.

However, the revolution in France was considerably more radical than in America. It entailed so much violence and demanded such drastic changes that some Americans were frightened.

A split occurred within the political elite, with Republicans taking the French side and Federalists supporting the British. President George Washington (1789-1797) sought to maintain a balance and was very wary of entangling the United States in European affairs.

By 1793, Britain had entered the international wars of revolutionary France. The United States remained neutral and managed to sign a treaty with the British, which strengthened commercial ties while securing the withdrawal of British forces from the forts in the Old Northwest. This treaty was designed by federalist leader Alexander Hamilton (c. 1755-1804) and vehemently opposed by the Jeffersonian Republicans.

Thomas Jefferson (left) and Alexander Hamilton (right)

While relations with Britain were improving, relations with France were increasingly hostile. The United States refused to make payments on its war debts, arguing that the debts were owed to the Kingdom of France and not to any Republican state.

Therefore, France allowed privateers to begin seizing American ships. Since the United States did not have a navy, hundreds of ships were taken without any effective response.

By 1798, the Adams administration decided to seek congressional authorization to revive the Navy and the Marine Corps, break off all treaties with France, and fight the French navy. The so-called Quasi-War of 1798–1800 followed.

The war consisted of a series of naval engagements, and by 1800 the activity of French privateers and warships along the American seaboard had declined significantly.

Nevertheless, the Federalist administration of John Adams became increasingly popular due to the passage of the Alien and Sedition Acts, introduced to silence dissenters and limit the rights of immigrants during the war.

PERIOD 2

1790-1877

Major historical events of the period:

1803 – Lewis and Clark Expedition

1807 – Embargo Act

1812 – War of 1812

1819 – Panic of 1819

1820 – Missouri Compromise

1823 – Monroe Doctrine is issued

1830 – Indian Removal Act

1846 – Wilmot Proviso

1846-1848 – Mexican-American War

1848 – Guadalupe Hidalgo treaty signed

1848 – California gold rush

1848 – Seneca Falls Convention

1854 – Kansas-Nebraska Act

1861-1865 – the Civil War

1862 – Homestead Act

1863 – Emancipation Proclamation

1864 – Sand Creek Massacre

1865 – the Thirteenth Amendment abolishes slavery

1876-1877 – Sioux War

1876-1890 – the Gilded Age

POLITICAL INSTITUTIONS, DEVELOPMENTS, BEHAVIOR, and PUBLIC POLICY: 1790 - 1877

The French Revolution's spread throughout Europe and beyond helped fuel America's debate not only about the nature of the United States' domestic order but also about its proper role in the world.

The French Revolution threatened the old order in Europe, which had been similarly challenged by the revolution in America. Thus, Americans at first viewed the Revolution with delight, hoping that it would usher in a new era of liberty and equality. The introduction of a constitution limiting the king's power was looked upon favorably.

However, the Revolution went much further than this. Soon France was embroiled in war, a republic was declared, the king was executed, and a reign of terror set in. The radicalism of the French Revolution even entailed the emancipation of slaves in the West Indian colonies. These new developments stirred debate and vigorous arguments between supporters and opponents of the Revolution across the Atlantic.

Illustration of an execution, Revolution Square, France

Federalists tended to support Britain, while the Republicans preferred republican France in the ferocious war going on in Europe. Republicans like Jefferson saw what was happening in France as part of a broader struggle against the old order. The Federalists believed that the radical tendencies of the French revolutionaries jeopardized the concept of social order altogether.

These developments brought many Americans to believe that some of their countrymen held opinions that were not only wrong but evil, and that such opinions had to be suppressed, as they were by the Alien and Sedition Acts. Each side began to see the other as a threat to what they thought the United States should be.

Although George Washington's Farewell Address warned about the dangers of divisive political parties and permanent foreign alliances, European conflict and tensions with Britain and France fueled increasingly bitter partisan debates throughout the 1790s.

The revolutionary wars in Europe created tensions between pro-French and pro-British factions in American politics. As such, international politics and questions of foreign policy played an essential role in dividing the American political elite into two camps and thereby constituting the first party system in the United States.

By 1796, political contests were no longer personal but rooted in organized efforts to further certain principles and promote specific interests. The political climate became more unpleasant, and several politicians and newspapermen were arrested under new laws limiting the right to dissent.

The election of 1800 showed the solidarity of the political system, as power passed peacefully from Federalist to Republican hands. Upon being elected president, Thomas Jefferson called for unity and reconciliation.

In the late 18th century, new experiments with democratic ideas and republican forms of government, as well as other new religious, economic, and cultural ideas, challenged traditional imperial systems across the Atlantic World.

The late 18th and early 19th centuries saw outbreaks of revolutions on both sides of the Atlantic Ocean, with profound and long-lasting consequences both in the Americas and in Europe.

The American Revolution occurred and was secondary in importance only to the French Revolution, which had the most significant effects due to the status of France at that time and the fact that the influence of France spread with its military expansion during the Revolutionary and Napoleonic Wars. In the Americas, Haiti was affected early on, and Spanish America somewhat later.

The timing of these events was not coincidental; the revolutionaries in different countries and colonies knew about each other and emulated each other. The ideals of republicanism, democracy, and human rights spread widely, threatening existing institutions such as monarchies, aristocracies, and influential state churches.

The revolutionaries professed Enlightenment beliefs, fighting for freedom, equality, and expanded opportunities for political participation and the rule of law. Their success demonstrated that starting from scratch with a brand-new system of government was possible and, in some cases, both useful and accessible.

Many new state constitutions and the national Articles of Confederation, reflecting Republican fears of both centralized power and excessive widespread influence, placed power in the hands of the legislative branch and maintained property qualifications for voting and citizenship.

The Articles of Confederation, adopted by the Continental Congress in 1777 and ratified by all thirteen states by 1781, created a U.S. government composed simply of a legislature. The legislature only had one chamber, and there was no executive or judiciary branch.

Members of the legislature were appointed, rather than elected, and each state had one delegate regardless of its population. This reflected the belief that the United States should be a decentralized confederation of states with limited powers, and that all other powers should belong to state governments. The appointment of delegates by state legislatures rather than election by the populace similarly reflected that the founders had limited faith in democratic electoral politics.

At the same time, state constitutions moved power from the executive branch to the legislative branch, due in large part to the bad experiences dissident Americans had had with British-appointed governors. Pennsylvania went so far as to abolish the office of governor and the upper house of the legislature, leaving only a unicameral legislature elected by all adult men who paid taxes.

The Pennsylvania constitution was far from typical, as most states placed significant restrictions on voting rights even for adult white men and even stricter restrictions on eligibility to hold elected office.

In most cases, voter qualifications were similar to those known from the British system, meaning that voters had to be free adult males who owned property and belonged to the established church in that state (in some states, there was no established church).

The limitation of voting rights to property owners was justified by the claim that only those who owned property were independent men with a genuine stake in society.

After experiencing the limitations of the Articles of Confederation, American political leaders wrote a new Constitution based on the principles of federalism and the separation of powers, crafted a Bill of Rights, and continued their debates about the proper balance between liberty and order.

The Articles of Confederation had limitations that, in the view of many critics, inhibited the development of effective governance and credible defense. The army was tiny and unpaid, and there was no navy.

In the case of foreign threats, Congress neither had enough money which was voluntarily donated nor the authority to tax the citizenry, which meant that no real preparations for war could be made. Many of the states failed to honor the Articles, developing their foreign policies and, in some cases, violated the terms of the peace treaty with Britain.

Two factors exacerbated the money problem. The currency had become practically worthless, and the states failed to pay their taxes, meaning that the national government was unable to pay foreign debts. By 1786, the United States was practically bankrupt.

In 1787, the Constitutional Convention assembled to solve the many outstanding problems of creating a viable federal government. Federal executive and judiciary branches were introduced, with a plethora of checks and balances to ensure that no branch of government would be able to overpower the rest.

The Constitution attempted to strike a balance between the rights of the states and the need for centralization and leadership. The new legislature was bicameral, with one popularly elected chamber where the states were represented according to population. The members of the other chamber, the Senate, would be elected by state legislatures, and all the states would have the same number of senators.

The Constitution was made the supreme law of the land, and the United States Supreme Court was given the authority to hear appeals in cases originating in state courts.

The Convention at Philadelphia, 1787

As some skeptics were critical of the new Constitution, especially the danger that a strengthened federal government might infringe on the rights of states and individuals, a series of amendments were later added.

These first ten amendments to the Constitution became the Bill of Rights, which secured for American citizens a variety of specific freedoms and protections essential in everyday life, the development of civil society, and legal proceedings.

Difficulties over trade, finances, and interstate and foreign relations, as well as internal unrest, led to calls for significant revisions to the Articles of Confederation and a stronger central government.

The Articles of Confederation limited the U.S. government to powers over diplomacy and Indian affairs, issuing currency, handling the mail, and controlling a virtually nonexistent army. With no executive or judicial branch, there was no system to enforce the limits placed on the power of the individual states. The problem of creating a unified and viable government was a serious one, mainly due to the lack of resources and the difficulty of making decisions, as all thirteen states had to agree on vital decisions.

Congress lacked the power to tax and received little from the states, who, in many cases, preferred to issue currencies and build their armies. They even imposed tariff regimes, placing tariffs on imports from other states. Both economic and foreign policy suffered from inconsistency and a lack of coherence.

When Spain restricted American navigation on the Mississippi River, the government lacked the means to do anything other than protest.

At last, the government even failed to defend itself. When Shays' Rebellion broke out in Massachusetts in 1786, it was struck down by mercenaries rather than the United States army. This embarrassment finally convinced political leaders that a new and more centralized constitution had to be developed.

Delegates from the states worked through a series of compromises to form the Constitution for a new national government while providing limits on federal power.

The new Constitution emerged from many compromises between the states. The first and most important was the so-called Connecticut Compromise, which combined two original proposals, the Virginia Plan and the New Jersey Plan. The Virginia Plan suggested that the population in Congress should be proportional to each state's population.

At the same time, the New Jersey Plan called for equal representation as in the system put in place by the Articles of Confederation.

The Connecticut Compromise combined the two by proposing a bicameral solution where representation in one chamber was equal for all states and, in the other, corresponded with the population.

The Connecticut Compromise solution then raised the question of the extent to which slave populations should be taken into consideration. The southern states insisted that slaves should be taken into consideration when calculating state populations, while the northern states rejected this proposal. In the end, a compromise was made in the form of the three-fifths rule: one slave would count as three-fifths of a free person.

The southern and northern states clashed again over trade regulation. Southern elites were fearful that northerners might seek to abolish the slave trade and impose tariffs that would hurt the southern export business. They wanted states, rather than the federal government, to regulate trade.

The northern states thought that the issue of trade regulation should be a federal responsibility. The Commerce Compromise meant that states would continue to regulate intrastate trade, but the federal government would regulate interstate trade.

The case for import duties was accepted, but it was stipulated that there would be no export duties and no ban on the slave trade for the next twenty years.

Calls for higher guarantees of rights during the ratification process resulted in the addition of the Bill of Rights shortly after the Constitution was adopted.

During the ratification process, some critics argued that the Constitution did not adequately enumerate the rights of people as a protection against government abuses. They felt that the federal Constitution should have a Bill of Rights attached to it, just like several of the state constitutions already in existence.

President James Madison (1751-1836; 1809-1817), who had been the primary formative influence on the original Constitution, initially felt that such an enumeration of rights might suggest that rights not enumerated were not protected.

James Madison, 1751-1836

The Bill of Rights 175th anniversary

James Madison Bill of Rights
$5 commemorative gold coin

Due to widespread skepticism, Madison finally proposed a series of amendments to the Constitution, of which ten were eventually adopted and became known as the Bill of Rights. These amendments barred the federal government (but not necessarily the states) from interfering with rights to free speech, free religion, and the right to bear arms.

The Bill of Rights also offers protection from illegal seizures, cruel and unjust punishment, and unfair trials, among many other rights. In keeping with the concept of natural rights, the Ninth Amendment specified that the people retain rights not explicitly enumerated in the Constitution.

As the first national administrations began to govern under the Constitution, continued debates about the relationship between the national government and the states, economic policy, and the conduct of foreign affairs led to the creation of political parties.

The relationship between the federal and state governments continued to be the subject of essential and heated debates in the late 18th century. When the Alien and Sedition Acts were passed during the undeclared war with France, legislatures in Kentucky and Virginia passed resolutions that held these laws to be unconstitutional, as they allowed the federal government to exercise powers not mentioned in the Constitution.

The Virginia version of the constitution authored by Madison argued that the government's efforts to clamp down on free speech and free press were perilous, as these were notably the necessary foundation for the defense of republican liberty and natural rights in general.

According to Madison, Congress had not given the national government the power to infringe on these rights. Jefferson, who drafted the Kentucky Resolutions, went even further, arguing that the states had the power to nullify (i.e., invalidate) laws that were passed by Congress, which the states found unconstitutional.

Before the outbreak of the Quasi-War with France, Madison and Jefferson took issue with the Proclamation of Neutrality issued by President Washington when war broke out between France and Britain in 1793. Alexander Hamilton offered arguments in favor of the proclamation based on constitutionality, international law, and political expediency.

Madison countered that a strict reading of the Constitution implied that Congress, not the president, should be responsible for foreign policy, and suggested that supporters of the Proclamation represented anti-revolutionary and anti-republican sentiments.

In general, these conflicts over foreign policy and constitutional matters contributed significantly to the development of two parties, with Republicans like Jefferson and Madison distancing themselves from leading Federalists like Adams and Hamilton. Another aspect of this conflict was disagreements over economic policy.

Hamilton presented ambitious centralizing financial plans that involved paying off debts incurred in the revolution by borrowing from the public in the form of issuing securities and suggested that only a central bank should be issuing currency. In this way, Hamilton sought to give the federal government financial credibility and make money available for investment in infrastructure projects.

Madison and Jefferson argued that this scheme was unconstitutional. Hamilton asserted that the good of the nation depended on using any means necessary to further its interests if the Constitution did not expressly prohibit a policy. Madison, taking a much narrower view of constitutionality, suggested that the federal government did not have the right to do anything that was not explicitly mentioned as one of its responsibilities in the Constitution.

During and after the American Revolution, increased awareness of the inequalities in society motivated some individuals and groups to call for the abolition of slavery and greater political democracy in the new state and national governments.

During the revolution, critiques of British governance often referred to the situation of American colonists as a form of slavery. This way of speaking, along with the universalist language of freedom and equality for all, caused some Americans to reconsider the institution of slavery as it existed within farms, plantations, households and shops around the country. Many began to doubt that differences in skin color alone could justify keeping an entire people in slavery.

Soon organizations working for the abolition of slavery were established, such as the Pennsylvania Abolition Society and the New York Manumission Society. In 1780, the Pennsylvania legislature passed a law that would allow "gradual emancipation" by declaring all children born of slaves free. The same act also banned the trade of slaves.

By 1788, eight states had abolished or suspended the slave trade. In the following decades, the northern states enacted laws of either gradual or immediate emancipation. However, the southern states—where slavery was more prevalent—did not follow the northern states' lead.

This led to mutual suspicion between the two sections, as when Abigail Adams questioned whether Virginians with their propensity to own slaves could love liberty as much as the people of New England. While First Lady Martha Washington (1731-1802) relied on slaves in the presidential household, First Lady Abigail Adams helped a young black man learn how to read and write.

The constitutional framers postponed a solution to the problems of slavery and the slave trade, setting the stage for recurring conflicts over these issues in later years.

Slavery was a severe problem for a country founded on ideals of freedom and equality. Founders like Washington, Jefferson, and Madison found slavery repugnant but held large numbers of slaves themselves.

The Founding Fathers did not see any practical way to end slavery. The Articles of Confederation did not mention slavery, and the Constitution failed to deal with slavery because of the divergent interests of the northern and southern elites.

In exchange for concessions in other areas, the southern founders even forced the representatives of the northern states to accept a clause about fugitive slaves in the Constitution. Northern states were obliged to track down fugitive slaves and return them to their owners. Over the years, the question of slavery reappeared intermittently and created significant tensions between the North and South.

The American Revolution and the ideals outlined in the Declaration of Independence had reverberations in France, Haiti, and Latin America, inspiring future rebellions.

The American Revolution inspired liberals, republicans, and nationalists in Europe and throughout the Americas. They saw the United States as an example of putting Enlightenment ideas into practice in the name of liberty and equality.

The Revolution encouraged the Irish to seek more freedom from the British and the Belgians to seek independence from Austria. The French Revolution became another example of a fight against privilege and tyranny in support of universal human rights.

However, when slaves in Haiti rebelled against their owners, the United States was not especially supportive. The American government cooperated with the Haitian revolutionaries when vocal slavery opponent John Adams was president, but the tide turned when Jefferson became president in 1800.

Southern slave owners found the spectacle of a slave rebellion and a republic led by blacks terrifying, and the United States did not recognize the independence of Haiti until 1862, long after France had done so.

When the Spanish colonies in South America sought independence in the early 19th century, they were keenly aware of the examples of both the United States and Haiti. They rallied around ideals of freedom and national independence while fearing that the government of Spain could not protect them against slave rebellions.

The disorganized state of the Spanish government during the lengthy revolutionary wars and Napoleonic Wars (1803-1815) in Europe made Latin American separation and independence possible.

The French withdrawal from North America and the subsequent attempt of native groups to reassert their power over the interior of the continent resulted in new white–Indian conflicts along the western borders of British—and later U.S.—colonial settlements and settlers were looking to assert more power in interior regions.

The French withdrawal from North America created something of a power vacuum in the borderlands between the British colonies and the territories previously claimed by the French. The backcountry was only sparsely settled, and conflicts between settlers and Indians multiplied as more whites sought lands in these areas.

The Paxton Boys of Pennsylvania, who became famous for their atrocities against local Indians, turned to put pressure on the colonial assembly, demanding that more be done to protect the settlers against Indians. The Paxton Boys murdered and scalped peaceful women, children, and older men to achieve their goals. This was only one example of the increasingly violent and brutal confrontation between whites and Indians as the rise in the European population encouraged migration into the interior.

Paxton Boys' massacre of the Indians at Lancaster

These confrontations continued to take place throughout the revolutionary period and into the national period. From the mid-1780s to the mid-1790s, a series of wars against the Indians played out in the areas to the west of the original thirteen colonies.

The 1794 Battle of Fallen Timbers was the turning point, a decisive victory for a professionally trained American army that was followed by major Indian concessions in the Old Northwest.

The United States policies that encouraged western migration and the incorporation of new territories into the nation extended republican institutions and intensified conflicts between American Indians and Europeans in the trans-Appalachian West.

Under the Articles of Confederation, the United States was unable to tax its citizens directly. To raise money, the Land Ordinance was passed in 1785. The Land Ordinance regulated the sale of western lands by the federal government and created a system for surveying public lands. The land was divided into townships that were six square miles, and these were, in turn, divided into thirty-six square sections.

Once townships and sections had been surveyed, they could be sold to settlers and speculators (the two were not entirely distinct categories, as most settlers also speculated in the long-term increase in land values). One section in each township was to be used to fund public schools in the area.

Once the land had been sold, authority devolved from the federal government to local inhabitants, encouraging a strong sense of local autonomy in western development. At the same time, local autonomy sometimes intensified conflicts between Indians and whites due to the lack of coherent and consistent policies toward the indigenous population.

Surveying the Northwest Territory, c. 1787

As settlers moved westward during the 1780s, Congress enacted the Northwest Ordinance for admitting new states and sought to promote public education, the protection of private property, and the restriction of slavery in the Northwest Territory.

The Northwest Ordinance of 1787 was of utmost importance because it defined the process of the westward expansion of the United States. It determined that the new nation would expand westward by creating new states, not by the extension of old states.

It gave Congress the power to create new states out of federal lands and outlined the political development of these states-to-be. When the proposed state had 5,000 adult males, they would have a territorial legislature but a federally appointed governor. Once the region had a free population of over 60,000, they could apply to become states.

The Northwest Ordinance followed the Land Ordinance in emphasizing the importance of public education. It also secured religious freedom and private property. More controversially, it also prohibited slavery in the area. In some areas, notably southern Illinois and Indiana, settlers still brought in slaves and fought to legalize slavery.

The Constitution's failure to precisely define the relationship between American Indian tribes and the national government led to problems regarding treaties and Indian legal claims relating to the seizure of Indian lands.

The Constitution did not deal directly with the question of how the relationship between the federal government and the Indians should be managed. However, an ordinance had already been passed in 1786, dividing U.S. lands into three districts with a superintendent for Indian affairs in each.

In 1790, this was followed by the Trade and Intercourse Act, which described the process of licensing traders who ventured into Indian areas. It sought to define the terms of land acquisition by prohibiting white settlers from direct purchase of Indian lands.

All land purchases had to go through the federal government. Also, the Trade and Intercourse Act stipulated penalties for Americans who committed crimes in Indian country. This law was followed by several other trade and intercourse acts in the years that followed, meant to strengthen the protection of Indians against criminal whites attacking them and taking their lands.

As national political institutions developed in the new United States, regionally-based positions on economic, political, social, and foreign policy issues promoted the development of political parties.

Even during the Revolutionary War, Americans had been divided between Patriots, Loyalists, and those who remained mostly aloof. After the war ended, divisions remained as some of the founders were highly skeptical of the new Constitution, becoming known as Anti-Federalists.

In the 1790s, political conflict in the United States intensified and became partisan. The Revolution in France and the continuing threat of war against either France or Britain put an enormous strain on citizens and members of the elite, with different feelings about radical republicanism and different interests to preserve concerning foreign policy.

Disagreements over economic and financial policy were equally vehement, pitting proponents of a commercial, manufacturing civilization against those who relied on the civic virtue of the independent yeoman farmer in a predominantly rural republic.

All these conflicts, to some extent, reflected the need to come to terms with the legacy of the American Revolution. The radical and violent example of the French Revolution and the general instability of politics at home and abroad made this discussion increasingly necessary and challenging.

It was apparent that the United States remained a tentative, experimental form of the republic that could not count on being left alone by the European powers. To some extent, this introduced an element of fear and apprehension into American political debate.

Although the father of the Constitution, James Madison, was an exception, most politicians, and Americans in general, did not believe that there was room for more than one legitimate political body in public life. As Patriots, they had assumed that all reasonable people would be on the same side politically. This made the development of a party system especially painful for the new republic, and opinions on both sides tended to be firm and unyielding.

Newspapers added to this by being overtly political and highly critical of opponents. The great hero of the American Revolution, president and father of his country, George Washington, was even attacked, vilified and ridiculed by the opposition press, sometimes seen as an enemy out to destroy liberty and the republic. Even worse, abuse was heaped on the main protagonists of the party struggle, such as Hamilton and Adams on the Federalist side and Jefferson and Madison on the Republican side.

For the 1796 election, the Federalists and Republicans both ran candidates at all levels from local to state and national. They had become more than mere factions, growing into influential political organizations based on firm principles. Even Madison, who had anticipated legitimate disagreement on political issues, had not expected anything other than temporary alliances built around controversial issues.

However, voters were inclined to take an active part in politics and were not content with merely deferring to the elite. Thus, a competitive party system sometimes marked by less than civilized debate and confrontation arose. The strength of this system was exposed when Adams replaced Washington, and later Adams by Jefferson. The peaceful exchange of power and position is a hallmark of political stability, despite Washington's insistence that parties were a grave threat to the republic.

The Federalists were supporters of centralization and a broad interpretation of the Constitution that would facilitate the use of government power to help the economy grow and develop. Those who supported Hamilton's policies promoting commerce, manufacturing, internal improvements, and national finance tended to support the Federalist Party. Merchants, creditors, and the urban middle class in the Northeast and New England were prominent among these supporters.

The opposition party that emerged during Washington's presidency was called the Democratic-Republicans, now sometimes called the Jeffersonian Republicans to distinguish this party from the modern Republican Party, which emerged in the 1850s.

Republican supporters were a diverse bunch, led by southern planters like Jefferson, Madison, and Monroe but also including farmers throughout the country.

Unlike the Federalists, who were typical of English descent, the Republicans were a more heterogeneous party with many German and Scotch-Irish voters.

James Monroe's southern plantation, c. 1810

In the 1796 election, the Federalists portrayed themselves as the more responsible party associated with the steady leadership of Washington. They suggested that Washington should be followed by Adams, lest dangerous radicals take over the government and bring the chaos and anarchy of the French Revolution to American soil. The Republicans, meanwhile, often portrayed the Federalists as enemies of freedom and equality, and as secretly scheming to introduce monarchy and aristocracy into the U.S.

Adams thus came into power in a divided country and at a challenging time, given the explosive international situation and continued harassment of American shipping by both sides of the European conflict. His response to the vehemence of his critics led to the severe abridgment of civil liberties through the Alien and Sedition Acts. It was a response that showed that the scope for legitimate opposition and debate was still being negotiated in the new republic.

President Adams's heavy-handed tactics were disliked by many voters, and the election of 1800 showed that Americans' desire to participate in and influence politics was more durable than ever. The emotional appeals of the Federalists, arguing that a victory for the ungodly Jefferson would ruin the country, were not successful.

The Republican insistence on curbing the centralization of political power was more effective. They criticized the Federalist military buildup, the encroachment on freedom during the Quasi-War, and the willingness of the government to borrow and spend. They argued that the government should become closer to the people by leaving more decisions to state and local governments. This message was highly popular. Jefferson and the Republicans won a decisive victory, and the party remained in control of national politics for the next quarter of a century.

The United States developed the world's first modern mass democracy. It celebrated a new national culture, while Americans sought to define the nation's democratic ideals and to reform its institutions to match them.

The search for a national identity characterized the first half of 19th-century American history. The Americas were an empty slate for the Europeans who had colonized them. This meant that the changes taking place in the newly christened United States of America were impacted by the unstable government and lack of infrastructure. Americans had to define a national identity based on their foundational democratic ideals, while rapid changes were occurring in the economy, territory, and population.

When the representatives from the colonies decided to declare independence from Great Britain, they created a unique opportunity for themselves. The government that followed would be wholly new and original. There were no laws, treaties, or agreements to which they must adhere.

While liberating, this lack of restrictions also meant that conflicts were frequent, as the founders tried to create the most agreeable government for each of the very different colonies. These colonies had been founded at different times with different charters.

Each Founding Father had been shaped differently by Great Britain's tyranny. This meant that one of the most challenging problems facing the newly created United States was establishing how to work together to achieve a common goal.

Drafting the Declaration of Independence, c. July 4, 1776

The nation's transformation to a more participatory democracy was accompanied by continued debates over federal power, the relationship between the federal government and the states, the authority of different branches of the federal government, and the rights and responsibilities of individual citizens.

The Declaration of Independence (July 4, 1776) is an excellent example of the early influences and struggles faced by the colonies. Written by a five-person committee, though usually attributed to Thomas Jefferson, the Declaration of Independence is heavily based on the significant political influences of the day, primarily the Enlightenment thinkers.

The declaration of "Life, Liberty, and the pursuit of Happiness" as fundamental human rights in the Declaration of Independence, for instance, is an echo of John Locke's *Second Treatise* (1689), where he explains that all men have a right to "their lives, liberties, and estates, which I call by the general name 'property.'"

Enlightenment concepts, such as fundamental human rights, spoke to the struggles that the colonies endured under King George III of England (1738-1820; 1760-1820), struggles that they hoped to eradicate from their government. Thus, the grievances listed against the King became the basis for the new government. However, even these were difficult to define.

Jefferson originally included an entire passage denouncing slavery and blaming the entire institution on George III, even though he owned slaves. This passage was struck from the final document to appease Southern representatives, who knew that an end to slavery would mean crippling the economic prosperity of the South. Eventually, the document was finalized and signed. War was upon the colonies, and while their soldiers fought for their independence on the battlefield, their next challenge would be framing the new government.

The Articles of Confederation served as the first constitution of the newly created United States of America. The Articles, like the Declaration of Independence, show the effects of Britain's rule. The founders created a confederation of states which functioned almost as individual countries. A weak centralized government loosely joined these.

A weak centralized government was to avoid the dictatorial control that King George had exercised over the colonies. The Articles of Confederation had a pronounced weakness. They allowed so many rights for each state that they also severely crippled the power of the federal government to enhance and protect liberty.

Postage with an image of the Founding Fathers drafting the Articles of Confederation

Thomas Jefferson (1743 to July 4, 1826), in his autobiography, noted the issue of funding the U.S. Treasury under the Articles of Confederation. Most representatives' arguments showed an acknowledgment that the Treasury needed to be funded but lacked any intent to promise funds from their constituents. It was challenging to achieve consensus when each representative wanted to promote the interests of their state over the interests of the new nation.

The event that best represents the country's inability to function uniformly is Shays' Rebellion in 1786 and 1787. Upset with the tax burden placed upon them to pay for the American Revolution, protesters began speaking out in Massachusetts. They soon moved on to physical protests outside of local courthouses. While these protests did not turn violent, they did stop the county courts from meeting and disrupted the flow of business.

Anger grew as change seemed unlikely, and eventually, a group of men from Massachusetts—many of them veterans of the American Revolution—marched on a federal armory under the leadership of Daniel Shays. The federal government was unable to respond without funding for a military. Therefore, the response was weak and highlighted for many the need for change. To what extent change was needed was another matter of contention.

The Constitution, despite being a short and concise document, is very well balanced. Some of the fears of the anti-Federalists were well-founded, and the framers of the Constitution took steps to address them. The primary safeguard is the system of checks and balances between the three branches. This was put in place to keep any one branch from gaining too much power.

For instance, Congress has the power to declare war, but the President does not. This would hopefully mean that all wars would have to be fully considered and debated before the U.S. military took action. However, in a state of emergency, the president can deploy troops for a limited time while seeking Congress's consent for further action. This way, the president cannot act alone on behalf of the nation, but still has the power to respond to unforeseen events.

Similarly, the president has the power to veto Congressional laws to protect against Congress, gaining too much political sway. Congress can override a veto to protect against a president who is trying to misuse his power. The Supreme Court is the final judge as to whether any law is constitutional or not. The Constitution protects against abuses of power like those seen in many of the monarchies of Europe at the time.

Once the Constitution was ratified, a list of ten amendments was added soon after. These ten amendments, the Bill of Rights, outlined the fundamental rights given to all citizens at the time of their ratification. The Bill of Rights includes the right to free speech, assembly, and religion. It grants all citizens the right to own weapons and to use them in defense of the country.

The Bill of Rights protects people against potential abuses of the military or police, like those that suffered under King George III. It is the Supreme Court's role to analyze and interpret the Constitution, its amendments, and the constitutionality of laws and judicial rulings.

The Bill of Rights is a collection of the first ten amendments, but there are twenty-seven amendments in total. Many of the amendments further regulate the three branches of government. As questions about a branch's role and power have arisen, amendments have been added to ensure that there are answers. For instance, Amendment XXII defines the term limits for presidents.

Other amendments are indicative of much more significant social changes, like Amendment XIII, which abolished the institution of slavery in the United States. These amendments are dynamic and subject to change. Amendment XVIII prohibited the buying and selling of alcohol, ushering in the era of Prohibition. Later, Amendment XXI was used to repeal Prohibition, making the sale and consumption of alcohol legal again.

State governments are modeled on this federal ideal, with a three-branch system and a state constitution. Each state has a governor that functions as the state's executive branch. Several presidents have first served as governors of their respective states, like former President Bill Clinton (1993-2001), who served as the governor of Arkansas.

States also have a legislative system, though these vary in the titles. Each state also has a state and the federal court system. The state court tries violations of state laws, while the federal court tries any cases which violate federal laws.

As constituencies and interest groups coalesced and defined their agendas, political parties, most significantly the Federalists and Democratic-Republicans in the 1790s and the Democrats and Whigs in the 1830s, were created or transformed to reflect and promote those agendas.

Two distinct political parties fought to sway public opinion on the matter of rewriting the Constitution: The Federalists and the anti-Federalists. The Federalists were led by John Jay, Alexander Hamilton, and James Madison. They believed that a stronger centralized government would better protect the fundamental human rights of the citizens and the liberties gained during the American Revolution.

The Federalists were well funded and organized. They had the support of respected political figures like George Washington and Benjamin Franklin. The anti-Federalists had legitimate fears about a strong central government. They pointed out that a strong centralized government would lend itself to the types of tyranny they had fought a war to end.

Federalist John Jay, 1745-1829

The ability of the president to veto decisions made by Congress, for instance, had few legitimate restrictions. They also worried about the lack of protected rights for the citizens. The anti-Federalists were less organized and funded than their Federalist counterparts. However, they were able to force the Federalists to reevaluate their agendas and compromise to achieve a more balanced constitution.

In the 1790s, immediately after the ratification of the Constitution, a new conflict between political parties arose. The Federalists and Democratic-Republicans had vastly different interpretations of the recently created legal system. The Federalists were focused on economic prosperity through the encouragement of wealthy investors, and therefore favored an alliance with Great Britain.

The Federalists believed that Britain, as a leading European government, would promote trade and encourage exports from the United States. They also felt that too much direct influence from voters would cause confusion in the government and that after being elected, all political figures should seek to distance themselves from their constituents.

Republicans viewed Federalist tactics as a holdover from colonialism and feared the political elite taking power on a national level. Therefore, they opposed connections with Britain, favoring the French instead, as former allies from the American Revolution. Republicans also sought to promote state and individual rights as opposed to the national rights that the Federalists focused on. This would keep the balance of power in favor of the individual states instead of allowing the federal government to have majority control.

These political parties were not stable. By the time Andrew Jackson (1767-1845) was entering the political arena (1796), a new set of political parties were quickly replacing the Federalists and Democratic-Republicans.

Democrats were in favor of reduced government spending and involvement. They found a ready constituency in those who were exposed by the market system, such as subsistence farmers.

Whig politicians wanted the exact opposite: increased government spending and regulation. They were most popular with the individuals who benefitted from a market system, particularly Northerners, who owned the means of production.

Supreme Court decisions sought to assert federal power over state laws and the primacy of the judiciary in determining the meaning of the Constitution.

One of the Supreme Court's most important decisions happened as a result of the Alien and Sedition Acts endorsed by Federalist President John Adams. The Alien Act allowed the government to remove (i.e., deport) citizens that were suspected of plotting against the government. This was an effort to discredit French citizens, as well as those that were vocal in their criticisms of President Adams (1797-1801). The Sedition Act that followed allowed the punishment of those who attempted to "stir up sedition" in the United States.

The passing of the Alien and Sedition Acts led to public outcry and widespread debate as to the constitutionality of such laws. Several of Adams' political opponents and critics were tried under the Sedition Act, including Matthew Lyon, a Republican representative from Vermont, and Thomas Cooper, who wrote publicly about the president's Alien Acts and military actions and questioned the constitutionality of both.

The Sedition Act and the political split with fellow Federalist Alexander Hamilton led to a defeat for Adams in 1800 to political rival and Democratic-Republican Thomas Jefferson.

Recognizing that his power was fading after the election of his rival, Adams wanted to make sure that his party still had power in Washington. Thus, one of Adams' last actions as President was the Judiciary Act of 1801.

The Judiciary Act of 1801 was a sweeping reform and expansion of the federal judiciary. The act added sixteen judgeships for the six judicial systems and gave them jurisdiction over all cases where constitutionality was called into question.

Thomas Cooper, 1759-1839

The Republicans were worried that this might empower the federal system and weaken the state court systems. They also worried that Adams would appoint his Federalist supporters to the positions, which is exactly what he did with less than three weeks left in office. This earned Adams' appointments the title of "Midnight Judges" and meant that although Jefferson and the Republicans were taking hold of the government, they would have a difficult time passing non-federalist legislation.

Jefferson stopped several of the commissions for the "Midnight Judges" before they were sent out, and in doing so, started proceedings on one of the most relevant judicial cases of the period. William Marbury petitioned the Supreme Court to force Secretary of State James Madison to send him his commission as Justice of the Peace in the District of Columbia. The court's decision for the case of *Marbury v. Madison* (1803) was not what Jefferson, or others, expected.

The Supreme Court decided in favor of Marbury and ruled that Madison's refusal to deliver the commission was illegal. The Supreme Court also stated that the Judiciary Act of 1789, which allowed an individual to petition the Supreme Court in this way, was itself unconstitutional because it extended the Supreme Court's jurisdiction beyond that laid out in the Constitution. This decision kept Marbury from his commission but also established the practice of judicial review.

According to *Marbury*, Judicial review allows the Supreme Court the right to review decisions made among the lower courts. If decisions are deemed unconstitutional, the Supreme Court has the jurisdiction to readdress the case. It also allows for the review of all legislation.

After the Panic of 1819 (a financial crisis that crippled the U.S. economy until 1821), the Supreme Court, led by Chief Justice John Marshall (1755-1835; 1801-1835), decided two famous pro-capitalist cases. In *Dartmouth College v. Woodward* (1819), the Supreme Court decided that the state could not control private corporations, even if the state had created them. Then in *McCulloch v. Maryland* (1819), the Supreme Court ruled that the states could regulate the Bank of the United States. These were important decisions because they established the limit of the government's power over private institutions and industry.

In 1830, the Indian Removal Act was passed. The act required the relocation of eastern Indians to a territory west of the Mississippi River. Activists and tribes protested the act. The Cherokee tribe contested it in court, and the Supreme Court decided in their favor in 1832. Chief Justice John Marshall ruled that the Indian tribes are "domestic dependent nations" and that the United States' function was that of a guardian. Later that same year, *Worcester v. Georgia* (1832) held that the states do not have jurisdiction over the Indian nations within their borders.

The heart of these rulings was that President Andrew Jackson's (1829-1837) removal of native people from their lands was an abuse of power, though not technically unconstitutional. The president ignored the Supreme Court's sentiment and continued the forced relocation of tribes. This laid the foundation for the United States' Native American policies. The idea of tribes as sovereign protected nations still legally holds.

Concurrent with an increasing international exchange of goods and ideas, more significant numbers of Americans began struggling with how to match democratic political ideals to political institutions and social realities.

Even though the Constitution had established the political future of the United States, there were still conflicts between factions and parties. The authority of the Supreme Court did not stop people from disagreeing with the decisions it reached.

With conflict occurring in the political arena, it was hard to create a stable social reality that reflected stated political goals. Many groups tried to arrange these conflicting ideas into some form of truth that supported the ideals of the country's founding documents.

Despite the outlawing of the international slave trade, the rise in the number of free African Americans in both the North and the South, and widespread discussion of emancipation plans, the United States and many state governments continued to restrict African Americans' citizenship possibilities.

As the American economy began to bounce back, social issues like slavery moved to the forefront of politics. Like the economy, slavery was a complex issue that opposing sides attempted to simplify. By 1808, it was illegal to import slaves into the United States from Africa or the Caribbean.

This meant that most slaves bought and sold after these times were born in the United States (although an illicit trans-Atlantic slave trade persisted after 1808). However, slaves born in America were not considered American citizens and held very few rights.

Many Southerners embraced slavery as the "peculiar institution of the South" and saw slavery as part of their regional identity. They relied on slaves as a form of cheap labor and a ready workforce. Slavery allowed for higher profits because the workforce did not have to be paid. That is not to say that all slaves were laborers. Some slaves served inside houses as domestic servants and companions. These slaves might be taught skills that were not accessible to other laborers. Domestic slaves, for instance, were the most likely to know how to read and write.

In the South, slave codes were published detailing the "rights" of slaves. These were manuals for slave owners and detailed how slaves could be legally treated. For instance, slave marriages were not considered legally binding so that those slave families could be broken up by their owners.

In the North, most states preferred to ignore that the problem existed. Many passed laws to discourage free slaves from settling in their state, like Ohio, in 1804. In 1817, the American Colonization Society was founded to try to help freed slaves return to Africa. While initially applauded as a way to assist the plight of African peoples, most people soon realized that the American Colonization Society was more worried about removing freed African Americans from northern states than improving the situation of those still in slavery.

Abolitionists fought against this negligence, trying to keep slavery an issue in the minds of the public. Many slaves, unwilling to live in the horrible conditions they were subject to, attempted to escape. If successful, the slaves would flee to Canada, where slave catchers were banned after 1819. If caught, slaves would be killed or returned to their owners.

Harriet Tubman, the Moses to her people

In 1804, the Underground Railroad was established in Pennsylvania by abolitionists hoping to help runaway slaves. The "railroad" was a connected line of safe houses where slaves could hide. They would be given food and shelter and transported from one house to the next, until free. The different station houses did not necessarily know each other. Conductors led runaway slaves, often runaway slaves themselves. Perhaps the most famous of these conductors was Harriet Tubman, who is credited with assisting over 300 slaves to freedom. She made at least nineteen trips to the South, never lost a passenger, and was never caught.

Regional interests continued to trump national concerns as the basis for many political leaders' positions on economic issues, including slavery, the national bank, tariffs, and internal improvements.

The issue of regional identity versus national identity was constant during the 1800s. Movements helping one part of the country were inevitably met by resistance from another part of the country. Slavery was seen as a necessity in the South but was abhorrent to northerners. The tariffs on imports and exports inevitably helped the North and West while hindering the potential economic development of the South, and internal improvements in the North tended to distance the South.

U.S. interest in increasing foreign trade, expanding its national borders, and isolating itself from European conflicts shaped the nation's foreign policy and spurred government and private initiatives.

To create an independent global presence, U.S. policymakers sought to dominate the North American continent and to promote its foreign trade.

The War of 1812, sometimes referred to as the Second War for Independence, was the result of Anglo-American tension that had been brewing since the American Revolution. The tension increased with the British impressment of American sailors during the Napoleonic Wars, one of the leading causes of the embargo in 1807.

As previously mentioned, Jefferson implemented the Embargo Act of 1807 in response to British ships bullying American vessels on the high seas. Jefferson intended this act to punish the British and French by withholding resources and thus convince them to leave American ships alone. This act put a strain on the relationship between America and the French and British and hurt American traders more than it hurt European traders.

James Madison, who succeeded Jefferson, mended the relationship with the French, but America's relationship with Britain remained tense, leading to the War of 1812. The British were also encouraging the resistance of Native Americans as settlers began to move west into the newly purchased Louisiana Territory.

In 1812, encouraged by the War Hawks in Congress, James Madison and Congress declared war on Britain. American troops were immediately dispatched to Canada (then a British colony) and were pushed back due to their under-preparedness.

The British had several successes in the war, including the capture of Washington, D.C., and the burning of the White House in 1814. The Americans held control of the Northwest Territory and had several naval victories.

War of 1812, Battle of New Orleans

When Fort McHenry in Baltimore withstood more than twenty-four hours of sustained bombardment, the British Navy moved south towards New Orleans. The Treaty of Ghent was signed at this point, and the war was supposed to be over.

However, communication was slow, and the British did not know that the war had ended when they attacked New Orleans, where American troops led by Andrew Jackson defeated them. The war and its consequences highlighted the need for America to become a player in the international community.

Following the Louisiana Purchase, the drive to acquire, survey, and open new lands and markets led Americans into numerous economic, diplomatic, and military initiatives in the Western Hemisphere and Asia.

Several of the international diplomatic initiatives during this period involved Great Britain. In 1842, Secretary of State Daniel Webster met with British Ambassador Lord

Atherton to negotiate on some key points. The issue of the Canadian border was quickly resolved by establishing a fixed latitudinal border and a discussion of actions to be taken in the event of an accidental violation.

The issue of the international slave trade was similarly finalized. The British agreed to stop searching American ships if the Americans agreed to police the coast of Africa to look for slave ships flying the American flag. With Anglo-American tensions relaxed, the two countries could focus on other areas, such as China.

However, tensions flared again in 1846 as the Oregon Territory became a pressing matter. In the end, England conceded its claim to some territory in exchange for uncontested control of the northern territories. With the border established from sea to sea in the North, America had almost established its present-day continental size.

In 1836, Texas successfully rebelled against Mexico and formed its own state. America, having just won a war for its independence, offered the new territory diplomatic recognition and otherwise left it alone until 1844, when President John Tyler started negotiations for annexation.

As a result, Mexico severed all economic and diplomatic ties with the U.S. Failing on the first vote; Texas was eventually added to the Union in 1845. Relations with Mexico tensed as a result, especially as the Mexico–Texas border had not been resolved before annexation.

Mexican American War, the battle of Palo Alto, May 8, 1846

When buying the disputed territory did not work, President Polk (1795-1849; 1845-1849) gained congressional support for a declaration of war against Mexico. After American troops captured Mexico City in 1847, the treaty to buy the disputed territory was reexamined. Mexico agreed to give the United States over half of its pre-war territory, provided that the United States pay Mexico $15 million and forgive $3.3 million in debts owed by Mexican citizens.

The United States sought dominance over the North American continent through military actions, judicial decisions, and diplomatic efforts.

In the 1820s, America began to look abroad at its influence in the international theatre. President James Monroe (1758-1831; 1817-1825), in the spirit of former President Jefferson (1801-1809), wanted to encourage other countries to leave the Americas alone as far as colonization was concerned. To this extent, and with the support of the British, he issued the Monroe Doctrine in 1823 during a State of the Union Address to Congress.

President James Monroe, 1817-1825

In 1823, nearly all Latin American colonies were moving towards independence. Monroe wanted to make sure that no one would step in and fill the void as the colonies established themselves as governments. Monroe made it very clear that any action to gain control of these colonies would be met with American intervention.

Monroe promised that America would not interfere with existing colonies, referred to as the Monroe Doctrine; it has been upheld by numerous U.S. presidents and still plays an integral part in American foreign affairs.

American groups and individuals initiated, championed, or resisted the expansion of territory or government powers.

After the acquisition of the Louisiana Territory, expansion became a certainty. In 1803, Thomas Jefferson commissioned the Corps of Discovery, better known as the Lewis and Clark Expedition. Meriwether Lewis (1774-1809) and William Clark (1770-1838) led the Corps over 8,000 miles from 1804 to 1806, to chronicle the land, plants, animals, and people in the new territory. During the journey, Lewis recorded everything in a detailed journal, so the expedition was well preserved for posterity. They were aided by several native tribes who provided supplies and assistance, as well as their guide and interpreter Sacajawea, a native.

Meriwether Lewis (left) and William Clark (right)

Their discoveries helped to expand the knowledge of the new territory, plants, and animals that had never been seen before. The expedition was heralded as a success, and Meriwether Lewis was given a governorship upon their triumphant return. Lewis and Clark had made it to the Pacific Ocean, and their example spurred others to turn west. Manifest Destiny, the belief that Americans were meant to conquer the entire continent from east to west, became a prevalent force in society.

Two issues held up the expansion of these western territories: the nation had to decide how to deal with Native Americans and the question of slavery.

Map of the general route followed by Lewis and Clark

With the expanding borders came public debates about whether to expand and how to define and use the new territories.

The federal and state governments had to negotiate to create an agreement as to the role that slavery should play in the West. The government had kept a delicate balance between the number of slave and free states, splitting the twenty-two states evenly. This peace was maintained until Missouri requested to join the Union as a slave state in 1819. A fierce debate ensued, as abolitionists fought the request. The government eventually decided upon the Missouri Compromise of 1820. Missouri would be a slave state while Maine, formerly part of Massachusetts, would enter the Union as a free state.

Furthermore, the compromise drew an imaginary line across the nation to separate free and slave states. Few people were happy with the compromise. Southerners protested that the federal government was making rules related to slavery, a state issue, and northerners disagreed with the compromise on the premise that it allowed for the expansion of slavery, even if only below the compromise line.

This uneasy peace existed for thirty years until it was repealed by the Kansas–Nebraska Act of 1854, which established the rule of popular sovereignty in both states. This meant that both Kansas and Nebraska could enter the Union as slave states even though they were above the compromise line.

Native American territories caused similar problems, as the tribes tried to establish their land and rules in the face of American migration. President Andrew Jackson (1829-1837) decided this issue with his Indian Removal Act of 1830, which required the relocation of eastern Indians to a territory west of the Mississippi River.

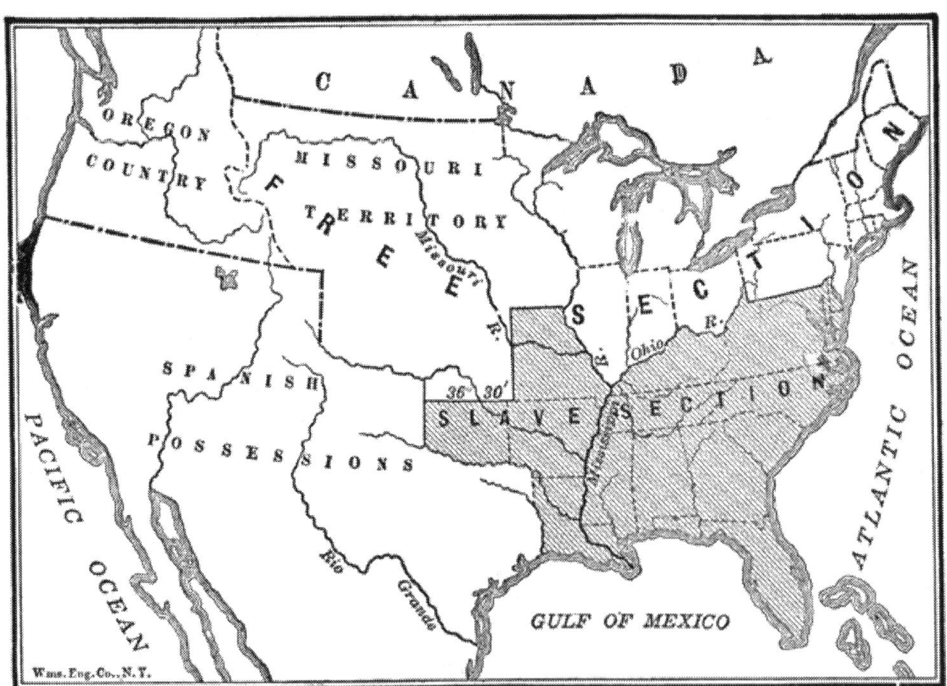

Missouri Compromise, 1820

Although heavily contested, the president ignored the opposition and pursued forced relocation of the American Indian tribes. While activists protested, few people were moved to do anything as the Native Americans' former territory became usable land for agriculture and settlements.

The federal government attempts to assert authority over the states brought resistance from state governments in the North and the South at different times.

While President Andrew Jackson (1765-1845; 1829-1837) sought to repeal parts of the American System such as the National Bank, Congress was considering another tariff, like President Adams' Tariff of 1828, which was called the Tariff of Abominations.

The new tariff was very similar. It was a protectionist tariff that attempted to protect local producers from foreign competition. It did this by taxing imported goods, which would raise their price and make buying American products more appealing.

The issue was that any tariff that taxed imports was going to benefit the North over the South. The North's products, like textiles, would be cheaper than foreign products, causing northern markets to flourish. Southern markets would suffer, mainly cotton, because foreign traders would be able to buy less of these products.

Southerners protested the tariff vehemently, but on July 14, 1832, Andrew Jackson signed it into law. The southern states, which were to be the hardest hit, were outraged. South Carolina particularly resisted the new tariff, and in the winter of 1832, the state government declared it null and void because it was unconstitutional.

In response, President Jackson issued a proclamation disputing South Carolina's ability to ignore federal law. Congress soon passed the Force Act, which would allow a military force to be used against any state that refused to comply with the tariff acts. As tensions grew, a deal was brokered by Henry Clay (1777-1852) and Vice President Calhoun (1825-1832).

The Compromise Tariff of 1833 gradually reduced taxes back to their set levels from 1816. This conflict quickly demonstrated the tensions that still existed between the federal and state governments. It also illustrated why regionalism was inherent in American culture.

Whites living on the frontier tended to champion expansion efforts, while resistance by American Indians led to a sequence of wars and federal efforts to control American Indian populations.

President Jackson's Indian Removal Act was signed into law in 1830. From 1831 to 1839, the Five Civilized Tribes of the Southeast (Cherokee, Chickasaw, Choctaw, Creek, and Seminole) were relocated to the "Indian Territory" west of the Mississippi River. The conditions of their removal are often associated with the Holocaust from World War II.

The Native Americans were forced from their homes with few possessions and marched over land to their new territory. Disease was rampant among the natives, who had no immunity to many of the European plagues, such as smallpox. Some protested the treatment of the Native Americans, but many were willing to ignore their plight in favor of the opportunities opened by their relocation.

Many tribes did not leave their land peaceably. The Seminole tribe in Florida participated in three different wars with the U.S. government to keep their land. The First Seminole War lasted from 1817 to 1818 and was a defense of tribal members. It was started when General Andrew Jackson, pre-presidency, attempted to recapture runaway slaves living with the Seminole tribe. The tribe was shaken by the encounter but defended its members.

Seminole War: an attack upon Fort King by the Indian forces under Osceola, c. 1840

The Second Seminole War (1835-1842) occurred in the wake of Jackson's Indian Removal Act. The tribe had large amounts of highly coveted land that they refused to leave. This time, when soldiers approached, the tribe hid in the Florida Everglades and engaged in guerrilla warfare against the U.S. army.

Their tribe's tactics were incredibly useful and might have continued that way if their leader had not been caught and ransomed back to them. After the Second Seminole War, many members of the tribe moved west. The Third Seminole War (1855-1858) was focused on convincing the last remaining band to move west. Eventually, the federal government paid them to leave.

The American acquisition of lands in the West gave rise to a contest over the extension of slavery into the western territories as well as a series of attempts at national compromise.

As northerners moved westward, a balance was maintained between the free and slave states. As slavery began to move westward, the nation had to decide what to do about slavery and the clear division in national attitudes. The federal government tried several compromises before tensions became too high for them to interfere directly.

The 1820 Missouri Compromise created a truce over the issue of slavery that gradually broke down as confrontations over slavery became increasingly bitter.

While the Missouri Compromise preserved peace in the United States for thirty years, the issues with slavery grew increasingly bitter over time. As slavery spread, so did the abolitionist movement and the firsthand accounts of cruelty under slavery. Freed slaves, like Frederick Douglass, became famous orators and writers, spreading awareness to their cause and painting a picture of slavery that turned many northerners against those in the South who practiced it. This, coupled with laws that allowed hunting parties to look for runaway slaves in the North, polarized the nation and caused a breakdown between the regions.

As over-cultivation depleted arable land in the Southeast, slaveholders relocated their agricultural enterprises to the new Southwest, increasing sectional tensions over the institution of slavery and sparking a broad scale debate about how to set national goals, priorities, and strategies.

As the South finally ran out of arable land, and many southerners were forced to move westward, the slavery issue sparked more public debate over how to redefine territory. The Kansas–Nebraska Act of 1854 established the rule of popular sovereignty in all new states as a way for the federal government to keep from alienating any side or faction. While a worthwhile attempt, the result was a race to populate the state with supporters on both sides before the votes.

Enthusiasm for U.S. territorial expansion—fueled by economic and national security interests and supported by claims of U.S. racial and cultural superiority—resulted in war, the opening of new markets, acquisition of new territory, and increased ideological conflicts.

During the early part of the 19th century, territorial expansion became a full-fledged activity in the U.S. effort to protect its states and to further its economic status. A critical factor that influenced expansion policies opened new markets and caused ideological conflicts was the invention of the cotton gin in 1793 by Eli Whitney (1765-

1793). This machine reduced the time required to separate seeds from cotton fiber, previously a laborious process that required manual labor and primitive tools.

The cotton gin increased the profitability of the cotton industry in the South, and the increase in profits led to a rise in slavery, which many historians cite as the main reason for the Civil War (April 12, 1861 to April 9, 1865). Due to the flourishing cotton industry, the American economy improved dramatically, and cotton was exported in plenty. While the South benefited from the exports, the North—particularly New England—benefited from the ample raw material supply for its textile industry.

The first Industrial Revolution (1790 to 1830) was also influenced by Whitney's production of muskets on a large scale, which was one of the earliest examples of the American mass-production system. The muskets were made of standardized and identical interchangeable parts, enabling faster assembly and repair. This led to the massive production of arms, which was highly profitable for the country.

Gathering cotton in the field of a plantation, c. 1793

The acquisition of new territory in the West and the U.S. victory in the Mexican-American War was accompanied by a heated controversy over allowing or forbidding slavery in the newly acquired territories.

The Mexican-American War (1846–1848) was the first armed conflict fought by the United States entirely on foreign land (although the U.S. had invaded Canada during the War of 1812, this was a part of a more massive war which was mainly fought in what is now the United States America). Texas, which was part of northern Mexico before 1836, had rebelled from Mexico to create the Republic of Texas, which was occupied in large numbers by white American settlers from the South. The Republic of Texas further served as a haven for the African American slaves who settled there because of Mexican antislavery laws. Nearly 5,000 slaves lived in this republic, but when Texas decided to allow slavery, these people lost their rights.

While at first, the United States had declined to annex Texas to the Union because of the reluctance of the political powers in the North against annexing another slave state, the annexation proceeded after Polk was elected president. He wanted to re-annex Texas and reoccupy the Oregon Territory. Polk also initiated talks on purchasing New Mexico and California. Mexico refused, leading to a declaration of war.

Representative David Wilmot, PA

While the war was brewing, David Wilmot (1814-1868) drew the Wilmot Proviso in 1846 to soothe the escalating tension between the North and South. According to the proviso, southerners could acquire new territories, but slavery would be banned in the newly annexed lands. The proviso was passed in the mostly-northern House, but the Senate did not acquiesce, so the proviso was not enacted.

Mexicans led by General Antonio López de Santa Anna (1794-1876), who later became the president of Mexico, could not defend their territory against the advanced artillery and superior rifles of the Americans.

The treaty of Guadalupe Hidalgo, signed in 1848, established the Rio Grande River as the new border between the United States and Mexico, and California and the remaining territories north of Rio Grande as part of the United States. The territories were sold for $15 million. Mexico lost New Mexico, Arizona, Nevada, Utah, and California – nearly one-third of its territories.

The Mexican-American War was controversial because it played a crucial role in expanding slavery. The North had been opposing the Mexican-American War, claiming that the South was trying to expand its slave power with the acquisition of new territories.

The end of the war resulted in a compromise between the North and the South, but the status of slavery remained undetermined, spurring an intense debate that remained unresolved until 1863.

The desire for access to western resources led to the environmental transformation of the region, new economic activities, and increased settlement in areas forcibly taken from American Indians.

During the early 19th century, the United States increased in both power and geographical size. The Louisiana Purchase more than doubled the size of the nation, and the fertility and beauty of the new lands led to more westward expansion.

Additionally, the Louisiana Purchase and the Treaty of Ghent—which ended the War of 1812—removed the foreign infringements in American territory. This proved detrimental to the Native Americans, as they had received protection from these foreign powers. While some of the Indian tribes ceded all their lands, many resisted the U.S. government.

While the Native Americans—especially the Cherokee—tried to resist the takeover of their ancestral lands by founding a nation of their own, the federal government used force and trickery to expel the Indians and exert its dominance over their lands.

With blatant disregard for the sentiments of the natives who had previously inhabited the lands, the government started using the land as if it rightfully owned it. The superior weapons and many armed troops made the settlers a dominant force, undefeatable to the Native Americans who did not have sufficient economic support or resources to fight.

The incessant westward expansion by the United States forced several Native American tribes to resettle further west by force or by reluctant submission. The Indian Removal Act of 1830, passed by the United States Congress under President Andrew Jackson, authorized the exchange of lands east of the Mississippi River for the lands on the western side. This act relocated over 100,000 Native Americans.

Although, in theory, the act was intended to be a voluntary submission of the Native Americans, immense pressure was applied to make them sign the removal treaties.

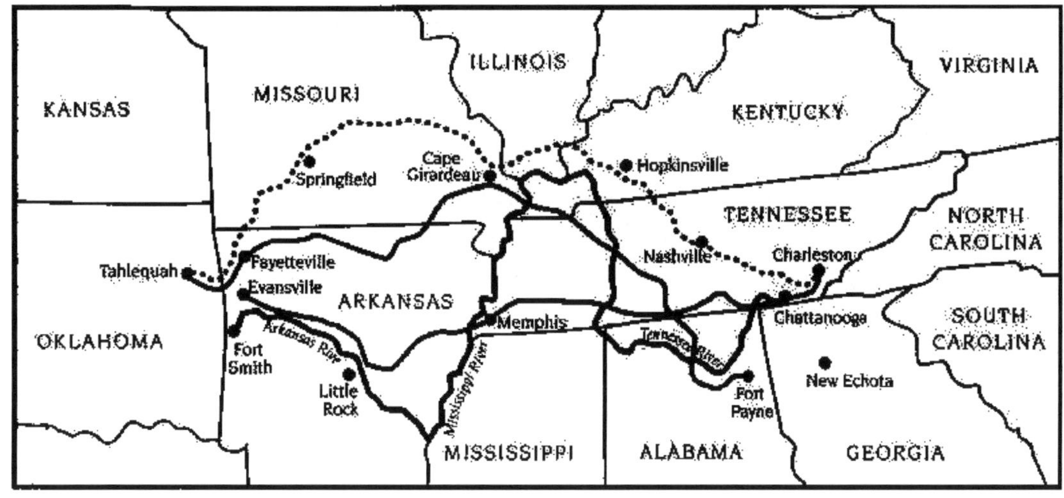

Map route of the Trail of Tears, the forced relocation of Native Americans in the 1830s

The Indian Removal Act spurred massive destruction of the tribes, and the assimilations that followed their removal were even more devastating. The reservations to which these tribes were restricted separated them from their traditional life and forced them to embrace the European American culture.

Those who acknowledged the U.S. supremacy accepted the teachings of missionaries, Christianity, and the inventions of white people. Some states even enacted laws forbidding the settlement of non-Indians on Indian lands to prevent white missionaries from helping the Indian resistance movement.

As the territorial boundaries of the United States expanded and the migrant population increased, U.S. government interaction and conflict with Hispanics and American Indians increased, altering these groups' cultures and ways of life and raising questions about their status and legal rights.

With a marked increase in the migrant population and expansion of territories westward, many conflicts and encounters arose with Native Americans and Hispanics, leading to questions of their legal rights and social status. Mariano Guadalupe Vallejo, born in California in 1808, was affected by the marginalization of his tribe in their land during the territorial expansion of the Union. Born into a Californio family (i.e., a Mexican family living in Alto California), he had been groomed to lead.

When Vallejo was fifteen years old, he joined the Mexican army. He took part in many Mexican and Indian expeditions and played a primary role in quelling the Indian revolts and establishing settlements to prevent Russian settlement in California. Vallejo identified himself with Mexican Liberals in their support of an efficient government that was independent of religious authority.

Vallejo favored the governing model of the United States and, in 1836, led a rebellion declaring California a free state. Although he supported the United States, he was poorly treated by American rebels in 1846. He was imprisoned by General John C. Frémont, leader of the Bear Flag Revolt. Vallejo's estate was damaged, and matters improved only when the rebels were replaced by U.S. forces under the leadership of Brigadier General Stephen Kearney.

Vallejo was made Indian agent for Northern California and was elected to the Senate in 1849. In the wake of the Treaty of Guadalupe Hidalgo, Vallejo lost most of his land. His life is an example of the fate suffered by many Californians under American rule. Despite their acceptance of the democratic U.S. government, they were treated as foreigners and could occupy only the lowest economic rung.

The Sand Creek Massacre was another effect of westward expansion on the country's Native Americans. Although the United States was engaged in conflicts with the Indian tribes due to territorial expansion, the 1851 Treaty of Fort Laramie ceded extensive territory to the Indians.

However, the terms of the treaty were renegotiated in 1861 by the United States after factors like the Pikes Peak Gold Rush in 1858. In 1861, the Treaty of Fort Wise was signed by Arapaho and Southern Cheyenne chiefs. This treaty reduced Native American land to one-third the original amount. The Indian chiefs had signed mainly to safeguard their people, but certain Lakota and Cheyenne tribes who called themselves Dog Soldiers opposed the treaty.

Eyewitness' depiction of the Sand Creek Massacre, November 24, 1864

In 1864, Colonel John Chivington, under orders from Colorado governor John Evans, attacked several Cheyenne camps situated in Colorado. More attacks followed in Kansas under the command of Lt. George S. Eyre. The Cheyenne attacked in retaliation, which further increased tension between the U.S. forces and the Indians.

On November 29, 1864, when most of the males were out hunting, the Colorado Territory militia, led by U.S. Army Colonel John Chivington, attacked the Indian villages of Arapaho and Cheyenne. Most of the people slaughtered were children and women. The massacre later came to be known as the Sand Creek Massacre.

Since the gold discovery in Native American territory, tensions prevailed between the United States and the Indian tribes. When the tribes refused to move their reservations as ordered by the U.S. Army, they were attacked by Custer in the Battle of Little Bighorn. Fought in 1876 near Little Bighorn River, the federal troops under the leadership of Lieutenant Colonel George Armstrong Custer (1839-1876) attacked Cheyenne warriors and the Lakota Sioux.

The Indian tribes fighting under Sitting Bull outnumbered the armed forces and overwhelmed them in what was later termed Custer's Last Stand. Nearly 10,000 Native Americans had joined the Indian camp at Little Bighorn River, which they dubbed Greasy Grass in defiance of the war department's order to move their reservations.

In the Battle of Little Big Horn, 3,000 Native Americans defeated 600 of Custer's men within an hour. The battle was the highest victory by the Native Americans against the invading U.S. army and the worst defeat for the United States in their fight against the Indians. In the wake of the war, the government increased its efforts and confined the Cheyenne and Sioux tribes to reservations.

States' rights, nullification, and racist stereotyping provided the foundation for the southern defense of slavery as a positive good.

The southern states' concern over their rights and their nullification of the laws against their economic growth led to the southern defense of portraying slavery as a sound system. One of the prominent southerners in this aspect was Democrat Senator John C. Calhoun from South Carolina (1782-1850; 1845-1850). A noticeable representative for the antebellum South, he had helped the United States during its war with Great Britain and served as secretary of war, vice president, and secretary of state.

Democrat John C. Calhoun, 1782-1850

Calhoun opposed the Mexican-American War and the annexation of California as a free state, and he was a renowned proslavery speaker. Calhoun initially supported the 1828 Tariff of Abominations, but after receiving criticism from the South, protested it.

Calhoun was elected as a senator for South Carolina (1845-1850) and defended the slave system against the growing antislavery protests. He dominated the American political scene from 1815 to 1850 with his gift as a debater on political, economic, social, and philosophical issues.

The proslavery sections also had support from racist minstrel shows. The shows featured blackface, a theatrical makeup where white performers used stereotyping and makeup to represent a black person. The shows were popular during the 19th century and glorified the slave stereotypes such as "dandified coon" or "happy-go-lucky darky" on the plantation.

The minstrel shows started in 1830 and stayed over one hundred years, becoming an essential tradition in American theater. The stereotypes embodied in the shows played a critical role in cementing as well as enhancing racist attitudes, images, and perceptions.

Repeated attempts at political compromise failed to calm tensions over slavery. They often made sectional tensions worse, breaking down the trust between sectional leaders and culminating in the bitter election of 1860, followed by the secession of southern states.

Northerners attempted several measures to reduce the tensions that prevailed between the North and the South over slavery and other issues, including more power for the southern states. The various attempts to solve the increasing sectional tendencies over slavery worsened the situation and led to the secession of the southern states.

National leaders made a variety of proposals to resolve the issue of slavery in the territories, including the Compromise of 1850, the Kansas-Nebraska Act and the *Dred Scott* (1857) decision. These ultimately failed to reduce sectional conflict.

The slavery conflict spurred by the annexation of territories in the wake of the Mexican-American War was resolved with the Compromise of 1850, which admitted California as a free state and allowed the territories of New Mexico and Utah to determine their slavery status by popular sovereignty.

The compromise aimed at settling the border dispute between Mexico and Texas in favor of the latter and ending the slave trade in Washington, D.C., making it easier for the South to regain fugitive slaves. This compromise led to the avoidance of slavery and regional issues for many years.

Bleeding Kansas: slavery debate in Congress, 1854

The Kansas-Nebraska Act—passed in 1854—allowed territory settlers to decide on slavery based on a popular sovereignty mandate. The bill overturned the Missouri Compromise and thus invalidated the boundary for the free and slave regions. Conflicts in the wake of this act led to what is called Bleeding Kansas, one of the causes of the Civil War in 1861.

This act, which tried to organize the western territories, led to sectionalism and railroad development. It also split both major political parties, leading to the creation of a third party and a worsening of relations between the North and South.

While Kansas was given statehood in 1861, southern states started to secede from the Union. The antislavery Republican Party lost the support of the Northern Whigs and independent Democrats, causing further division within the political parties.

The *Dred Scott* (1857) case was instrumental in Abraham Lincoln (1809-1845; 1861 to April 14, 1865) being elected president in 1860. Dred Scott was a slave who had gained his freedom via the American legal system. In 1857, the United States Supreme Court denied his plea for freedom, stating that a black man could not become a citizen. The abolitionists in the North were outraged by this turn of events.

The second party system ended when the issues of slavery and anti-immigrant nativism weakened loyalties to the two major parties and fostered the emergence of sectional parties, most notably the Republican Party in the North and the Midwest.

The anti-immigrant support and slavery issues that could not be adequately resolved led to the disintegration of the second party system and the formation of sectional parties, such as the Republican Party. While the issue of slavery was the focus, there were economic and social changes that the country had undergone during the 19th century, leading to the reordering of the political system based on separate lines.

During the compromise of 1850, the Democrats and Whigs were the only parties with voter loyalty. In the North, Democrats supported the compromise, and Whigs opposed it. In the upper South, Whigs supported the compromise, and the Democrats opposed it. This competitiveness continued with the Fugitive Slave Law, but the two merged to find a solution to the sectional conflict.

The changing economic structure made the traditional stand of the parties irrelevant, and the Whig ideals became less compelling in the wake of the gold rush in California (1848-1855) and the diversion of European investments to America. The Whigs' support of the high tariffs lost its appeal to the textile manufacturers of the North, as they wanted safety from foreign and local rivals.

The issue of the railroad also caused competition between regions as opposed to political parties. The state constitutions that were introduced from 1848 to 1852 resulted in the weakening of party machinery, as they had fewer opportunities to strengthen party loyalty. The biennial legislative system further reduced the capacity of the political system to pass laws and generated party allegiance.

Concerning nativism, the Democrats welcomed immigration, and the Whigs opposed it. The Whigs were forced to get help from the Catholic immigrants in the presidential election of 1852 to get a favorable vote. The election was the death knell for the Whigs, as they won only in four states. The Democrats won with a 2–1 majority in both Houses. This was mainly due to the controversy over slavery.

The party's decline in the South after the Compromise of 1850, its loss of support in the North, and dissension within the party cadres over the support of the Catholic immigrants all led to the downfall of the Whig Party. This led to the fragmentation of the second party system and realignment efforts for the formation of new parties.

Lincoln's election on a free-soil platform in the election of 1860 led southern leaders to conclude that their states must secede from the Union, precipitating civil war.

Prairie lawyer Abraham Lincoln (1809-1865) enjoyed a short span in Congress (1847 to 1849) and later embraced his law practice fully. He joined the Republican Party in 1856 during a time when sectionalism was at its peak. The debates over the Kansas-

Nebraska Act, slavery, and the role of the territories in these issues made him prominent nationally. However, he was unpopular in the South due to his antislavery ideals.

Lincoln was disliked by the South even before his taking office as president in the year 1861. According to the South, he was an abolitionist and a fanatic of the caliber of John Brown. The South considered him a Republican who would not fear to override the laws and constitution to arrive at a compromise of any nature. During his presidential campaign, Lincoln refrained from announcing any policies, fearing that they may be misunderstood in both the North and South.

President Abraham Lincoln, 1861-1865

The secession crisis emerged because of a disagreement over the validity of the election outcome (Lincoln was elected with a thin minority of the vote and less than half of the Electoral College votes) and, more importantly, a disagreement between north and south about the appropriate boundaries between state and federal governmental powers.

Southerners advocated strong states' rights, while northerners favored a robust federalist system. Despite being elected by a majority of voters, Lincoln's authority was rejected by southerners. Their threats of secession were a way to pressure Lincoln and the Republicans into accepting state autonomy.

The secession crisis was not new in 1860; it had already existed for over a decade. While the Compromise of 1850 had put down some of the ardor in the discord, the growing unrest among the southerners made them repeatedly resort to the threat of secession.

The secession issue caused both the slaves and southern landowners to evaluate the changing political scene. The entire social system of slave and master had been challenged after Lincoln's election. The collapse of the prevailing political system made the slaves look for new opportunities.

The slaveholders wanted the secession because they saw it as a positive step towards maintaining the stability of the master-slave balance. Northern intervention into their political and economic situation increased unrest among the slaves, and the deteriorating relationship between the masters and slaves led to their support of secession.

In 1860, Lincoln won the election without the support of the southern states. To preserve the Union, Lincoln decided to fight secession rather than accept it. Lincoln believed in preserving the union of the North and South by prudent and, at times, forceful execution of power. His use of flexible tactics in an inflexible pursuit of reunification helped the North win the war. Lincoln's wise judgments on when to use or avoid military force (such as the intense military domination in Maryland and the moderate handling of the opposition in Kentucky) helped the North gain victory and prevent secession.

The Union victory in the Civil War and the contested Reconstruction of the South settled the issues of slavery and secession. However, they left many unresolved questions about the power of the federal government and citizenship rights.

While the victory of the Union upheld the antislavery stand, helped resolve slavery issues and further put a stop to any idea of secession, unresolved issues remained regarding the extent of power wielded by the federal government and the rights given to the citizens.

Some of these issues included the northern states' failure to return fugitive slaves, the northern support of abolitionists and insurrectionists such as John Brown, and the religious and political beliefs of the North, which were not accepted by the southerners. The South was also against the idea of granting citizenship rights and voting rights to the slaves.

The North's more considerable manpower and industrial resources, its leadership, and the decision for emancipation eventually led to the Union military victory over the Confederacy in the devastating Civil War.

There are many reasons the Confederacy lost the Civil War (April 12, 1861 to April 9, 1865), but the main reason is that the North had more guns and men. The Union had overwhelming numbers of men, resources, and luck on its side, making it a very tough fight for the South. The large social divisions within southern society are also cited as a reason for the Confederacy's defeat. Southern society was rife with racial, class, and even regional antagonisms, all of which contributed to the fall of the South. These factors, together with the lack of resources, arms, and men, enabled the northern defeat of the South.

Both the Union and the Confederacy mobilized their economies and societies to wage war even while facing considerable home front opposition.

While it is broadly believed that the Union's resources were the main reason for their defeat of the Confederate army, some historians insist that it was the Confederate's approach that led to their defeat.

The Union had several advantages:

- The Union had 22 million people against 9 million in the South (of whom only 5.5 million were white).
- The firearm manufacturers in the North had a higher capacity than those in the South.
- A robust naval blockade prevented the South from getting materials.
- Four slave states—Kentucky, Maryland, Missouri, and Delaware—supported the Union.
- Some people within the Confederate states were not fully supportive of its cause.

Despite their many disadvantages, southerners were confident the Confederacy would win the war. The 750,000 square miles occupied by the South were considered a huge asset, making it difficult to occupy and conquer.

Battle of Fort Sumter during the Civil War, 1861

The South had the advantage of defending their land instead of invading the North. Additionally, the rifles in use were best suited for defensive rather than offensive tactics.

Geographically, the rivers flowing through North Virginia made it difficult for the Union armies to conquer Richmond, the capital of the Confederates.

Finally, while the northerners were engaged in the war in pursuit of a reunion, the southerners had a more needy cause, that of defending their homes and lands, making their fight more psychologically immediate.

The Confederate victory in the initial major battle at Manassas confirmed Confederate supremacy, and expert opinion contends that had the Confederate forces been more proactive and brought Britain on their side, they might have been more successful.

Therefore, a combination of missed opportunities and lack of luck is also cited for the downfall of the Confederates.

Lincoln's decision to issue the Emancipation Proclamation changed the purpose of the war, enabling many African Americans to fight in the Union army and helping prevent the Confederacy from gaining support from European powers.

Lincoln's Emancipation Proclamation was a critical document that changed the objective of the war. It is also one of the least understood documents in U.S. history. The Emancipation Proclamation was issued twice, first in 1862 and again in 1863. It applied only to the states that rebelled and intended to restrict the Confederacy. While at first, the cabinet did not support the proclamation, it later did so after witnessing the victory at Antietam and noting Lincoln's continued commitment towards executing its ideals.

While the initial aim of the Civil War (April 12, 1861 to April 9, 1865) was safeguarding the Union from disintegration, freedom for the slaves became the primary objective after the Emancipation Proclamation was issued. Another advantage of the Emancipation Proclamation was that it prevented foreign nations from supporting the Confederates, as the European nations were against slavery.

The proclamation also helped African Americans to participate in their fight for liberation. Nearly 200,000 African Americans served the Union navy and army by the end of the Civil War. The Emancipation Proclamation encouraged citizens to advocate and accept the abolition of slavery in both the North and South.

Although Confederate leadership showed initiative and daring early in the war, the Union ultimately succeeded due to improved military leadership, more effective strategies, key victories, more considerable resources, and wartime destruction of the South's environment and infrastructure.

Events like Gettysburg and Sherman's March to the Sea reinforced the fact that the Union had won because of their plentiful resources, key victories, effective leadership, and efficient strategies. While the Civil War—like any other war—did not have one single moment that turned out to be the turning point, it did have many crucial moments that, in retrospect, clearly indicated the way it would end.

General Lee's (1807-1870; 1862-1865) repulse of McClellan's army in Richmond in 1862, the victory of the Union in Antietam, the Emancipation Proclamation, and the successes that ensued at Gettysburg and Vicksburg in 1863 all transformed the fight significantly.

General Robert E. Lee, 1807-1870

Lee's defeat at Gettysburg showed that victory was imminent for the Union. The clear defeat and massive damage incurred by the Confederates, together with the final capture at Vicksburg, demoralized them and restored control of the Mississippi River to the hands of the Union.

The March to the Sea is another landmark event that strengthened Union supremacy. Led by General William T. Sherman, the Union army destroyed most of Georgia and captured Savannah from the Confederates in 1864. While Atlanta was a Confederate stronghold, Sherman had the needed supplies and troops to defeat the Confederates and destroy Georgia.

The Civil War and Reconstruction altered power relationships between the states and the federal government and among the executive, legislative and judicial branches, ending slavery and the notion of a divisible union but leaving unresolved questions of relative power and largely unchanged social and economic patterns.

The Civil War and the period of Reconstruction (1865-1877) that ensued changed political relationships and power dynamics in all aspects, including the legislative, executive, judicial, and federal government policies. It also marked the end of slavery and the division of the Union. However, it did not resolve the questions related to the control of power and the change in the economic and social patterns.

Reconstruction entailed the first step taken by the United States to develop an interracial democratic system. The war also resulted in the ratification of the Thirteenth, Fourteenth, and Fifteenth Amendments of the Constitution, which declared slavery a federal crime and brought in a new dimension to citizenship and universal male suffrage. This promised new powers and an active role by the government in enforcing the amendments.

The Thirteenth Amendment abolished slavery, bringing about the war's most dramatic social and economic change, but the exploitative and soil-intensive sharecropping system endured for several generations.

The Thirteenth Amendment (ratified December 6, 1865), passed in 1865 by the House of Representatives, abolished slavery in the United States and all places subject to its jurisdiction. During the war, the purpose of the struggle changed from the restoration of the Union to freeing the slaves. This prompted Lincoln to issue the Emancipation Proclamation.

The Thirteenth Amendment was not accepted in 1864, as the Democrats were worried about the rights of the states. Lincoln's election, along with Republican majority votes in both Houses, helped in passing the Thirteenth Amendment successfully in 1865, leading to the eradication of slavery, which had left behind an indelible mark in the history of the United States.

The amendment was ratified eight months after the war ended. The Thirteenth Amendment represented the resolution of the long, drawn-out struggle for the freedom of the slaves. When the war started, some northerners were against it, as they saw it as a crusade to end slavery. While most of the Democrats and conservative Republicans in the North opposed the expansion of slavery, they were against abolishing it entirely.

However, in the wake of the First Battle of Bull Run in Virginia (July 21, 1861), they reconsidered the role slavery played in the conflict. By 1862, Lincoln was convinced that without abolishing slavery, the war did not serve any purpose.

First Battle of Bull Run, stand of the Union troops at the Henry House, July 21, 1861

Therefore, after the big victory at the Battle of Antietam in Maryland, Lincoln issued the Emancipation Proclamation, declaring that slaves in all the rebelling territories would be declared free. The move was symbolic, as it freed only the slaves in the regions outside the control of the Union. However, it changed the main objective of the war from a reunification effort to the destruction of slavery.

Lincoln strongly believed in the need for a substantial constitutional amendment to end slavery ultimately. While Congress debated several proposals in 1864, which included incorporating provisions that would prevent discrimination against blacks, the Judiciary Committee of the Senate was the body that provided the final language of the amendment. The conditions were drawn from the 1787 Northwest Ordinance, which had banned slavery from the region north of the Ohio River.

The Thirteenth Amendment was passed in 1864, and the victory of Republicans in the election guaranteed its successful implementation.

The Radical Republicans wanted the complete abolition of slavery, while the Democrats wanted restoration of the states' rights. Lincoln's victory in the election ensured that the ratification of the amendment was done smoothly.

When the House passed the amendment in 1865, it was sent to the states.

After Georgia ratified the Thirteenth Amendment on December 6, 1865, slavery ceased to be an institution in the United States.

Efforts by radical and moderate Republicans to reconstruct the defeated South changed the balance of power between Congress and the presidency. These Republican efforts yielded some short-term successes, reuniting the union, opening political opportunities, and other leadership roles to former slaves and rearranging the relationships between white and black people in the South.

With the end of the war, the fight for power emerged with renewed vigor as the moderate and Radical Republicans tried to change the power balance between the president and Congress. This led to positions of leadership and political significance among the former slaves. Notable among the Republicans were Hiram Revels, Blanche K. Bruce, and Robert Smalls.

Republican Hiram Revels (1827-1901; 1863-1865) was the first African American to become a member of Congress when he was made a senator of Mississippi, filling in for Jefferson Davis, the former senator, and Confederate president. He was part of the committee of Labor and Education in the District of Columbia. While Revels was not predominantly for racial equality, he opposed the segregation of schools in Washington, D.C. He was also an advocate for the black people banned from working in the Navy Yard in Washington because of their racial identity.

Republican Robert Smalls (1839-1915; 1862-1868) was an African American Congressman who represented South Carolina from 1882 to 1883. He was enslaved until 1862 when he piloted a Confederate ship into Union waters. Smalls became actively involved in politics and, in 1870, was an influential leader in South Carolina. He was against segregation in railroads, eating establishments, and the military, and he opposed the western emigration of African Americans in America as well as their emigration to Liberia.

Republican Blanche K. Bruce (1841-1898; 1875-1881) escaped slavery during the initial phase of the Civil War. He has the distinction of being the first African American to serve as Mississippi senator full-term and head a Senate session. Bruce wanted better treatment of the Native Americans and advocated army desegregation. He was part of the committee to improve navigation on the Mississippi River.

Radical Republicans' efforts to change southern racial attitudes and culture and establish a base for their party in the South ultimately failed due both to determined southern resistance and to the North's waning resolve.

Despite several arduous efforts by the Republicans, especially the Radical Republicans, resolving slavery failed to bear fruit as the South steadily resisted all the moves towards altering their racial attitude. The sectional wounds wrought by the war failed to heal during Reconstruction (1865-1877).

While the North tried to bring the South back into the Union and give it equal footing by reviving its economy and rebuilding the southern landscape battered by war, the deep divisions in the federal government prevented the attainment of these goals.

Furthermore, the assassination of Lincoln led to Andrew Johnson—a proslavery leader—becoming president. Andrew Johnson (1808-1875; 1865-1869) started a Reconstruction plan that was against rights for the freed slaves. While the Confederates tried to enter the power positions in the government, the Republicans who had a dominant role in Congress refused to yield.

President Andrew Johnson, 1865-1869

While the Radical Republicans opposed the southerners, moderates and conservatives wanted the southerners to be admitted. The Radical Republicans were committed to the total emancipation of slaves and equal treatment and enfranchisement of freed slaves. During its formation in the 1850s, the Radical Republican Party—consisting of northern industrialists, altruists, practical politicians, and former Whigs—was not committed to abolitionism. However, it did attract some of the most fervent antislavery advocates.

While President Abraham Lincoln insisted that restoring the Union was the main aim of the Civil War, abolitionists in Congress wanted emancipation included as well. The Radical Republicans formed the Joint Committee of the Conduct of the War due to agitation over the poor performance of the Union army and the lack of attention given to emancipation. The Radicals favored including black troops and eventually broke with Lincoln over his Reconstruction policy and his reluctance to enforce the speedy abolition of slavery.

The areas in the South under military control were subjected to Reconstruction under the command of Lincoln, who had planned on including only 10 percent of the southern electorate for forming the government. The Radical Republicans were not satisfied with Lincoln's Ten Percent Plan. They produced the Wade Davis Bill, which required fifty percent of the white male population of a state to take an oath of loyalty and excluded an increasing number of Confederates from taking part in the restored governments.

Portrait of Lincoln surrounded by Civil War scenes, c. 1865

When Lincoln vetoed the bill, the Radical Republicans were enraged and launched an effort to deny Lincoln a second-time nomination. While they welcomed Andrew Johnson when it was clear that he pursued the same lenient policies in Reconstruction (1865-1877), they formed the Joint Committee on Reconstruction to ensure that Reconstruction was under congressional control rather than presidential control. They passed several measures to safeguard the political involvement of blacks in the South despite Johnson's vetoes.

Despite the Radical Republicans' efforts, white control of southern governments was gradually restored. The African Americans were frightened and prevented from participating in the polls by terrorist organizations such as the Knights of the White Camellia and the Ku Klux Klan.

Furthermore, the North lost its initial zeal over the continued military occupation of the southern states, and Reconstruction efforts failed by the end of 1877. One reason for this failure was Northern politicians' lack of cohesiveness as a group.

Their commitment to emancipation and ending racial discrimination were the only threads that held them together. They were not united over other critical issues such as labor reform, protectionism, and hard or soft money.

In the wake of the Civil War, the economic prosperity of the North—where the industrial inventions and output increased enormously—also led to a further divide between the North and the South. The subsequent depression and the northern boom served to make the Reconstruction efforts fail.

Additionally, some of the white supremacy factions combined with Black Codes to dominate the freed slaves and deny them civil liberties. The Supreme Court rulings also limited the rights of the African American population.

The disparity in the sharecropping system pushed the African Americans into debt, which evoked their dependence during slavery. They remained an oppressed community and were afforded only second-class citizenship until the 20th century.

Post-Civil War migration to the American West, encouraged by economic opportunities and government policies, caused the federal government to violate treaties with American Indian nations to expand the amount of land available to settlers.

As the Civil War came to an end, the West was sparsely populated. There were notable settlements in Texas and lands promised to Native Americans taking up most of Oklahoma and Kansas, but other sections of the West were considered wild and unsettled. This was quickly remedied with the conception of a transcontinental railroad, which would provide the people, goods, and services necessary for the westward expansions called for by the government. During the 1870s and 1880s, the West grew at an alarming rate, causing many more to settle west of the Mississippi.

Using the railroad companies and governmental policies, the United States created large land grants that angered many settlers in the West. Examples of this can be seen throughout the Gilded Age (1870s to 1900), where disgruntled settlers attacked land grant sites, cutting off railroads and temporarily stalling the progress made by these steam giants. Such opposition did not change the policies of the U.S. government, which sought to settle the wildlands of the West at any cost.

As the expansion continued, it seemed inevitable that it would be at the expense of Native American populations, who had been promised lands after being displaced from the East Coast following the initial American expansion of the Atlantic Seaboard.

In hopes of bringing an end to Native American aggression, the United States sought to enact several treaties to eliminate coercive actions. These included the Medicine Lodge Treaty signed in 1867, in which the federal government recognized the Great Plains as individual tribal lands allocated by the federal government.

Other treaties of the period included the Fort Laramie Treaty signed in 1868, which concluded warfare along the Bozeman Trail and promised vast areas of Wyoming, Montana and the Dakota territories, including the Black Hills, to the Lakota people.

Many of these treaties would eventually be violated as the U.S. government failed to secure enough land in the western regions not already promised to the Native American populations. Land grants in the West given to railroad companies greatly influenced this process and would become commonplace along the frontier and in the settled West.

Additionally, the practice of land-grant colleges during this period strained the territorial resources available, while also establishing sixty-nine colleges. The Native American and Mexican populations, who believed the U.S. government would expand their territories until all other settlers were expelled and replaced with American frontier men and women, frowned upon the use of such policies, but were powerless to stop them.

The long-term implications for such policies can be seen today, especially in the western portion of the United States, where Native American tribes maintain their traditions and culture on the reservations surrounded by the unfamiliarity of the contemporary United States.

Such policies also brought criticism on many Americans both during the period and in later decades; policies regarding Native American programs and assistance have not seen much progress.

The U.S. government generally responded to American Indian resistance with military force, eventually dispersing tribes onto small reservations and hoping to end American Indian tribal identities through assimilation.

As a result of westward expansion, the American government was again forced to enact domestic policies to address growing concerns over its interactions with Native American populations. In the early part of the 19th century, many Native American tribes had been allowed to remain on their native lands, with intermittent regulation attempts by the U.S. government.

By the mid-19th century, the government had changed its policies to limit Native American access to land; they enacted the concentration policy, which removed Native American populations from areas white settlers wished to inhabit.

Following the Civil War, regiments of soldiers, most notably those led by Generals William Sherman, P. T. Sheridan, and George Custer, took up military offensives against Native American tribes.

The policy of forcefully dispelling resistance was commonplace in the U.S. military during this period. It can be seen in the Sioux War (1876–1877) and Nez Perce conflicts, culminating in the battle at Wounded Knee in 1890.

In hopes of maintaining their livelihood and traditions, many Native Americans took up arms against the military forces and called upon their deities in hopes of evading assimilation.

One notable example of the resistance movement by Native Americans comes from the Nez Perce tribe, initially located in the Northwest, mainly in Oregon. This tribe, led by Chief Joseph, fought to maintain their lands in Wallowa Valley; however, they were repeatedly engaged by American military forces and were eventually defeated in 1877.

The government initially promised relocation to ancestral lands, but instead placed the remaining tribal members in malaria-infested camps in Kansas and Oklahoma, decimating the population. To avoid a similar outcome, many Native Americans began practicing ghost dancing as a means of avoiding forced relocation.

On the eve of each new moon, many Native American tribes would practice this ritual, which eventually caused disturbance amongst white settlers. The authorities intervened, causing deaths and further soured the relations.

Gilded Age politics were intimately tied to big business and focused nationally on economic issues—tariffs, currency, corporate expansion, and laissez-faire economic policy—that engendered numerous calls for reform.

The domestic politics of the United States during the Gilded Age (1870s to 1900) focused primarily on economic and social transitions produced as a result of the unregulated markets and the tremendous expansion of the industrial capacities of the factories where most Americans now worked.

After years of struggling to subsist in their new urban surroundings, many in the working and immigrant classes began seeing the role of the government as too limited and accommodating the members of big business.

Regarding corporate expansion, the American public had seen the rise of empire and monopoly in the United States through the railroad and steel companies dominated by the Vanderbilt and Rockefeller families.

The banking industry of this period had been wholly influenced by J. P. Morgan (1837-1913), who stabilized the financial markets many times before finally being defeated by the chaos of the Great Depression. These hands-off policies in the manufacturing, production, and economic sectors would end, for the most part, in the early years of the 20th century.

Tariffs were also an area of concern for many factory workers and consumers during this period, as well as factory and manufacturing owners. While the use of tariffs benefited the owners, it had the opposite effect on consumers, who typically belonged to the working class.

The two types of tariffs included revenue tariffs, which fund agencies, and protective tariffs, which allowed American companies the ability to compete with the prices and services of foreign companies at the expense of the consumer. Such policies were heavily influenced by the business elite and caused division between the management and working classes.

The currency was another topic of interest and contention during this period, causing the further division of Americans, this time into supporters and opponents of soft currency. In 1873, The Fourth Coinage Act was enacted to create the gold standard, which was opposed by those who argued silver was a more logical choice given that the mines were already producing vast silver reserves.

Corruption in government—especially as it related to big business—energized the public to demand increased popular control and reform of local, state, and national governments, ranging from minor changes to major overhauls of the capitalist system.

Leading up to and during the Gilded Age, many Americans perceived the government's role as one that enforced law and order but stopped short of ensuring the social welfare of the American population.

However, this idea began to change in the late 19th century and caused many to embrace new ideas surrounding the regulation of business and corruption by local, state, and federal officials.

One notable incident that caused many to support regulation was the American transcontinental railroad scandal, where the Union Pacific and Crédit Mobilier companies had engaged in an interlocking directorate.

After further investigation, it was discovered Union Pacific had paid Crédit Mobilier at highly inflated rates, making the supply company rich at the expense of the American public and Union Pacific shareholders.

East and West shaking hands at the laying of the last rail of the Union Pacific Railroad, 1869

Many Americans who lacked support from the government turned to the neighborhood and fraternal organizations that provided services to those typically neglected by state and federal institutions.

As these organizations grew, they became substantially more powerful and were able to influence and infiltrate the political entities of the cities for which they provided services. Such influence and lack of federal or state regulations quickly led to corruption, "under the table" dealings and the establishment of the "good ol' boy" network.

As Americans saw this corruption, now fully integrated within the government system, they began to embrace ideas of socialism, which before had been entirely out of the question.

Reformers working against machine politics, most notably those embraced by William "Boss" Tweed at Tammany Hall in New York, were able to convince the American population of the need for reforms.

ECONOMIC DEVELOPMENTS:

1790 - 1877

The expansion of slavery in the lower South and adjacent western lands, and its gradual disappearance elsewhere, began to create distinctive regional attitudes toward the institution.

Unlike the southern elite of the antebellum era, who tended to glorify slave society, most early American leaders from both the North and South saw slavery as distasteful and outdated. They envisioned that slavery would eventually die out on its own. The Virginian founders who later became Presidents (including Washington, Jefferson, Madison, and Monroe) were all slaveholders with interest in the gradual abolition of slavery.

The Northwest Ordinance also banned slavery in the vast northwestern territories of the United States without much protest from southern politicians. Southerners were content that it would be challenging to grow competing tobacco in the new territories without slave labor.

The introduction of new breeds of cotton and the invention of the cotton gin allowed for explosive growth in cotton agriculture in the South. At the same time, the mechanization of textile manufacturing, the first stage of the Industrial Revolution, led to a vastly increased demand for cotton, especially in Britain. As new cotton lands opened in the West, slaveholders in the East saw the value of their slave property increasing as the prices of slaves rapidly increased.

Eli Whitney watching the cotton gin, c. 1793

Meanwhile, slavery was disappearing in the North. During the Revolutionary War, blacks in New England were agitating for emancipation. During the 1780s, several states passed laws of gradual or immediate emancipation, and by 1804 all the northern states had taken such steps.

Vermont had joined as a free state, and the new states carved out of the Northwestern Territory would become free states as well. However, Kentucky and Tennessee entered the Union as slave states, and the lands to the southwest were prime candidates for cotton plantations worked by large numbers of slaves.

Founding Father Benjamin Franklin

Boston-born Benjamin Franklin (1706-1790), a former slaveholder, became one of the most vocal opponents of slavery. In 1790, the octogenarian petitioned Congress, proposing that slavery should be abolished throughout the United States. Quakers from Pennsylvania were also agitating for the same policy. Their petitions provoked great anger and controversy in the House of Representatives.

Southern representatives argued that slavery was justified by the Bible and economically necessary in the South. They also feared that any debate on this topic might inspire slave rebellions. Some northern representatives claimed that slavery was not protected by the Constitution and directly contradictory to the message of the Declaration of Independence.

As a response, both South Carolina and Georgia made threats to secede from the union. To avoid disintegration, hostilities, or possibly even civil war, Madison brokered a solution that suggested Congress had no right to abolish slavery, as it was a state matter.

Slavery continued and expanded into the new lands to the west of the original southern states. By the time of the Civil War, twice as many slaves had been taken from the Eastern Seaboard into the new states as had arrived from Africa in the whole of colonial and national history. This expansion of slavery and slave-owner power and wealth would become the most divisive political issue of 19th- century United States.

With the acceleration of a national and international market economy, Americans debated the scope of the government's role in the economy. At the same time, diverging economic systems meant that regional political and economic loyalties often continued to overshadow national concerns.

As the government and the country started to grow, the United States had to deal with its place in the world as an economic market. By 1805, constant conflict between Britain and France was starting to put military, financial, and social pressure on America.

When British ships began targeting American vessels on the high seas and abducting American soldiers using the practice of impressment, Jefferson implemented the Embargo Act of 1807, which prohibited American goods from being exported overseas.

The intention was to withhold several of the raw materials that the British and French relied on economically, like cotton. Jefferson hoped that this would pressure both countries into leaving American vessels unmolested. Sadly, the act did more to hinder American growth than French or British aggression due to stockpiles in Europe. James Madison eventually repaired the relationship with the French, but not with Britain, setting the stage for the War of 1812.

While the Embargo Act made sense from a national standpoint, most of the states were against it because it would hurt them individually. Many of the northern states were unsuited for the agricultural specialization that flourished in the South.

They were less arable, and the lack of slaves meant that labor was more expensive. Eventually, the northern states began to industrialize, building factories that supplied the country with materials that had been previously supplied by Europe.

At the time of the War of 1812, Europe was supplying most farming tools and weapons to the United States. The North also protested vehemently, because the northern states were heavily involved in the shipping industry. They stood to lose a significant amount of money because of Jefferson's embargo.

In the South, agriculture was the primary profession. Products like tobacco and cotton made southern plantations very lucrative. This was due in part to the cheap labor provided by slavery. Southerners primarily sold goods to Europeans, although, as the North industrialized, clothing factories began competing for southern cotton. This meant that both regions were opposed to the idea of the embargo because it gave them less of an opportunity to market and sell their goods.

Disputes like this between state and federal governments persisted, as regional interests continued to differ from overarching national plans.

Transporting cotton

A global market and communications revolution, influencing and influenced by technological innovations, led to dramatic shifts in agriculture and manufacturing.

The early 1800s saw some significant shifts in technology and business. Suddenly, machines that could do the work of multiple men, with less strain and effort, were available. This rocked the market foundation of the country and opened the door for several possibilities. These changes were rapid and far-reaching, affecting everything from where new communities settled to gender roles and family relationships.

Two major problems were facing the early U.S. agricultural market: communication and transportation. With long-distance communication existing only in the form of letters, it was challenging to determine markets for products and establish fair buying and selling practices.

For example, a tobacco farmer in North Carolina may not have wanted to sell his tobacco in North Carolina because most of the other farmers in the state also grew tobacco, saturating the local market.

This meant that the farmer had to find a different market for his goods to profit. The farmer's market options were limited due to the difficulty of transportation. If the farmer could not get his items to a new market, they were virtually worthless.

All of this changed as infrastructure created safer and more comfortable transportation and with the creation of the telegraph by Samuel Morse in 1844.

Samuel Morse making the telegraph, 1844

Innovations, including textile machinery, steam engines, interchangeable parts, canals, railroads, and the telegraph, as well as agricultural inventions, both extended markets and brought efficiency to production for those markets.

America's development was very dependent on technological innovation. Samuel Slater, for instance, is often referred to as the father of the American factory system.

After covertly memorizing the setup of a British textile mill, Slater came to the United States and put his mill into practice. While he used methods already conventional in Britain, they were new to Americans and revolutionized how northerners looked at their labor force.

Slater further changed the factory system by constructing a small town for his factory. By employing families and housing them at the factory, Slater believed he could improve production. This system gave families an option outside of semi-subsistence farming—the typical lifestyle, at the time—although most factory families obtained some of their food through farming.

Samuel Slater, 1768-1835

Other innovators focused on agriculture. Cyrus McCormick (1809-1884) is not well known in the modern era, but his company became part of International Harvester in 1902, which still supplies farming equipment today. McCormick's invention, the mechanical reaper, meant that harvesting was no longer limited to the amount that could be cut by hand.

Beyond that, McCormick created an entire industry, including creditors and a service department utilizing the new concept of interchangeable parts. His business model is still relevant in a modern market, and many enterprises follow a similar plan.

John Deere (1804-1886) started his company with the manufacture of plows that could tackle the prairie lands where grassroots made the sod thick and difficult to penetrate. His innovative design began what is still a successful agricultural business.

Increasing numbers of Americans, especially women in factories and low-skilled male workers, no longer relied on semi-subsistence agriculture but made their livelihoods producing goods for distant markets, even as some urban entrepreneurs went into finance rather than manufacturing.

The Slater method of employment, in which entire families were housed and taken care of by the factory, was later adapted in Massachusetts by Frances Cabot Lowell (1775-1817), who employed farm girls and young women instead of whole families. The girls were housed in supervised dormitories and were provided with educational and cultural opportunities. While this type of situation often raises suspicion as to working conditions and pay, the Lowell system was extremely beneficial to its workers.

Lowell women at the loom, c. 1810

Lowell drew in a ready and willing labor force by hiring young women, typically from rural communities, where they would not have had many opportunities to better themselves. Lowell's system had an impact on the Women's Rights Movement, helping to encourage more women to join political movements, empowering them to demand rights and education equal to their male counterparts.

With the progression of the market and the development of new factories, the discovery of anthracite coal deposits in Pennsylvania was a blessing to the nation. As industrialization continued, it became apparent that there were not enough trees to power the growing factories. Coal was a good solution, especially anthracite, with its high carbon content that allows it to burn longer than most other types of coal.

Finding ways to mine and transport coal proved difficult. It took an entire generation to prepare the mountainous areas of Pennsylvania for coal mining. Canals were built to connect the coal mines with cities that needed their product.

Eventually, railways replaced water transportation, which meant that more coal could reach the market at a higher speed. It also meant that coal tycoons, having control of the product and the means of transportation, could sway the future of entire regions.

Regional economic specialization, especially the demands of cultivating southern cotton, shaped settlement patterns and the national and international economy.

Many scholars believe that multiple variables affected where and when settlement occurred in the United States during the 1800s. Before 1815, settlements were relatively slow to expand and branch out, particularly beyond the Appalachian Mountains, because there was very little immigration due to wars in Europe and the War of 1812 in America. Following the war, immigration to the United States increased rapidly, with the promise of new land in the Louisiana Territory.

Southern cotton furnished the raw material for manufacturing in the Northeast. In contrast, growth in cotton production and trade promoted the development of national economic ties, shaped the international economy, and fueled the internal slave trade.

One of the country's most important agricultural products was cotton. While important before the Revolutionary War, cotton became one of the most influential American products in the world after Eli Whitney developed the cotton gin in 1793. Whitney's machine allowed cotton production to increase at unheard-of rates: nearly 800 percent in the first decade.

King Cotton, as it was called, was an excellent money-maker that created high competition and provided good returns on investment. It did not spoil the way produce did, and could, therefore, be sold in domestic markets and overseas. Typically, cotton was grown in the South and sold to factories in the northern states, or to England, whose thriving textile factories could not be adequately fed by European wool. If sold to England—and, on average, 80 percent was—cotton was transported on northern shipping vessels. This meant that the North also prospered from the sale of cotton.

Picking cotton, c. 1790

The increase in production also meant an increase in labor; slavery became even more deeply ingrained into the southern economy as new labor forces were always needed to keep up with growing demand. Slave ships illegally transported cargo from Africa and the Caribbean to southern markets.

Many slave women were encouraged or forced to produce children. Poor farmers, those who did not own slaves and could not afford to buy them, often stopped planting other crops to focus on cotton. Southerners were eventually forced to seek out new farmland as their one crop system quickly drained the land of its resources. This eventually raised the question of whether slavery should be allowed to spread into new territories and is why the cotton gin is often cited as a cause of the Civil War.

Despite some governmental and private efforts to create a unified national economy, most notably the American System, the shift to market production linked the North and the Midwest more closely than either was linked to the South.

Cotton wasn't the only thing tying the North and South together. John Quincy Adams, son of former President John Adams, focused on America's internal integrity using the American System.

Secretary of State Henry Clay (1777-1852; 1825-1829) created the American System consisting of three main pieces: a tariff that was designed to promote American industry, a national bank to help establish productive business and enterprise, and federal monetary support for infrastructure to help agriculture reach new, more profitable markets inside the United States.

While the American System was not very popular, especially with Adams' political opponents, it did achieve significant strides in infrastructure. The Cumberland Road, also known as the National Road, connected the Potomac and Ohio Rivers and allowed for westward expansion at an exponential rate.

Adams also commissioned a series of canals that opened America's waterways to encourage economic growth. This was partially due to the *Gibbons v. Ogden* (1824) Supreme Court decision, which allowed the federal government the right to regulate interstate trade. As railroads and canals made interstate commerce easier, the county's prosperity continued to grow. By the time Adams left office, the national debt had been reduced to one-third of its size.

Adams hoped that its continued economic growth could unite America, but many people, particularly southerners, disliked his American System because it limited the number of markets for products like cotton. This meant a limit on competition and price.

The North was not as impacted because it could adapt its shipping industries inward. The North and western territories grew closer as more commerce and movement opened between the two. The South, in comparison, stayed relatively isolated by its beliefs and its economic and infrastructural differences.

Efforts to exploit the nation's natural resources led to government efforts to promote free and forced migration of American peoples across the continent. Also, new ideas defined and managed labor systems, geographical boundaries, and natural resources.

Natural resources were abundant in the Americas. Virtually untouched, America had immense forests that could be turned into boats or tools. They could be shipped to Europe where lumber was more expensive and far less plentiful.

Abundant supplies of fresh, clean water supported the creation of new towns and communities while also allowing for faster travel of people, resources, and news.

America also had vast untapped mineral wealth, including coal, iron, copper, silver, and gold. As each of these resources was discovered, an industry grew to harvest it for consumption elsewhere. These jobs were dangerous but profitable, so a steady supply of labor was almost always on hand.

Disease and bodily harm created concerns about job safety, and regulation became a topic of national interest.

The economic changes caused by the market revolution had significant effects on migration patterns, gender and family relations, and the distribution of political power.

Businesses tended to differ from region to region, depending on the type of environment. For instance, in the agricultural areas, cities were very far apart, as settlers claimed the land for farming.

In areas where the growing season or land was not conducive to agriculture, people tended to band together to form larger cities for economic growth and prosperity. This meant that the societal makeup for these different areas differed significantly.

The market revolution helped to widen a gap between rich and poor, shaped emerging middle and working classes, and caused an increasing separation between home and workplace, which led to dramatic transformations in gender and family roles and expectations.

With the rapid changes happening to industry, workers started to band together to form protective agencies called unions. Unions were focused on improving conditions for workers by creating safer working conditions and offering fair wages.

In 1834, the National Trades Union made a short appearance, yet most unions functioned better on the local level than the national level.

Intensified by expansion and deepening regional divisions, debates over slavery and other economic, cultural, and political issues led the nation into civil war.

The expansionist policies and worsening divisions regionally led to contested debates over slavery and its abolition. In addition to the raging slavery issue, the cultural, economic, and political changes that occurred during the period led to civil war. These issues included the abolition of slavery, the control of governments, nullification, and sectionalism.

The institution of slavery and its attendant ideological debates, along with regional economic and demographic changes, territorial expansion in the 1840s and 1850s, and cultural differences between the North and the South, intensified sectionalism.

The central conflict that separated the North and South and increased sectionalism between them was the slavery debate. The United States was not able to bring about a balance between the northern free states and the southern slave states, although there were numerous legal documents signed in attempts to resolve the issue.

The South was also feeling dominated by the North due to the increase in the northern population. This limited the chance of getting a president who supported the pro-slavery policies of the South.

The South had to face increased tariffs as it mostly relied on agriculture and plantations. The North was mainly industry-based and thrived on manufacturing. The South needed more land to arrive at a better economic balance with the North. The economic disparity between the two sections increased tensions and led to the Civil War.

The North's expanding economy and its increasing reliance on a free-labor manufacturing economy contrasted with the South's dependence on an economic system characterized by slave-based agriculture and slow population growth.

The main economic difference between the North and South was the labor systems they employed. While industry played a vital role in the North, with commerce taking priority, the South was mainly agricultural. The Southern economy was based on plantations that relied on slaves as cheap labor for their production of cotton and tobacco. The expanding economy in the North and its dependence on the free-labor manufacturing economy led to a sharp divide between the North and South.

Sectionalism, a term used to describe the needs of one section of a nation being given precedence over the needs of the entire nation, was rife during the period before the Civil War. The antislavery stand of the North remained a significant cause for sectionalism. Additionally, each section wanted to pass laws that benefited their land. This resulted in the free states supporting the North and the slave states supporting the South. The westward expansion further widened this divide.

Tariffs, which were imposed on imports, affected the South more heavily, as southerners relied on importing goods from Britain and exporting their cotton overseas. While the North wanted the tariffs to safeguard their industries, the South opposed the tariffs, and tensions rose between the two.

The South argued their right to a nullification of the tariffs and antislavery laws that the North was intent on passing. Even before the Civil War, the relationship between the North and South had worsened due to taxes. While the taxes imposed on the imported goods by Congress helped the industrial development of the North, it crippled the economy of the South, because, with its agriculture-targeted economy, the South needed to import machinery from foreign countries.

Southern industry

During the 1850s, when the recession was at its peak, Congress raised the tax on imports from 15 percent to 37 percent. In response, the South threatened to secede from the Union. The North was livid, as southern secession would significantly reduce foreign trade and strike a heavy blow to the American economy. Secession would mean that the coastwise trade, which the South dominated, would also leave the Union.

Therefore, the shipping would remain idle without the involvement of the South. Given all these economic implications, the Union decided that war was the only remaining alternative to a situation that would land them in financial ruin.

On the cultural front, the North was against slavery, and the South thrived on it. The northern culture depicted the southerners as un-Christian sponges and decadent people. When the Free Labor Movement–supporting the Republican Party won the elections, and Abraham Lincoln was made president of the Union in 1860, southerners interpreted the move as a coup d'état by the northerners.

The war was instigated by the cultural and economic fear of the people. Contrary to popular belief, slavery was not the only issue. Although the Republican Party was against slavery, it was not abolitionist. Abraham Lincoln's Emancipation Proclamation of 1862 supported the freeing of slaves only in the regions occupied by Confederate forces. All the other slave-holding states, which had been supporting the Union by fighting for it, were exempted.

Lincoln had addressed the issue directly, saying that he did not have the right or inclination to interfere with slavery. He said that if he could have saved the Union from division without freeing any of the slaves, he would undoubtedly do it, but that it was not an option. According to Secretary of State William H. Steward (1801-1872; 1861-1869), the Emancipation Proclamation was meant to emancipate slaves in regions where the Union could not help them and keep slaves in bondage in regions where they could easily be set free.

The rise of big business in the United States encouraged massive migrations and urbanization, sparked government and widespread efforts to reshape the U.S. economy and environment, and renewed debates over U.S. national identity.

The emergence of entrepreneurs, corporate conglomerations, innovators, and economic and social reformers embodied the spirit of the Gilded Age (1870s to 1900) and set the United States on a trajectory for the political, economic, and social system existing today. Following the damage and desolation of the Civil War, it was challenging to define the American spirit and national identity. This changed as Americans moved into the 20th century. Twentieth-century Americans were confident, resourceful, and urbanized, and they began to call into question social oppression involving gender and racial discrimination.

In response to these transitions, the U.S. government set out to expand into its western lands, address workplace misgivings and lack of regulations, and embrace the newly expanding consumer and production cultures. Americans began to question the government's land-use practices and, for the first time, were concerned with massive conservation attempts, highlighting the change in American planning from reactive policy agendas to those crafted with the future in mind.

The rise of big business in America determined the national identity associated with the United States heading into the 20th century. Without this boost in industrialization and manufacturing capacities, it is difficult to say whether the United States would have acquired and maintained its position as a global power in the 20th and 21st centuries. This exceptional rate of growth was crucial for the economic reforms in the early years of the 20th century under the Progressive movement. The major political players of the late 19th century envisioned an economic market with no restrictions, and it was because of their laissez-faire economic policies that many Americans began to question the level of control and influence these magnates held over the American political system.

Mr. and Mrs. Goodhue Livingston and Mrs. Vanderbilt,
the wealthy elite of the American Gilded Age, c. 1900

Large-scale production—accompanied by massive technological change, expanding international communication networks, and pro-growth government policies—fueled the development of a "Gilded Age" marked by an emphasis on consumption, marketing, and business consolidation.

As the entrepreneurial spirit swept across America, both the government and the public struggled to adjust to the fundamental changes in urban development and technological innovations. The improvement of workplace technology, such as conveyor systems, expedited the time required to produce goods, causing an influx of goods and later services.

To meet these demands, the American perception regarding consumerism had to change. As more Americans required more goods, the market became less saturated and more stable, propelling the economic machine of the late 19th century.

In addition to consumer trends and exponential growth in production capabilities, the American public also witnessed the beginning of monopolies with the emergence of company trusts and interlocking directorates. Such consolidation of business by buyout processes caused the wealthy elites in America to increase their fortunes while also limiting access to such ambitions.

While the entrepreneurial spirit was never more evident than in this period, it is also true that the former wealthy class did not welcome newcomers and were resistant to embrace the nouveau riche of the Gilded Age (1870s to 1900).

In addition to technological achievements, the Gilded Age was also responsible for explosive expansion in various areas, the evolving economy, urban dwellings, and city living as well as the unparalleled growth in the West. These transitions and their initial successes caused the U.S. government to promote further growth, which would have catastrophic results for the Native American populations of the United States.

In this period, many saw the displacement and resettling of Native Americans as a necessary sacrifice for the American dream, and in many cases as an opportunity to give an uncivilized population the proper training and resources to live in the 19th century.

The lasting influences of this period are all-pervasive and have had a direct impact on the economic and social systems we see today. The Gilded Age of business expansion and the American spirit of Nationalism was vital in the development of today's perception of the American dream.

Following the Civil War, government subsidies for transportation and communication systems opened new markets in North America. At the same time, technological innovations and redesigned financial and management structures such as monopolies sought to maximize the exploitation of natural resources and a growing labor force.

In hopes of reunifying the United States following the disastrous Civil War, many believed growth and expansion—which would connect the Atlantic and Pacific coasts—were necessary. To accomplish this monumental task, the U.S. government began investing in the transcontinental railroad, which would be a source of communication, travel, and much-needed work for minorities and whites.

To promote the success of the railroads, the government and railroad companies used land grants and other incentives to lure workers out west. Leaflets and brochures widely distributed in both the United States and parts of continental Europe proved to be a very successful advertising tactic.

The draw of land and better wages following the economic and political uncertainties of the earlier 19th century caused many working-class citizens, both native-born and immigrant, to support westward expansion, thus promoting the success of the railroad and—by default—the federal government.

As the industrial magnates of this period realized the opportunity for financial return from the new railroads, many jumped on the expansion projects, attempting to corner sectors of the market such as ownership of the only railway leading into New York City. This type of economic strategy saw the emergence of the first monopolies, which were able to dictate the labor policies of the railroads while also greatly influencing the political landscape of the period.

The lasting influence of such political agendas and strategies can be seen in the monopolies created during the Gilded Age, as they were the first of their kind and incredibly influential.

However, the backlash these same monopolies experienced just a few years later reflected the social upheaval average Americans experienced during this period and served as a precursor to the social revolutions of the 20th century.

Business leaders consolidated corporations into trusts and holding companies and defended their resulting status and privilege through theories such as social Darwinism.

As the magnates of the Gilded Age experienced periods of criticism, many were quick to use the ideas of social Darwinism, which had transformed the social sciences also beginning in this period, to secure their new status within the political and economic systems.

The most notable entrepreneurs of the Gilded Age included John D. Rockefeller (1839-1937) and J. P. Morgan (1837-1913). These men initiated the economic production and markets of the late 19th century and forever transformed the notion of the American dream and the accumulation of wealth during the Gilded Age.

Some of the business practices of the Gilded Age would be considered illegal in today's markets. The use of interlocking directorates and the buying up of corporations under parent umbrellas to create monopolies were all new ideas in this period. Such tactics were wildly successful for those managing the companies.

However, this was typically at the expense of shareholders and, sometimes, the American public. Business dealings, such as the Union Pacific interlocking directorate scandal, caused great dissatisfaction and mistrust between the working class and the ruling or business class. These sour relationships would continue until the late 20th century, where, for the first time, progressive activists and presidents sided with labor instead of its big business partners.

John D. Rockefeller, c. 1900

John D. Rockefeller (1839-1937), born into a modest family in New York, became one of the leading magnates of this period and spent much of his time acknowledging and defending the fortune he had amassed. In 1870, Rockefeller struck liquid gold and was able to quickly after that establish the Standard Oil Company, which at the time was valued at one million dollars.

Rockefeller perfected the use of trusts to weed out and eliminate his competition in the oil markets. By 1877, Rockefeller controlled close to 95 percent of the oil refineries operating in the United States. After eliminating his competition, such as the Vanderbilt family, he was able to exercise a monopoly on the global petroleum market.

As leaders of big businesses and their allies in government aimed to create a unified industrialized nation, they were challenged in different ways by demographic issues, regional differences, and labor movements.

As industrial and manufacturing giants dominated the political landscape of the period, they were met at times with strong opposition from the immigrant classes as well as the emergence of labor unions and planned strikes. These had a drastic impact on the future of labor movements in America.

As immigration labor fueled the railroad expansion, which would unify the country through transcontinental means, it was also the first to experience labor strikes as a result of the newly formed unions.

One drawback of exponential labor reserves—as seen in the immigration explosions of the late 19th century—was that it made workers expendable and decreased their wages. Keeping vocational practices in this light caused increased social tensions and issues within the railroad companies, which further soured the relationship between workers and management.

These first influential labor movements allowed many Americans the right to go on strike or demand better workplace conditions concerning health and safety. These concepts became the common workplace expectations of all Americans leading into the 20th century, forever altering the conception of union and labor movements in America.

The drastic increase in labor movements and strikes highlights an American landscape amid a tumultuous and challenging transition.

Labor and management battled for control over wages and working conditions, with workers organizing local and national unions or directly confronting corporate power.

As the industrial and manufacturing giants of the period amassed wealth and influence, the working classes struggled to be protected or fairly represented. To combat this social and economic issue, many social activists emerged to fight for the rights of the working class.

Workplace conditions in 1866 led to the first labor union, the National Labor Union, which supported implementing an eight-hour workday, the use of greenbacks, the enforcing of health and safety regulations, and the repealing of laws that made importing labor easier. This latter concern embodies the sentiment of nativism, which spread during this period.

In 1869, the Knights of Labor was formed, which encompassed both skilled and unskilled laborers. They worked toward equal pay amongst genders—a revolutionary concept at the time—as well as an eight-hour workday, codes for health and safety in the workplace, and the use of greenback or soft currency to expand the supply of currency being circulated while also elevating pressure on debtors.

Other notable labor unions of this period include the American Federation of Labor (AFL), which was founded in 1886 and was an example of the emergence of craft unions. The establishment of such unions would become common in the early 20th century, as many more Americans began to embrace the idea of organized workers bargaining with management and going on strikes when an agreement could not be reached.

Knights of Labor pentagram

Mary Harris Jones (1837-1930), often referred to as "Mother Jones," was also an influential character of the labor movements of the late 19th century. She was an Irish American immigrant who worked tirelessly for the advancement and protection of industrial workers.

Aside from planning and implementing vast strikes, Jones was also the co-founder of the Industrial Workers of the World in the early 20th century, which fought against child labor and the exploitation of the industrial workforce.

Some significant strikes of this period included the Great Strike of 1877, where the workers of the Baltimore and Ohio railroads went on strike following a drastic pay cut of almost 10 percent. The strike ended with the intervention of federal troops sent by President Hayes.

Despite the industrialization of some segments of the southern economy, a change promoted by southern leaders who called for a "New South," agrarian sharecropping and tenant farming systems continued to dominate the region.

As a result of the Confederate defeat in the Civil War, many southerners began to question the economic practices of the past, specifically the economy's sole reliance on cotton. With the emergence of the "New South," many had hoped to see a diversification of the goods and services offered there.

As the southern markets and goods expanded, the South found a new market in which to invest: northern exports. Many northerners imported the tobacco grown in the South as well as industrial exports such as lumber, iron, and coal.

Though some called for the industrialization of the South, this seemed rather unlikely, as the society was agriculturally based and continued to be so after the Civil War. The introduction of secondary crops such as tobacco, rice, and sugar cane all reestablished the agrarian traditions of the past.

Supported by people such as Seaman Knapp, who perfected the cultivation of crops in the South, the newly formed local and state governments were able to establish and expand agriculture education and production programs aimed at assisting those farming in the New South. This was particularly important, as much of the New South's tradition and the effects of Reconstruction (1865-1877) still centered around the implementation of an agrarian society, rather than one dominated by the industrial and manufacturing movements seen elsewhere.

In addition to agricultural transitions (moving away from cotton and into tenant farming), the New South explored industry in cities such as Birmingham, Alabama. Here southerners found natural resources of iron, limestone, and eventually coal, all of which were extremely important to the economic development needed in the South following the disastrous Civil War and the railroad and manufacturing booms experienced in the North, Midwest and the western territories.

Other industries that expanded during this period included lumber exports of prized southern pine trees—which were found to be in high demand around the country—and new markets for paper, clay, and glass production.

While the New South struggled to shed its image of outdated agrarian life, it became clear that the impact of industrialization in the Midwest and Northeast had influenced some southern politicians, but not enough to transform the economic landscape of the southern states.

It should be noted that the reemergence of the South as a sustainable, operating entity was a vast accomplishment of the Reconstruction period and the capitalist system, and greatly influenced the future of political and social reforms, or lack thereof, in the region.

SOCIAL DEVELOPMENTS: 1790 - 1877

Protestant evangelical religious fervor strengthened many British colonists' understandings of themselves as a chosen people blessed with liberty. At the same time, Enlightenment philosophers and ideas inspired many American political thinkers to emphasize individual talent over hereditary privilege.

The Puritans had always tended to see themselves as a chosen people sent to the New World on a divine errand. However, social and political changes had transformed Puritan thinking by the 18th century. Some conservatives, called Old Calvinists, continued to cling to old beliefs and practices.

Many influential clergymen, called the Old Lights, were eager to increase the appeal of the church to the population at large, opening membership and preaching a more liberal doctrine.

The Great Awakening of the 1730s and 1740s brought new development, the evangelical New Lights, who built on old-fashioned Puritanism but set out to bring compelling, individual experiences of salvation to people throughout the colonies.

The Protestant clergy played a crucial role in preparing the colonial population for war against Britain, responding to British policies with severe denunciations, and suggesting that Britain was doing the work of Satan and referring to the king as the "Whore of Babylon." In retrospect, some Loyalists even claimed that the fervor and influence of Protestant preachers were the main reason behind the success of the Patriots.

At the same time, Enlightenment philosophers also influenced American political thought. Social contract theorists (e.g., John Locke and Jean-Jacques Rousseau) based their notion of political legitimacy on the idea that men were naturally free and equal. They suggested that differentials in power and status should be based on talent, character, and merit rather than traditional and hereditary privileges that had previously been ascribed to divine providence.

Similarly, Adam Smith (1723-1790) argued that economic privileges and monopolies should be abandoned in favor of free competition on open markets, allowing skilled individuals of any background to pursue their economic interests. He argued that market mechanisms would ensure that this pursuit of individual enrichment would also lead to better allocation of resources and a more prosperous economy.

Profile of Adam Smith, c, 1790

While the new governments continued to limit rights to some groups, ideas promoting self-government and personal liberty reverberated around the world.

Although the United States was a sparsely populated country very far away, Europeans were impressed and heavily influenced by developments in North American during and after the American Revolution.

The Declaration of Independence codified a new way of discussing human rights, and many in Europe adopted the language and ideas of American revolutionaries. The French Revolution was, in part, inspired by the American precedent.

The United States was the "first new nation," created, as it seemed, by the application of philosophy and principle rather than justified by tradition and heredity. The notions that government should be based on the consent of the governed and the preservation of liberty, and that monarchs who failed to do so could be disposed of, were powerful ideas that inspired enthusiasm in some and animosity in others.

Meanwhile, the language of freedom and equality did not grant freedom and equality for all in the United States. Women did not have the same rights as men, and slavery and the removal of Indians from their territories remained vital elements of the new American reality.

Migration within North America, cooperative interaction, and competition for resources raised questions about boundaries and policies, intensified conflicts among peoples and nations, and led to contests over the creation of multiethnic, multiracial national identity.

After the revolution, Americans tried to create a unified national identity founded on ideas of equality, civic virtue, and commercial success. At the same time, the country was deeply divided along cultural, geographic, economic, and racial lines. To some extent, the identity of Americans, or preferably white property-owning male Americans, came to rely on subjugating and demonizing others, including women, Indians, blacks, and poor whites. The evolution of the media facilitated this process by allowing a broad audience to seek an understanding of their superiority that was rooted in guilt, fear, paranoia, and violence.

As migrants streamed westward from the British colonies along the Atlantic seaboard, interactions among different groups that would continue under the independent United States resulted in competition for resources, shifting alliances, and cultural blending.

Even in colonial times, white settlers were trickling through the mountain passes and into what is now Kentucky and Tennessee as well as deeper into the South and the Ohio Valley. The viability of their settlements was threatened by the Proclamation of 1763, by Spanish and French designs on the area and by Indian resistance to their occupation of the land. These areas were characterized by instability, overlapping authority, conflicts, and cultural mixing. Due to the brutality of military action and massacres both during and after the Revolutionary War, they were also marked by hatred between peoples.

Migrants from within North America and around the world continued to launch new settlements in the West, creating new distinctive backcountry cultures and fueling social and ethnic tensions.

Large numbers of colonists in the British colonies were not of English origin but instead hailed from other parts of Europe. Thus, white culture in North America was diverse from the beginning. One crucial cultural influence was that of the Scotch-Irish Protestants from Northern Ireland. Many of these immigrants settled in western Pennsylvania and later traveled along the Appalachians into the southern backcountry.

The immigrant's emphasis on herding cattle and pigs, and isolation, leisure, and hunting, rather than community, hard work, and farming differentiated them from the English colonists. They were also significantly different in their other habits and values, which, along with the deep class divide of southern society, often led to conflict with other segments of the white population.

Differences between the coastal areas and the backcountry prevailed in the North as well. In rural New England, the economy was still based on subsistence agriculture after the Revolutionary War. When merchants and tax collectors began to demand that debts and taxes be paid in hard currency, many farmers in the hill country were unable to pay and ended up losing their land and other valuables.

In 1786, armed groups of men in Massachusetts began to close courts to stop creditors from enforcing judgments against debtors. When the legislature answered by passing laws to prevent further mob actions and even suspended habeas corpus, organizers in western Massachusetts began to mobilize to overthrow the government. They were led by Daniel Shays (1747-1825), a veteran of the Revolutionary War. In the absence of an army, the state's merchant elite organized mercenaries to defeat the rebellion.

Since thousands of people had taken up arms against the state government, Shays' Rebellion was an important factor in convincing members of the political elite that a more centralized and powerful federal government was necessary.

Shays' Rebellion, portraits of Daniel Shays and Job Shattuck, leaders of the Massachusetts Regulators

The Spanish, supported by the bonded labor of the local Indians, expanded their mission settlements into California, providing opportunities for social mobility among enterprising soldiers and settlers that led to new cultural blending.

In the 1770s, the Spanish sent explorers into California, and by 1776 they established San Francisco. The fierce resistance of the Yuma Indians closed the overland route to California from the 1780s to the mid-19th century, forcing colonists to arrive by sea. Nevertheless, the Spanish established more than twenty settlements along the coast from San Diego to San Francisco. There was virtually no white settlement in the interior.

The mission towns, located about a day's ride apart, were usually manned by a couple of friars and a handful of soldiers. The labor in the settlements was done by Indians who were either forced or persuaded to join the missions and hunted down if they tried to run away. The Indians were treated as slaves, even though they were not legally slaves.

Eventually, the missions claimed vast lands—as much as one million acres per settlement. Soldiers and ambitious colonists could receive huge land grants virtually for free, and even foreigners could be granted lands if they were determined to become Spanish and Catholic.

Mission Indians of Southern California

Despite these opportunities, the number of migrants to California remained low. Therefore, the culture of the area was heavily influenced by the Indians. The dependence on local materials constrained even the architecture of the Spanish missions and artistic renderings in the churches show the influence of Indian styles.

California also developed its version of the Spanish vaquero, or cowboy, with his way of training horses and a unique way of life.

New voices for national identity challenged tendencies to cling to regional identities, contributing to the emergence of distinctly American cultural expressions.

Having secured independence from Britain, some Americans were eager to define their new national identity as Americans. Especially among the elite, many saw this as a necessary condition for building a united and cohesive nation across a vast geographical expanse. It was important that this new culture be republican, and that American art and architecture have a distinctly republican flavor.

The image of George Washington became especially popular as Washington was considered the most celebrated American and a prime example of the virtuous republican citizen. His image appeared not only in paintings but in china and engravings. After his death, authors also began to publish biographies of Washington.

Engraving of George Washington, 1732-1799

In addition to visual artists and literary figures, American inventors, architects, scientists, and philosophers also contributed to the new American culture. Education was especially crucial in shaping a national, republican identity. In this case, education did not just mean schooling, but more generally being exposed to art, culture, and knowledge in specific ways that promoted civic virtue.

Enlightenment ideas and women's experiences in the movement for independence promoted an ideal of "republican motherhood," which called on white women to maintain and teach republican values within the family and granted women a new importance in American political culture.

The American Revolution altered women's lives as well as men's. Many women oversaw the household and the family when the husband and other males left, and some adopted republican principles to demand greater equality for women. First Lady Abigail Adams (1744-1818) suggested that her husband, Founding Father John Adams (1735 to July 4, 1826), should "remember the ladies."

Abigail Adams

In general, the Revolution and the republican ideology underlying it suggested a critique of all authority, hierarchy, and traditional constraint, which encouraged women to take on new roles and have opinions of their own. However, the most critical role of women in revolutionary ideology was as mothers of virtuous male citizens.

Since women had the primary responsibility for rearing, nurturing, and educating children, they needed to have the proper virtue and a republican outlook. Academies were built to prepare American women for this role, which some historians call "republican motherhood."

While extending the rights, opportunities, and importance of women, this way of thinking also cemented the division of appropriate activities between men and women, emphasizing that the proper arena for a woman was the private sphere of the home.

Many white Americans in the South asserted their regional identity through pride in the institution of slavery, insisting that the federal government defend slavery.

Proponents of slavery ignored the pathos-driven arguments of the abolitionists and focused instead on what they considered practical reasons for slavery. They claimed that slavery was a historical constant. Slaves had existed in all significant societies since ancient times as a form of fast and cheap labor. Proslavery advocates pointed out that slavery made economic sense. The Egyptians had used slaves to build the pyramids, and the Americans used slaves to pick plants, which would surely whither on the vine if slavery was ended.

They also argued that not only were slaves necessary to the continued economic growth of the nation but that if all slaves were freed, there would be a substantial social impact. Slaves were not citizens and had no rights, these proslavery advocates argued that emancipation would disrupt the running of society and create widespread unemployment as slaves entered the workforce and competed for jobs.

Supporters of slavery also turned to the Bible for justification of their views. They argued that several Christians had slaves, and God still supported them. King Solomon, the blessed king of the Israelites, had owned slaves. Similarly, the Ten Commandments chastised those who coveted their neighbor's possessions, and supporters of slavery interpreted "possessions" to include slaves. Therefore, they argued that God both condoned slavery, and condemned attempts to take slaves away from their owners.

Furthermore, by bringing slaves to America and educating them in the Christian faith, many slave owners thought that they were saving their slaves from hell. Senator John C. Calhoun claimed in a proslavery speech to the Senate, "Never before has the black race of Central Africa, from the dawn of history to the present day, attained a condition so civilized and so improved, not only physically, but morally and intellectually."

Calhoun went on to describe slavery as an institution "indispensable to the peace and happiness of both" races. Slavery, according to him, was a better condition to live in than the ignorance of their native Africa. Calhoun insisted that southerners stop apologizing for the institution of slavery, and his comments defined the proslavery arguments for the next several decades.

Resistance to initiatives for democracy and inclusion included proslavery arguments, rising xenophobia, anti-black sentiments in political and popular culture, and restrictive anti-Indian policies.

While groups like the abolitionists looked at the founding documents and concluded that all humans—not just whites—had rights, many people had the opposite sentiment. Many citizens were concerned about what the inclusion-based policies of the federal government would mean if extended to all people, especially the rights afforded to citizens.

Thus, a rise occurred in anti-black and anti-Indian sentiments. If these groups were made citizens, they would be able to vote, and that would change the political field. Similarly, as land opened in the West, xenophobia spread. Americans began demanding that the federal government deal with the waves of immigrants traveling to America.

While Americans celebrated their nation's progress toward a unified new national culture that blended Old World forms with New World ideas, groups of the nation's inhabitants developed distinctive cultures of their own.

Although America tried to cultivate a cultural identity separate from the rest of the world, the creation of purely American art forms took time. Americans had not been around long enough to break away from traditional art forms, and it was trendy to mimic the highly elegant styles of Europe.

This changed during the first half of the 1800s, primarily as a reaction to the opening of the western territory and the development of so many regional identities, which were then expressed and preserved.

Groups of American Indians, women and religious followers developed cultures reflecting their interests and experiences, as did regional groups and an emerging urban middle class.

The early 1800s saw distinct cultures emerge within numerous communities. For the Native Americans, this was a resurgence of traditional values. Through trade with the Europeans and Americans, many tribes had changed and adapted their cultural practices. They used new agricultural methods, learned to read and write in English, and adopted new technology at the expense of some of their traditional practices.

Many natives encouraged a shift back to older ways. For instance, in 1811, three Cherokee in Georgia reported that they had seen a vision denouncing European goods. The Cherokee deities were unhappy with the way Cherokees had allowed settlers to treat animals and the land, demanding that they return to the old ways.

Women also saw a surge in culture as they began to realize their place in the new nation. While less volatile than slavery, gender equality was another polarizing issue of the time. Women in the early 1800s did not have a place in the public sphere and were often considered an accessory to their husband's image. This trope, often known as "the cult of domesticity," strictly defined gender roles for women and men.

As abolitionism spread, women began their fight for rights. They questioned their subservience to men and felt that the abolitionist movement should be extended to include all human rights. This created a split in the abolitionist movement, particularly over whether women could serve as officers and speakers.

When Elizabeth Cady Stanton (1815-1902) was snubbed at the World Slavery Convention in London, she joined with Lucretia Mott and Susan B. Anthony (1820-1906) to create a separate women's movement.

Susan B. Anthony

The resulting Seneca Falls Convention in New York established the women's movement in earnest. The convention encouraged speakers to share their perspective on a woman's rights in the United States, and delegates drafted a Declaration of Sentiments based on the Declaration of Independence.

The Declaration of Sentiments demanded specific rights and improvements for women, including protection in the event of divorce (especially with custody laws that tended to grant the father custody), equal property rights to men, fair wages, and access to higher-level professions. The primary demand and the vehicle through which women sought to achieve these changes, was suffrage.

The right to vote would allow women to pursue the changes they wanted on a national level and would grant them an equal say in other political issues, like slavery. While the women's movement was separate from the abolitionist movement, there was still significant support for abolition amongst the delegates.

Sojourner Truth demonstrated this relationship at a women's rights convention in 1851 when she gave her famous speech, *Ain't I a Woman?* In the speech, she reminds her fellow women that the fight for women's rights does not end at suffrage for white women but is for all women. Later, this issue would divide the organization.

Enslaved and free African Americans, isolated at the bottom of the social hierarchy, created communities and strategies to protect their dignity and their family structures, even as some launched abolitionist and reform movements aimed at changing their status.

Slaves and free African Americans were creating their own culture during this period. In 1794, Richard Allen created the first black denomination: the African Methodist Episcopal Church. Spirituals were sung in the fields as slaves worked to create a sense of community and family. They also had the dual role of acting as coded messages for runaway slaves. *Follow the Drinking Gourd*, for instance, explains how to travel north to freedom by following the Big Dipper (Ursa Major), which includes the North Star.

Runaway and freed slaves began sharing stories that detailed their lives under former masters. Frederick Douglass wrote arguably the best known of these works: *Narrative of the Life of Frederick Douglass, An American Slave* (1845). This text and others like it were published in the North. These writings opened the eyes of many northerners to the evils of slavery by making slavery about a person instead of an institution

Frederick Douglass, 1818-1895

Other African Americans served as an example of what freed slaves could be. Most notable amongst these are James Forten (1766-1842) and David Walker (1796-1830). Forten apprenticed with a sailmaker in Philadelphia and took over the business when the owner passed, refusing to make rigging for any slave trading vessels. He was an inspiration to the African American community and actively fought for an end to slavery.

Forten opposed the American Colonization Society on the basis that he was an American and belonged in the United States. Forten also financially supported William Lloyd Garrison's abolitionist paper, *The Liberator* (1831-1865). Several similar publications spread across the northern states and provided a vehicle for abolitionists to band together.

David Walker published his thoughts on slavery in *An Appeal to the Colored Citizens in the World,* which he then smuggled into the South using sympathetic sailors as contacts. Slaves who read his works—writing that defended them against slavery in the South and discrimination in the North—were uplifted and inspired. Slaveholders soon had a bounty on his head, but he refused to flee to Canada and insisted on staying in the public eye. Another publisher, Elijah Lovejoy, was eventually killed for publishing anti-slavery messages.

Many white abolitionists encouraged the spread of African American art forms to polarize the issue further and encourage more people to join the abolitionist movement. However, even amongst abolitionists, there was discord.

For example, with *The Liberator* (1831-1865), Garrison intended to bring abolitionists together and spread their ideas. Nevertheless, Garrison (1805-1879) scorned the idea that solely political action would have any impact on ending slavery. This put him in direct opposition to the Liberty Party, who tried to influence abolitionist change using the existing political system.

Harriet Beecher Stowe, 1811-1896

Others thought that by emulating and popularizing slave narratives, they could gain attention. Harriet Beecher Stowe wrote one of the most famous pieces of literature from this period, *Uncle Tom's Cabin* (1852). Her take on the slave narrative style was widely popular and earned her, and the abolitionist movement, a wealth of support. Some of the more extreme abolitionists took after John Brown.

Brown attacked the federal arsenal at Harpers Ferry, Virginia, with the intent to lead slaves in an armed insurrection. Although Brown's actions shocked and were criticized by many, they earned him a great deal of respect from others.

With the opening of canals and new roads into the western territories, native-born white citizens relocated westward, relying on new community systems to replace their old family and local relationships.

As with the utopian communities, new areas in the western territories created connections outside of the familial to encourage migrations. Small towns and communities were typically close-knit, as the individuals living there relied on each other for continued survival. This meant that fellowship through uniting ideas, such as religion, tended to take the place of the familial relationships, and life in town would revolve around these uniting opinions and goals.

Emigrants to the West

Migrants from Europe increased the population in the East and the Midwest, forging strong bonds of interdependence between the Northeast and the Old Northwest.

Most of the immigrants moving into the western territories were Europeans because trade with China was tentative at best, and Africa was still off-limits due to the legislation regarding the slave trade. These European settlers typically started in the northern states, where the shipping business made it easier to travel from Europe. Then they set out west, typically among easily traveled paths like rivers or established trails. Similar groups tended to stay together, and scholars believe they may have sought locations that reminded them of their original homeland.

The South remained politically, culturally, and ideologically distinct from the other sections while continuing to rely on its exports to Europe for economic growth.

While the population in the North continued to grow and change, the population in the South stayed reasonably similar. This gave rise to a unique class system that further separated the North and South. While the North had industrial empires like those of the railway barons, the South had developed a landed gentry or aristocracy amongst those that could afford large plantations and the slaves to work them.

Below this class were those that could afford some slaves, but not as many as were needed to turn the massive profits of the genteel southerners. Below them were those that were too poor to afford any outside labor. Called "white trash" by their neighbors, these citizens were almost at the level of freed slaves. This social system baffled and deterred northerners and immigrants, allowing the South to strengthen its ties with Europe further.

The westward expansion, migration to and within the United States, and the end of slavery reshaped North American boundaries. It caused conflicts over American cultural identities, citizenship, and the question of extending and protecting rights for groups of U.S. inhabitants.

The westward expansion and migration within the country, the influx of immigrants, and the end of slavery changed the social boundaries in North America. This created several conflicts due to the various cultural identities, issues of citizenship, and protecting the rights of all the different groups of inhabitants—Asians, African Americans, Hispanics, and Native Americans. The unresolved slavery issue and voting and citizenship rights for immigrants and former slaves were significant issues that had significant economic, religious, and political impacts on the nation.

Substantial numbers of new international migrants—who often lived in ethnic communities and retained their religion, language, and customs—entered the country prior to the Civil War, giving rise to a major, often violent nativist movement that was strongly anti-Catholic and aimed at limiting immigrants' cultural influence and political and economic power.

During the pre–Civil War period, many international migrants entered the United States, including more than one million Germans, over three million British, and four million Irish.

Prior to 1845, only Irish Protestants migrated to the United States. After 1845, Irish Catholics started migrating in huge numbers mainly due to the Great Famine.

Italians, Greeks, Hungarians, Poles, and other Slavic nationals migrated to America after 1880. These immigrants served to make up the bulk of the American labor pool and were instrumental in making the country a leading economic giant worldwide.

The nativist, or Know-Nothing, movement of the 1850s had opposed the German and Irish Catholic immigration. The movement was powered by fear within the nation of the domination by Catholic immigrants who were considered opposed to American values.

While the movement did not meet with much success, it was joined by many of the Protestant groups and middle-class people who were unresolved over the slavery issue. The Know-Nothing movement aimed at purifying American politics by ending the Irish Catholic influence. The movement wanted to uphold Republican values and curb naturalization and immigration.

U.S. political poster for the Know-Nothing Party

The anti-Catholic sentiment that began with the influx of Irish Catholics in the 1840s resulted in the conviction that Catholic children needed to be educated in public schools to learn American values.

The Irish Catholics—despite opposition from the Protestants—built their parochial schools on a national scale and formed the Catholic Educational Association, which was later called the National Catholic Educational Association. Piety, strict discipline, and orthodoxy were prominently taught.

The Catholic schools were founded in reaction to the increasing number of schools publicly funded by Protestants. The American Bible Society in 1840 declared that the Bible be read in each classroom.

In 1875, a constitutional amendment was called for by President Grant, who favored the Know-Nothing Party, for prohibiting the use of public funds for sectarian schools and making free public schools mandatory.

The amendment was motivated by anti-Catholic views and the fear that the ambition, superstition, and greed, which were believed to be fueled by the Catholic Church, would go against values of intelligence and patriotism. This led to Grant's support of public schools that were free of pagan, sectarian, or atheistic teachings.

Although the amendment was defeated, it laid the groundwork for the Blaine Amendments, which were incorporated into the thirty-four state Constitution over the next few decades. The Blaine Amendment passed in 1880 forbade the use of tax money to fund the parochial schools or parish schools operated by the Irish to protect their Catholic religion, culture, and language.

Asian, African American, and white peoples sought new economic opportunities or religious refuge in the West, efforts that were boosted during and after the Civil War with the passage of new legislation promoting national economic development.

The white, African American and Asian populations had migrated to the West to capitalize on the plentiful economic opportunities there as well as to seek religious refuge. The Mormons' history is one stark example of a religious exodus across the continent and the successful establishment of a strongly religious society.

The Mormon Church originated in western New York. Joseph Smith Jr. (1805-1844), a fourteen-year-old migrant farmer's son, claimed to have experienced supernatural revelations and spiritual visitations that led to the establishment of the Mormon Church. This Church was later named the Church of Jesus Christ of Latter-day Saints.

Smith's first vision, 1820

Mormonism attracted antebellum crowds in New York, who began to be inexplicably drawn by the promises of buried treasure, mystical visions, and magical talismans that Mormonism portrayed. Smith offered hope and promise to a weak, weary, and persecuted group of people who were in search of divine manifestation.

The antebellum people were economically backward when compared to the industrially rich northerners, and they were easily enticed by the promise of emancipation offered by the Mormons. The movement was threatened by local authorities and moved to Kirtland, Ohio, where the first temple was built, and later to Missouri and Illinois when the government ordered their extermination.

Smith was shot in 1844 by a mob while he was in prison. The anti-Mormon protests were mostly due to the struggle for political and economic power, as people believed that the Mormons with their large number of followers could upset the balance.

The Mormon practice of polygamy also fueled the protests. Early 19th-century American society supported monogamy, individualism, and private property. However, since these principles contrasted with Mormon values, they did not accept Mormonism. The Mormons' main objective was to establish God's kingdom on Earth.

Another event that influenced the economic growth of the United States was the gold rush of 1848. Before the peace treaty with Mexico, gold had been discovered in California in 1842 by Francisco Lopez, a Californio.

The announcement of a further discovery of gold by James Marshall in 1848, in the San Francisco newspaper *The Californian,* spurred on a gold rush in which people from all over the country landed in California with shovels and picks.

Gold washing in California, c. 1848

The gold rush (1848-1855) also attracted people from China, Latin America, France, Germany, Australia, and Britain. The population of San Francisco spiked from 459 to 20,000 in just a few months and transformed it into an ethnically diverse, violent, and unruly society. This sparked many murders of Native Indians, Mexicans, immigrants, and white people.

The Homestead Act of 1862 was passed due to land distribution issues that had been occurring prevalently in the wake of westward migration. The land policies before the act made it financially impossible for prospective homesteaders to acquire land.

All this changed due to the Mexican American War in 1846. Popular pressure occurred to alter policy according to the evolving demographics, improving the economy, and shifting the social climate of that period.

The rise in the prices of wheat, corn, and cotton helped the southern plantations dominate the small-scale farmers. The displaced farmers moved westward to unoccupied forested land, which had more affordable conditions.

Those settling in the West during this period demanded preemption, which allowed them to settle land initially and pay later. This was opposed by eastern economic forces, as they feared that the cheap labor available for their industries would be lost.

The unprecedented high number of immigrants to America also settled in the West, drawn by its economic prosperity. The advanced transportation in the form of roadways and new canals reduced the dependence of the West on the New Orleans harbor. Furthermore, England's repeal of the Corn Laws opened new markets for American agricultural exports. Thus, the West faced a high influx of local and immigrant people in search of fertile land.

Despite these improvements, the homesteading laws were opposed on different fronts. The North bemoaned the loss of cheap labor, and the southern states were worried that the settlers would form new antislavery states. This led to homestead laws being proposed and defeated three times in 1852, 1854, and 1859. In 1860, the Homestead Bill passed by Congress was vetoed by President Buchanan (1791-1868; 1857-1861).

While the new allocation methods were chaotic and arbitrary, resulting in frequent disputes over borders, the Homestead Act had a tremendous political and regional impact. When President Abraham Lincoln signed the Act in 1862, eleven states had defected from the Union.

The southern states' removal from the Union led to the act finally passing and being signed as law. The new law established filing for application, improving the land, and filing for title deed as its threefold process.

While initially, the physical frontier conditions prevented people from making a claim, the Frontier Railroad Act led to new railroads and easy access to goods, tools, weapons, and other necessities for the homesteaders. Such resources allowed homesteaders to improve their facilities by building towns, schools, and eventually new states.

Abolitionists, although a minority in the North, mounted a highly visible campaign against slavery, adopting strategies of resistance ranging from fierce arguments against the institution and assistance in helping slaves escape to a willingness to use violence to achieve their goals.

The sectional conflicts and reform movements that happened during the early part of the 19th century focused on slavery and led to the abolitionist movement in the North. This movement aimed at abolishing slavery and represented the best efforts by the North to defeat the pro-slavery southerners.

Southerners resisted this movement, and sectional conflicts grew. The abolitionist movement fought for the immediate emancipation of slaves and the ending of segregation and racial discrimination. Immediate emancipation differentiated abolitionists from the antislavery advocates whose moderate stand encouraged gradual emancipation.

The abolitionists also differed from the free-soil advocates who wanted to restrict slavery to the existing areas and prevent it from spreading west. Radical abolitionism was also encouraged partly due to the Second Great Awakening fervor, which motivated people to support emancipation based on religious conviction.

Abolitionist ideas became more prominent in the churches and politics in the North during the 1830s, creating more animosity between the North and South and eventually leading to the Civil War.

Of the numerous abolitionists, some notable personalities include:

- William Lloyd Garrison. Garrison was the publisher of the newspaper *The Liberator* and the most vocal of the abolitionists, writing in a blunt and coarse language that struck at the core of the matter.
- Fredrick Douglas. Born as a slave, Fredrick Douglas became an author, orator, and reformer and devoted his entire life to the abolition of slavery and the pursuit of rights for black people.
- Harriet Tubman. This African American helped free hundreds of slaves and was the leader of the Underground Railroad, helping slaves flee to the free states or Canada.
- Sojourner Truth. Like Tubman, Truth was born a slave without any formal education. She ran away from her master and became a preacher, attacking the organized religious beliefs that favored the whites and the privileges they were given.
- Nat Turner (1800-1831). This preacher and black slave led one of the most famous slave revolts in the history of the United States. In 1831, he and seventy other slaves killed sixty whites in Virginia, including his master, Joseph Travis. Turner was captured by Virginia militia and hanged, and this led to southern states passing stricter laws for controlling slaves, especially the slave preachers.

Nat Turner and his confederates in conference, c. 1831

The constitutional changes of the Reconstruction period embodied a northern idea of American identity and national purpose. They led to conflicts over new definitions of citizenship, particularly regarding the rights of African Americans, women, and other minorities.

The failure of Reconstruction was due to the South interpreting its efforts as a northern concept. Furthermore, the North did not have any clear plan for properly implementing Reconstruction. This led to the failure to reintegrate the South with the Union and to conflicts related to the rights of African Americans, minorities, and women.

While at the end of the war, it seemed that the freed slaves were given equal rights to whites, racism prevailed. Thus, Reconstruction failed to integrate freed slaves into society.

Although citizenship, equal protection of the laws, and voting rights were granted to African Americans in the Fourteenth and Fifteenth Amendments, these rights were progressively stripped away through segregation, violence, Supreme Court decisions, and local political tactics.

The Fourteenth and Fifteenth Amendments were adopted as part of the Reconstruction efforts. These were aimed at eliminating discrimination over the right to vote based on racial identity or previous servitude conditions. Before the amendments, the states were in control of determining the qualification of voters.

Adoption of the Thirteenth Amendment, c. 1865

While support for the amendments was an effort to help the freed slaves, there was a deeper reason behind it. The black votes from the South would gain the majority for the supporters of the amendments.

The main reason for the Fifteenth Amendment was that the Republicans wanted the support of black votes to gain a position of power in both the North and South. While the Fifteenth Amendment was temporarily and moderately successful in providing voting rights to the blacks living in northern and southern states, opposition to the amendments started in the Confederate states.

Voter intimidation, poll taxes and grandfather clauses were used to limit the voting rights of freed slaves. In the latter part of the 1870s, the southern governments nullified the Fourteenth and Fifteenth Amendments, stripped the privileges given to the African Americans, and engaged in numerous discriminatory practices including literacy tests, violence, and intimidation to prevent them from using their right to vote.

While the Fifteenth Amendment banned any explicit disenfranchisement based on racial factors or prior enslavement, the southerners used three overlapping alternative methods to disenfranchise blacks between 1868 and 1888. These methods included violence, illegal tactics, and massive fraud, such as the cumulative poll tax by Georgia.

The Supreme Court supported this disenfranchisement by gutting all the federal laws passed to protect the blacks. It undermined the federal executive powers that protected the voting rights of the blacks and refused to acknowledge racial discrimination, even if it was proven to allow constitutional violations by citing specious reasoning.

The women's rights movement was both emboldened and divided over the Fourteenth and Fifteenth Amendments to the Constitution.

While the Thirteenth Amendment abolished slavery, the complete elimination of racial discrimination was not possible due to the conflicting interests, motivations, and goals that prevailed during the Reconstruction period. The status of the freed slaves was unclear, and they did not receive proper legal protection to counter southern coercion.

The Fourteenth Amendment was passed in the wake of the *Dred Scott* (1857) decision, which occurred before the war and had declared black slaves as nonpersons. The amendment sought to restore their status as citizens with natural rights, recognize their allegiance to the country, and give full representation in the legislation, so that southern efforts to keep them permanently oppressed could be thwarted.

For women's rights advocates, the Fourteenth Amendment came as a big disappointment. Based on Section One of the Fourteenth Amendment, women were given the right to vote, but the Republicans, while supporting the protection of freed slaves, did not want to support women's suffrage. This was solved by the introduction of Section Two, which specified the counting criteria of the inhabitants of a state for legislative representation.

The three-fifths clause of the Constitution was amended, and the specification of voting rights and citizenship to black males denied women their right to vote. This enraged women's rights activists. Most of the Congressmen who had supported the rights of black men now opposed the women's right to vote, and the women's rights activists turned their attention to gaining women's suffrage rather than broader reforms.

The women's suffrage movement in America was founded by women who were actively involved in abolition and temperance movements. Founded in the mid-19th century, the women's rights movement met in Seneca Falls, New York, in 1848 to discuss women's rights. They passed a resolution to secure the elective franchise and discussed equal rights to employment and education.

Although the Seneca Falls Convention was ridiculed by the public and several supporters of the woman's rights movement refrained from supporting them, their resolution marked the beginning of the woman's suffrage movement in the country.

The first national convention on women's rights was held in 1850. It continued annually, improving the focus on the women's suffrage movement. When gender was not specified in the Fifteenth Amendment during Reconstruction, the National Women's Suffrage Association was formed. Founded by Elizabeth Cady Stanton and Susan B. Anthony, the association tried to push for women's suffrage via the U.S. Constitution.

The Civil War Amendments (13th, 14th and 15th) established judicial principles that were stalled for many decades. The court's decisions undermined civil rights.

While the Reconstruction amendments—namely the Thirteenth, Fourteenth, and Fifteenth Amendments—adopted in the wake of the Civil War helped to implement the Reconstruction of the South, they were also a historic step towards developing a single national identity for all Americans.

The Fifth Amendment had provided a due process clause to protect the natural rights of citizens and limit the powers held by the government. The clause did not restrict the powers of the states, making it easy for them to violate the amendments, and natural rights were only partially protected.

The Fourteenth Amendment remedied the situation by extending the prohibition of natural rights violations to the states. The language of the Fourteenth Amendment clearly states that the natural rights clause should extend protection not just to citizens, but also to all persons who are part of the immunity clause or privileged beneficiaries.

Based on the equal protection clause, the government has two tasks in its function of securing rights for the people: it should not infringe upon or threaten the rights of citizens, and it should take decisive measures to protect the persons within its governing territory.

While the due process clause addresses the former function, the latter is ensured by the equal protection clause. The states, however, were not duty-bound to protect rights, as the original Constitution did not make it mandatory. States were thus legally free to deny rights by their own measure or by failing to prevent others from violating rights.

The amendments were required because the earlier protection clause did not have a reliable standard for protecting all persons. While Congress seriously considered language akin to the full protection of laws, these were not clear-cut standards, as they left room for violation.

Equal protection provided a manageable standard, offering protection similar to that given to the most favored members of the community. By enforcing these amendments, the courts and Congress arrived at an enforceable standard.

The immunities and privileges clause does not guarantee natural rights, as it applies only to citizens, thereby lacking the universal natural right provision. Similarly, the Fifteenth Amendment is not favorable for protecting natural rights and only involves the right of a citizen to vote. This amendment denies states the right to abridge laws on a racial basis concerning the right to vote. However, states may abridge the right-to-vote clause on any basis other than racial discrimination.

Historians have identified four different categories of rights, which were debated in the nineteenth century: civil, social, political, and natural. Each stakeholder had different claims and statuses to protect. While natural rights are for all human beings, political rights are not universal, and eligibility is subject to the decision of the community.

The Fifteenth Amendment states that race is not a valid reason for determining the right to vote, but it leaves other ways of denying the right to vote (such as literacy) open. Thus, the actual intention of the amendment was circumvented for several years by crafty exploitation of such loopholes states used to deny minorities the right to vote.

While these amendments aimed at giving freedom, rights of citizenship, and voting to the slaves, they were slowly but effectively eroded by the federal court rulings and state laws – called "Jim Crow laws" after a mythical southern white racist – during the latter part of the 19th century.

Women were prohibited from voting, which led to Susan B. Anthony trying to vote in the presidential election of 1872 as an act of agitation against the rules. The Jim Crow laws passed by some states limited the rights of former slaves.

Furthermore, the *Slaughterhouse* (1873) and *Plessy v. Ferguson* (1896) Supreme Court cases undermined the rights given by the amendments. The freed slaves enjoyed the full effects of the rights only after the passing of laws such as the 1964 Civil Rights Act and the 1965 Voting Rights Act.

As cities grew substantially in both size and number, some segments of American society enjoyed lives of extravagant "conspicuous consumption," while many others lived in relative poverty.

The explosion of city living also brought to light the drastic and deplorable contrast between the wealthy elites and the working classes, which had never been more evident than it was during this period. As thousands of workers flooded into the city, it quickly became apparent that many did not have the resources or services necessary to live in these urban metropolises.

Due to a lack of space, the tenement houses were crowded and typically had communal bathrooms. The sewer and water facilities provided by the city were typically overloaded and unable to provide service to all those living in the cities, much straining the sanitation system. The trash piled up on the streets of New York, and Chicago health concerns mounted, partially due to the spread of communicable diseases such as tuberculosis.

The child mortality rate was extremely high in Chicago. Poverty and low standards of living caused many to despise the wealthy classes who, during this period, lived in a new sense of luxury. As a result of continued income inequality, many living below the poverty line joined neighborhood gangs, such as the Hell's Kitchen Gang or the Rock Gang, who subsided by shoplifting and other petty thefts.

In contrast to the slums many Americans inhabited in the city, the wealthy class had experienced an incredible increase in their standard of living. Leisure activities such as shopping and listening to the radio preoccupied many upper- to middle-class Americans. The introduction of vast department stores, theme parks, theaters, and operas had inspired many city dwellers to enjoy the benefits of urbanization, in contrast to the poor living conditions of those beneath their social status.

This was one of the first periods when working-class Americans were able to transition into the middle class, allowing for further consumerism. The term "millionaire" was coined earlier during the 19th century but was not actively used until this period, which should give some insight into the levels of excess and decadence experienced by the American elites. One such example of over-the-top opulence came from a formal dinner party thrown by the wife of a railroad tycoon in honor of her dog, who entered the party wearing a $15,000 (today approximately $384,000) diamond-crusted collar.

The social structure of this period, highlighted by the great income gap, influenced the social reforms of the period, but it is difficult to say how great of an impact it had. While many people were continuing to work towards better workplace treatment and more efficient city services, others continued to live below the poverty line.

It is also interesting to note that regardless of the manufacturing and technical accomplishments of this period, the European elites still looked down at Americans as wealthy barbarians, who had undoubtedly achieved innovative technologies but lacked social sophistication and grace.

The westward migration, new systems of farming and transportation, and economic instability led to political and popular conflicts.

The expansion of westward migration opened several new transformations in farming, mining, and ranching markets. Such expansion became possible only with the introduction of mass transportation through the transcontinental railroad.

With the implementation of the Homestead Act in 1862, the government stopped selling land as a means of revenue. Instead, it used it as a tool to encourage the settling of the West mainly by farming families and those moving west to find their Gilded Age niche, such as ranching, mining or working as a cowboy.

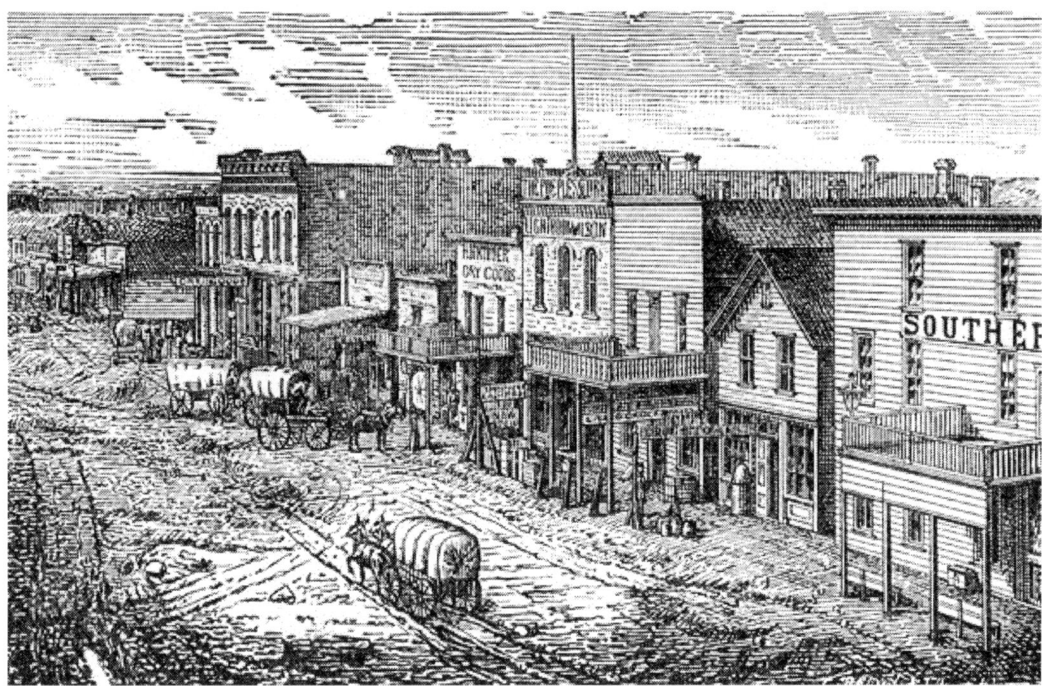

Western Expansion: street in Abilene

The main detriment of farming on the Great Plains during this period was the unpredictability of the climate, which could have disastrous effects on the crops and economic sustainability of the farm.

In addition to difficulties with the weather, the political landscape of the West was barren, and a lack of law and order pervaded the West, leading many to enact forms of vigilante justice. This was especially the case in disputes between ranchers and homesteaders, who, during this period, still shared prairie lands on the open range.

Women experienced more significant roles of independence and equality in the westward expansions than those living in the urbanized Northeast. The ratio of men to women in some frontier settlements in the West was more than 100–1. This gender differential afforded women many more privileges and the respect of their peers as they worked side by side with men in the farms and western communities.

The establishment of trading hubs on the Pacific Seaboard, such as San Francisco, embodied the West's diverse population, which was made up of nearly half immigrant populations, including but not limited to Hispanic, Asian, and European backgrounds.

Such diversity culminated in sources of conflict, including anti-immigration sentiment against Chinese populations in California, most notably in San Francisco, as well as Hispanic-Anglo aggression along the southern border of the United States.

Government agencies and conservationist organizations contended with corporate interests about the extension of public control over natural resources, including land and water.

As the American industries exploited the natural resources of the Midwest and West, some thought that action by the federal government was necessary to preserve national resources, including land and water. The difficult westward expansion had taught settlers the importance of protecting resources like water for future generations of farmers.

One of the first steps toward such conservation was the formation of the Office of Commission of Fish and Fisheries, also known as the Fish Commission, which was signed into law by Republican President Ulysses S. Grant in 1871 (1822-1885; 1869-1877).

Fisheries were one of the first renewable resources to receive the attention of the federal government, because Americans saw a drastic decline in the fisheries' production, calling into question the sustainability of fishing practices.

Farmers adapted to the new realities of mechanized agriculture and dependence on the evolving railroad system by creating local and regional organizations that sought to resist corporate control of agricultural markets.

The transitions experienced by farmers during the late 19th century varied and sometimes met with considerable pushback; one notable example of this was the farmers' dependence on rail transportation of goods to East Coast markets. This new relationship was not welcomed by most farmers operating in the Great Plains and eventually led to several opposition movements including, but not limited to, the Grange and Populist movements.

The Grange movement, also called the Patrons of Husbandry, was founded in 1867 and meant to facilitate the advancement of agricultural technologies, while also voicing social and economic concerns of the farmers operating in the Midwest.

As the government faltered in addressing the economic, political, and social concerns of farmers, the Grange movement saw a drastic increase in membership during the 1870s. Farmers were particularly upset with the rising costs of transporting goods by train, as well as the fact that the government opted for gold-backed currency instead of silver.

Grangers adopted the slogan "I pay for all," which embodied their stance as the breadwinners of American society where farming was the cornerstone of the American industries and progress during this period.

Such policies, along with failing crops, decimated the farming populations of the 1870s, leading farmers to support Populist and later Progressive movements that were concerned with the well-being of the American farmer.

U.S. postage stamp honoring the Grange movement

Business interests battled conservationists as the latter sought to protect sections of unspoiled wilderness through the establishment of national parks and other conservationist and preservationist measures.

As industry and manufacturing giants dotted the American landscape following the Civil War, it seemed a new war on natural resources and conservation had been declared. The industrial magnates of the period exploited and sought the natural resources of continental America in hopes of continuing their dominant role within the new economy.

However, many conservationists, who sought policies more in line with preserving and maintaining the natural resources and unspoiled wilderness of the United States, quickly opposed this.

The exploitation of natural resources by business interests centered mainly on iron ore, coal, oil, and lumber. Iron ore was used to create steel and pig iron, which was used by the railroad companies and in the building of urban bridges and buildings. Coal was needed to propel the steam engines in the railcars, after replacing the use of wood as fuel.

Other industry machines also used coal as a fuel source, making it a necessity of the Gilded Age (1870s to 1900). Oil was used as a form of kerosene to lighthouses and cities during this period. It also created a new industry, petroleum refining, which would later evolve into multi-billion-dollar corporations. Lumber was also sought during this period.

International and internal migrations increased both urban and rural populations, but gender, racial, ethnic, religious, and socioeconomic inequalities abounded, inspiring some reformers to attempt to address these inequities.

As Americans entered an unprecedented period of economic and social development, it became clear that reform was on the horizon, and many social groups, including women, the working class and immigrants would benefit from these eventual reforms.

Late 19th-century America had unregulated work environments, overzealous and sometimes corrupt politicians, and a population unhappy with the influx of recent immigrants. These divisions highlighted the difficulties faced by average Americans but also showed the abundant and varying solutions and perceptions of the American public.

In hopes of addressing forms of racial discrimination, many abolitionists and former slaves worked tirelessly to end the racial norms of the Civil War era utilizing organizations and support groups whose goal was to help assimilate former slaves into post–Civil War America.

Socioeconomic inequalities were addressed by attempts to reform the workplace, guaranteeing shorter workdays, protection of wages, and the formation of unions.

Religious rivalries and oppression were seen during this period, which is to be expected given the transition from traditional Victorian values into more modern interpretations of religion and science. Many people immigrated during this period to experience greater freedoms of religion and escape persecution in their native lands, examples being Russian Mennonites and migrant Mormons, who made a home for themselves in Utah.

While many embraced the transitions of the period, others worked tirelessly against such changes, arguing the tradition and cultural norms of the early 19th century were not broken and certainly did not need fixing.

Increased migrations from Asia and southern and eastern Europe, as well as African American migrations within and out of the South, accompanied the mass movement of people into the nation's cities and the rural and boomtown areas of the West.

As America began its transition westward or into urban centers, many immigrants from around the world looked to the United States as a means of accomplishing dreams unattainable in their native lands. Many immigrants moving from Europe and Asia sought better economic and vocational conditions.

In contrast, others looked for expanded religious freedoms as seen with Eastern Orthodox and Jewish immigrants of the period. African Americans, who had survived slavery and the Civil War, looked for the freedoms and equality promised by the Emancipation Proclamation.

As America experienced the boom of initial urbanization, many immigrants and minority groups looked to these cities and vast economic opportunities for better wages and the amenities of city life. While many groups that had previously experienced discrimination were able to find work, social and class expectations still stifled the ambitions of many living in the city.

The westward expansion proved a little less rigid in class and social structure, allowing many African Americans and immigrant classes to hold various jobs, including those which would have previously been designated strictly for white males. Such examples included mining, ranching, and homesteading. These initial opportunities would become the foundation of further calls for equal job opportunities as well as equal rights and protection within the political system.

The implications of such expansion were critical to propelling the United States into a more developed, unified country following the ravaging it had experienced during the Civil War. It also allowed many Americans to find opportunities previously unavailable, perpetuating the American dream of a new wave of citizens.

The competition for land in the West among white settlers, Indians, and Mexican Americans led to an increase in violent conflict.

As Americans began their massive westward expansion, it quickly became evident that these exploits would be undertaken at the cost of great violence and instability. The Homestead Act in 1862 had given many white settlers the upper hand over Mexican or Native American settlements, which dotted the western landscape.

HOMESTEAD.

Land Office at Brownville Neb
January 20th 1868.

CERTIFICATE, No. 1

APPLICATION, No. 1

It is hereby certified, *That pursuant to the provisions of the act of Congress, approved May 20, 1862, entitled "An act to secure homesteads to actual settlers on the public domain,"* Daniel Freeman *has made payment in full for* S½ of NW¼ & NE¼ of NW¼ & SW¼ of NE¼ *of Section* Twenty six (26) *in Township* four (4) N *of Range* five (5) E *containing* 160 *acres.*

Now, therefore, be it known, *That on presentation of this Certificate to the* COMMISSIONER OF THE GENERAL LAND OFFICE, *the said* Daniel Freeman *shall be entitled to a Patent for the Tract of Land above described.*

Henry M. Atkinson *Register.*

Certificate of the first homestead according to the Homestead Act, 1868

At the height of the farming and mining booms of westward expansion, the Great Plains also experienced a period of open range policies. During this period, farmers, cowboys, homesteaders, and native populations struggled to maintain boundaries, which culminated in frontier justice such as vigilante courts and killings.

Between the 1870s and 1880s, cowboys, ranchers, and farmers embraced the cattle industry with no feeding pattern, which would be unsuccessful and caused the end of open range farming and ranching.

CULTURAL and INTELLECTUAL DEVELOPMENTS: 1790 - 1877

During the 18th century, new ideas about politics and society led to debates about religion and governance and ultimately inspired experiments with new governmental structures.

By the 18th century, science had begun to vastly increase human understanding of nature, which led Enlightenment thinkers to conceive of the idea that the social and political world could also be understood, explained, and improved with the use of rational thought.

Increasingly, intellectuals and activists questioned authority and doubted the legitimacy of existing social arrangements, including government structures. Along with this new, more critical mode of thinking came suggestions for new models of government and society.

Enlightenment thinkers tended to favor systems based on freedom, toleration, equality, and consent. The opponents often argued that reason alone could not build a better society than the wisdom of the ages, and saw in some of the excesses of the French Revolution a confirmation of the dangers of a political system based on reason rather than tradition.

The colonists' belief in the superiority of republican self-government based on the natural rights of the people found its clearest American expression in Thomas Paine's *Common Sense* and the Declaration of Independence.

Thomas Paine (1737-1809) was an important intellectual figure during the American Revolution. Paine's pamphlet *Common Sense* (January 10, 1776) offered a blistering attack on the king and the concept of monarchy, suggesting that the people of the colonies had been forced to rise against the king to preserve their natural right to freedom.

In Paine's opinion, the government was a necessary evil at the best of times, always impinging on the rights of men. Only a republican government based on consent could avoid the kind of tyranny King George III (1738-1820; 1760-1820) was trying to impose, so a complete break with history and tradition was necessary. Paine's style of writing was so direct and straightforward that it gained wide circulation in virtually every class of society, reaching anyone interested in political ideas and not just the educated elite.

In breaking with the established rule of tradition and monarchy, the founders who penned the Declaration of Independence wanted to go beyond the ancient rights of Englishmen and the existing constitution. They made the natural rights of men to life, liberty, and the pursuit of happiness a new foundation of political legitimacy.

They explained that when a government such as the British threatened these rights, the inhabitants of the colonies had every right to resist and even overthrow the authorities. Instead of conceiving of rights as something dependent on a given political system, Jefferson, the principal author of the Declaration, thought of these rights as natural and "unalienable," and insisted that any legitimate political system must be set up to preserve those rights.

The Second Great Awakening, liberal social ideas from abroad, and romantic beliefs in human perfectibility fostered the rise of voluntary organizations to promote religious and secular reforms, including abolition and women's rights.

While less politically charged than many other conflicts during the time, religion was rapidly changing during the early 19th century. Before the American Revolution, most people belonged to one of three major Protestant denominations: Congregationalists, Anglicans, and Quakers. Congregationalist churches were the descendants of Puritan churches, and Puritan influence on America can still be seen in many American ideals, such as hard work and community.

The Anglican Church was the American branch of the Church of England. After the Revolution, they were known as Episcopalians. The Quakers were a "peace church" like the Amish. After the American Revolution, the major denominations changed, and the three foundation denominations gave way to evangelical Methodism and Baptists, as revivals swept the nation. This period is known as the Second Great Awakening.

At the heart of the Second Great Awakening were revivals. These were large meetings, typically held in fields where a preacher, or several preachers, would stand and speak. Charles Finney, sometimes called the Father of Modern Revivalism, was one such preacher. He shared his faith at revivals, and his style impacted the movement. Finney also allowed women to pray out loud in public meetings of mixed gender, which was not done during the period due to the cult of domesticity and public understanding of gender roles.

Charles Finney, 1792-1875

Charles Finney created what he called the "anxious seat," which was a place for non-Christians who were considering converting. They could sit in the anxious seat to receive prayers. He also made a habit of censuring individuals by name during his services and preaching extemporaneously for an audience. Using such methods, the energy of the crowd was masterfully controlled by these speakers.

An account of a 20,000-person revival in Kentucky reads:

> *The noise was like the roar of Niagara. The vast sea of human beings seemed to be agitated as if by a storm. I counted seven ministers, all preaching at one time, some on stumps, others on wagons...Some of the people were singing, others praying, some crying for mercy. A peculiarly strange sensation came over me. My heart beat tumultuously, my knees trembled, my lips quivered, and I felt as though I must fall to the ground.*
>
> —James Finley

The ministers at these revivals reached out to their audience at the emotional level and upheld ideals that the average person could agree with. Evangelical churches generally favored ordinary people over elites. They felt that a truly pious individual was more capable of leading others to salvation than a formally trained minister, like those required by many traditional churches. These open policies meant that many flocked to the Evangelical faiths.

While these religious revivals did not directly threaten any established order, they did encourage activism on a wide scale. The movement stressed the concept of free will and a person's choice to accept their lot in life or work to better their position. It was a very optimistic outlook, allowing the choice of religious salvation instead of the fatalistic views held by other denominations. However, it was also one that encouraged conflict with social norms.

White women, who were invited to take leadership roles for the first time, found themselves in a position to enact social change for women's rights. African Americans were also allowed to participate in the new religion actively. The stressing of individual salvation caused many to question the religion-based proslavery arguments. While this period is characterized by conflicts over slavery, women's rights, and Native American's rights, great strides were made in other forms of activism.

In 1837, Horace Mann (1796-1859), often called the Father of the Common School, used his position as the secretary of the newly-created Massachusetts Board of Education to enact significant education reform. He started the Common School Movement to ensure that all children would have a primary education at the expense of the state.

Horace Mann, c. 1855

Mann believed that society could only flourish when all citizens were literate and had a general understanding of civics. He argued that it was only with an educated public that a democracy, dependent upon the will of that public, could reach its fullest potential. Mann was involved in creating teacher training schools, called normal schools so that professionals would educate children. He also actively recruited and trained women for what was, at the time, an all-male vocation.

While Horace Mann championed the education system, Dorothea Dix was trying to bring social reform to the treatment of the mentally ill. In Massachusetts, in 1841, while teaching Sunday school at the East Cambridge Jail, a women's prison, Dix discovered that the living quarters for the prisoners were not hospitable, especially those holding the mentally ill. Many of the rooms had no heat, for instance. Outraged by the way these women were being treated, she petitioned the courts for an order to improve the standard of living in the prisons.

Concerned about the plight of others, Dix traveled around the state to research the living conditions in prisons and poorhouses. This led to her eventually writing a proposal for the Massachusetts legislature, which would expand and improve the State Mental Hospital at Worcester. Satisfied with her work at home, Dix began a national tour to improve conditions for all patients. Her continued success at the state level encouraged her to move into the federal arena.

In 1848, she requested an endowment to be put aside for the treatment of the mentally ill, the deaf, and the blind. Both the House and the Senate passed the bill, but President Franklin Pierce (1804-1869; 1853-1857) vetoed it. Discouraged but not defeated, Dix began to travel internationally, recommending reforms worldwide.

Frances Wright, 1795-1852

Scottish born Frances Wright (also known as Franny Wright) was a proponent of utopian communities and believed that they could be used to resolve the American issue of slavery (the term "utopian" comes from Sir Thomas More's (1478-1555) *Utopia* (1516), theorized as the perfect society). These settlements tended to experiment with different models of government, marriage, labor, and wealth to find the perfect society.

In 1825, Wright published *A Plan for the Gradual Abolition of Slavery in the United States without Danger of Loss to the Citizens of the South*. In the text, she urgently suggests that land is put aside to create a colony for freed blacks based on the utopian communities of the time.

Wright was so sure that her plan would work that she invested her own money in a 640-acre tract located in present-day Tennessee. She called the land Nashoba and populated her colony with slaves that she bought and freed in exchange for being a part of her colony. Soon after the colony was founded, however, she was forced to leave.

When she returned, she found it destroyed. Still insistent that her plan could work, she published a well-received newspaper article defending her idea, and in 1830 she planned for the Nashoba slaves to be emancipated to Haiti.

Several other utopian communities existed during the period. Few had any lasting impact on society, but each experimented with different social structures, an indicator that the young country was still trying to define itself. In 1841, Brook Farm was founded by Unitarian Minister George Ripley.

Known as the Transcendentalist Romance, the community was the first purely secular utopian community. The foundational idea was that by living together, farming together, and sharing their labor, members would have more time to spend on academic pursuits.

The community disbanded relatively quickly when finances became an issue. Nathanial Hawthorne, an influential Romantic writer, was one of the community's founding members.

Nathaniel Hawthorne, 1804-1864

Author Louisa May Alcott spent seven months of her childhood at Fruitland, a utopian community founded by her father and Charles Lane. Though it claimed to be based on principles of gender equality, Alcott's scathing reflection detailed a very different story. New Harmony, in Indiana, was a more fruitful endeavor.

Founded by social reformer Robert Owens, the community was populated by scientists and succeeded in establishing a center for scientific discovery outside of the Northeast. It disbanded after four years.

The Shakers are a utopian group that still exists today. Shakers practice celibacy and communal ownership of goods. Both aspects were typical of religious utopias. However, they also believe in strict gender roles and keep the sexes separate. Their prosperity is based mainly on a source of income, namely furniture design, and manufacture.

A new national culture emerged, with Americans creating art, architecture, and literature that combined European forms with local and regional cultural sensibilities.

As the country struggled to establish a national identity amongst the chaos of conflict, artists adapted original American styles. It became fashionable to document scenes of everyday life for different classes and in different regions. As territory opened in the West, landscapes became the dominant art form. Styles like the panoramic landscapes of the Hudson River School showed the country's beauty and vitality.

The Tonalism and Luminism movements invoked a spiritual serenity in landscapes, reflecting the ideas of westward expansion and Americans as the chosen people. Artists were expressing the serenity of an America that was embroiled in conflicts and searching for its place in the world. They were, in a sense, capturing those fundamental ideals that founded the nation.

Painter John James Audubon (1785-1851) established a very different style and body of work that still managed to capture the myth of America. His goal as a painter was to capture the majesty of the numerous American birds accurately. While this may sound simplistic, it made him incredibly famous in the United States and abroad. His birds managed to capture the majesty and youth of America.

In addition to painting, Audubon practiced science. Audubon made the first American bird bands and used them to track and identify a group of Eastern Phoebes that returned annually to his neighbor's yard.

John James Audubon

Passenger pigeon by John James Audubon

Romanticism, a great literary style characterized by philosophical idealism, gave way to one of the first American literary styles, known as transcendentalism. Though it is sometimes mistaken for religion, transcendentalism is about interpreting relationships.

Transcendentalist authors were trying to encapsulate the same mythology as visual artists of the period; they wanted to verbally define what it meant to be an American and write about the spirit of America.

The most famous transcendentalists are Ralph Waldo Emerson (1803-1882) and Henry David Thoreau (1817-1862). Emerson's essay *Self-Reliance* (1841) is still widely read and speaks to the inability of humans to obtain meaning from one another. Emerson wrote that the truth had to come from the individual. Thoreau's best-known work is his essay, *Civil Disobedience* (1849). In it, he encompasses many of the same ideas that Emerson illuminated.

His most well-known excerpt is his description of the night he spent in prison following his refusal to pay taxes to fund a war that he did not support. In the excerpt, Thoreau mocks the idea that a man whose conscience is clear could ever be "imprisoned." He, like other transcendentalists, valued the mental over the physical and therefore felt that his pure "body" could never be touched.

Ralph Waldo Emerson (left) and Henry David Thoreau (right)

Perhaps the premier artistic style to impact the early history of America was neoclassicism, characterized by a renewed interest in classical forms and ideas. It can be seen in stunning variety in America during the early 19th century.

Many of the political ideas from the Enlightenment had their roots in Greco-Roman culture. Epics, a literary form used by Greek and Roman poets, became popular and compared well with the slave narratives and westward expansionism of the day.

Even the buildings that housed the government showed an obvious homage to the Greek and Roman ruins. One of the most noteworthy members of this movement was Thomas Jefferson, who was an accomplished architect in addition to being a leading statesman.

Jefferson wanted his admiration of the Roman Republic to be manifested, not only in the political institutions of the new nation but also visually in the nation's public buildings, to remind the citizens that they lived in a Republic.

The White House uses the same style of columns as the Pantheon in Rome. Neoclassicism serves as an excellent metaphor for the early American people. They were attached to the past to remain connected to their ideas, yet they were prepared to change.

The idea of Manifest Destiny, which asserted U.S. power in the Western Hemisphere and supported U.S. expansion westward, was built on a belief in the particular virtues of the American people, their destiny to expand throughout the continent, and a sense of American cultural superiority. This helped shape the era's political debates.

Manifest Destiny fueled western territorial expansion. The term Manifest Destiny was first coined in 1845 by John O'Sullivan (1813-1895), editor for *The United States Magazine and Democratic Review*. It was proclaimed as an effort to expand the continent, which was gifted by Providence to help the multiplying millions of Americans flourish.

Manifest Destiny encouraged the belief that the American settlers were destined to expand and move across the New World to spread their culture, traditions, and institutions, and to enlighten the primitive nations of the world. Some American settlers considered the Hispanics and Indians as inferior beings who needed to be cultivated.

The settlers considered Manifest Destiny the best way to bring order to the country and remake the world in a way that mirrored their image. This belief that the American people had the mission of imposing their virtuous life on others led to westward expansion, the acquisition of new territories, and war with Mexico in the 1840s.

John O'Sullivan, 1813-1895

O'Sullivan's article focused on the recent Texas annexation and hinted at further annexation of the territories acquired during the Mexican-American War through negotiations with the British for Oregon and the proposed annexation of Cuba from Spain.

Western expansion had some resistance from the people of the East, who worried that their dominant role in national affairs would be restricted by expansion.

Regardless, in his address in 1844, President James K. Polk (1845-1849) reiterated the commitment of the nation to the expansion of existing territories and acquisition of new ones to strengthen the bonds of the Union, provide security and economic development opportunities and grant its people more agricultural land.

The new cultural and intellectual movements advanced innovation.

The Gilded Age—which ranged from 1876, at the end of Reconstruction, to 1890—was a period of exponential growth and innovation in America.

Below are some of the most notable inventors of the period:

- Nikola Tesla (1856-1943) invented the first motor that transformed alternating current (AC) electrical power into a usable mechanical force.
- Alexander Graham Bell (1847-1922) invented the telephone in 1876, which revolutionized communication in America.
- Thomas Edison produced the first record player or phonograph in 1877 and the light bulb in 1879, culminating his lifelong achievements with the establishment of the first direct current (D.C.) electric power station in Manhattan in September of 1882.

Thomas Edison, 1847-1931

DIPLOMACY and INTERNATIONAL RELATIONS: 1790 - 1877

The continued presence of European powers in North America challenged the United States to find ways to safeguard its borders, maintain neutral trading rights, and promote its economic interests.

Independence brought several foreign policy problems to bear on the American experiment. American ships were no longer sailing under British flags. Until the Jay Treaty of 1795, they were restricted from selling their goods in the British West Indies, an essential market for foodstuffs and other agricultural products for southern planters and farmers. American sailors even risked being taken as slaves by North African pirates.

On the mainland, Britain and Spain retained vast territories in North America and often acted in a hostile fashion. The British refused to vacate the forts in the Old Northwest for more than ten years after the end of the Revolutionary War, citing the failure of the new republic to compensate Loyalists for losses due to confiscation during the revolution.

The Jay Treaty also resolved this problem. Similarly, Spanish authorities refused to accept American sovereignty south of the Ohio River and closed the Mississippi River to American traders. They even got involved in secret conspiracies with prominent Americans to secure the Old Southwest for Spain.

However, Florida and Louisiana were peripheral parts of the sprawling Spanish Empire in the Americas, and the differences over borders and trade were eventually settled in Pinckney's Treaty, signed in 1795.

As western settlers sought free navigation of the Mississippi River, the United States forged diplomatic initiatives to manage the conflict with Spain and to deal with the continued British presence on the American continent.

The Jay Treaty, signed by the United States and Britain in 1794, resolved some of the outstanding issues of contention that had lingered since the end of the Revolutionary War. The architect behind the treaty was Federalist Alexander Hamilton, who sought rapprochement with the British and expansion of American trade. To Hamilton, the moment seemed opportune, as Britain had become involved in a new war with France.

The treaty was a victory for the United States because it finally ended the British occupation of the forts in the Old Northwest. The departure of the British was especially significant because it demoralized Indians who had hoped to stop American expansion into their lands. At the same time, the treaty was a consequence of the defeat of the Western Confederacy of tribes at the Battle of Fallen Timbers.

As the Indians seemed unable to resist the American military, the British no longer had any real role to play in the area. The British justification for holding on to the forts had been unpaid wartime debts related to the confiscation of Loyalist property; both parties now agreed to send this matter to arbitration.

The Battle of Fallen Timbers, 1794

The Jay Treaty made the Spanish fear a future alliance between the United States and Britain. Spain had closed navigation on the Mississippi to Americans, but now agreed to reopen commercial channels and negotiate boundaries. By 1795, this resulted in Pinckney's Treaty, where Spain ceded control of most of what is now Mississippi and Alabama to the United States.

Navigation rights were restored, and the Spanish pledged not to incite and arm the Indians against the United States. Thus, by playing the European powers against each other, the Washington administration managed to tighten the country's grip on frontier territories and reduce the risk of outside powers intervening in its dealings with the Indians. This facilitated the ongoing westward expansion of the United States.

The United States became more connected with the world as it pursued an expansionist foreign policy in the Western Hemisphere and emerged as the destination for many migrants from other countries.

During the period from 1844 to 1877, a series of events and issues, including the expansion policy of the United States and the growing unrest among antislavery organizations, led to the Civil War.

During 1844, when James K. Polk was elected president of the United States, the country attracted migrants due to its lucrative economic development policies. Polk supported expansion, as the Democrats believed in republican virtue being upheld only when more lands were opened for the yeoman farmers.

Furthermore, the Texas annexation and the acquisition of Oregon County were aimed at increasing the country's influence on the continent. While organizations against slavery existed before this period, they gained political mileage only after 1840, when the Liberal Party grew discontented with abolitionist organizations and began to fight slavery via political methods.

US interest in expanding trade led to economic, diplomatic, and cultural initiatives westward to Asia.

Previously, the American economy was based mainly on small-scale agriculture and local commerce. By the middle of the 19th century, America had turned into a capitalist marketplace. The Industrial Revolution changed America's economy and boosted urbanization, while agricultural development spread to the West. As settlers moved towards the West, their conditions improved, and they flourished as hunters and farmers.

The cheap land and plentiful resources attracted new settlers, and merchants and artisans followed farmers towards the western occupation. Chicago, Illinois, which in 1830 had been a trading village, became the richest and largest city by the time its original settlers breathed their last. The Preemption Act of 1836 allowed people to stake claims on land, and after 1862 people could acquire their land just by occupying it and making improvements.

The steel plow, invented by John Deere in 1837, made it easier for farmers to plow their land, while the mechanical mower and reaper invented by Cyrus McCormick in 1834 replaced manual scythes and sickles for large-scale agricultural practices. Soon mechanical seeders and threshers were introduced. The technological innovations and persistent westward movement resulted in large-scale commercial activity in the West.

The transportation revolution also helped the country economically. The pony express, steamboats, and clipper ships were some of the inventions that helped bind the nation together and connect it with other parts of the world. The clipper ships first launched in 1845 had tall masts, several sails, and could sail faster than a steamer in a good breeze.

They carried highly demanded tea from China to America and transported goods to prospective merchants in California. The transportation revolution integrated the continent into a single economic and cultural entity and instilled a more profound nationalist spirit.

In addition to its westward expansion within North America, the United States also wanted to extend its base overseas, especially in Japan, for three reasons. First, the United States needed a coaling base (i.e., a fueling port) for its steamships. Since Japan was located in the same latitude as San Francisco, it served as an ideal location for a coaling base.

Although Hawaii was used as a coaling base already, the U.S. navy wanted another port in the East. Secondly, an American presence in Japan would ensure that shipwrecked sailors reaching Japan received proper treatment. Lastly, the United States sought to increase its revenue by trading with other countries.

Before Commodore Perry's mission to Japan in 1854, only the Dutch could land their ships on Japanese soil, and all other countries were prohibited. After a few visits to Japan, Perry convinced the Japanese to sign the Treaty of Kanagawa in 1854, enforcing the Japanese provision of food, water, coal, and other needed supplies to the American ships that docked in Nagasaki. Ultimately, Japan consented to trade with the United States, ending two hundred years of isolation.

Commodore Oliver Hazard Perry, 1785-1819

The treaty brought in enormous amounts of foreign money and significantly damaged the Japanese economy. It paved the way for Russia, France, the Netherlands, and Great Britain to also sign unequal treaties with Japan, resulting in Japan having fewer rights than the foreign nations. Furthermore, the treaty helped to overthrow the Shogun government in Japan, which had previously been considered an undefeatable force.

Religion, particularly evangelical Protestantism, was involved mainly in the nation-building and internal expansion process in which the Americans were immersed during the entire 19th century, instigating the foreign missionary movement.

The foreign missionary movement increased in intensity in the wake of the Civil War, when the critical issues of national unity and slavery were, to some extent, settled. This movement was in full bloom after 1900. It progressed until the 20th century, imprinting its presence in all the continents of the globe with its unique American mix of national, religious, and civilizing objectives.

The early Puritan ideas of 1600, which stressed the "Errand into the Wilderness" along with the "Errand to the World" concept of the 19th century, led to the missionaries forming voluntary associations based on religion. The missionary movement evolved via internal expansion before it moved overseas. The initial challenge westward expansion presented to missionaries was providing the growing cities and towns with ministers and churches.

Methodists were exceptionally skilled at missionizing and forming new congregations via their adaptable structure and circuits. The Presbyterians, Baptists, and Mormons also expanded westward. Thus, the internal religious expansion was successfully implemented except in California. Here, the Protestants did not have a big success in integrating their religion.

The internal missionary efforts focused on the Native Americans, with many missionary groups supporting the Native Americans in their fight against the federal government. The missionary movement's interaction with the Native Americans involved both cultural sensitivity and high-handedness on the part of the missionaries, and religious conversions and resistance by the Native Americans.

The other area of focus for the missionaries included the African American slaves, wherein they tried to carry out their religious goals while alleviating the racist attitude of the whites and the poverty-ridden state of the blacks.

The foreign missionary movement grew based on the mission efforts and expansion policies of the Protestants within the United States. The initial step started with the formation of the American Board of Commissioners for Foreign Missions (ABCFM) in 1810 in New England.

Like the London Missionary Society, its British chapter formed two decades back, the organization belonged to the voluntary, nondenominational category and was not managed by any ecclesiastical group. The ABCFM played a significant role in all the missionary efforts of Americans overseas.

Businesses and foreign policymakers increasingly looked outside U.S. borders to gain more considerable influence and control over markets and natural resources in the Pacific, Asia, and Latin America.

As the United States began its inward expansion, many influential businessmen and politicians were also looking into the global system in hopes of finding influence, resources, and alliances.

To establish the United States as a real-world power, the industrial machine had to influence foreign markets in Asia and Latin America. Following this expansion-style foreign policy agenda, the United States was extremely interested in securing the natural resources required to sustain the industrial and manufacturing boom of the Gilded Age.

With the expansion of manufacturing and production, the United States and its business magnates were looking for fresh markets. Some of the most notable examples of this were the investments in Asian and Latin American countries to gain influence within the regions.

By undertaking these investment and export opportunities, the United States was setting the foundations of its 20th-century foreign policies, while at the same time creating a more pronounced rivalry between the United States and European counterparts. Such foreign policy decisions is a foreshadowing of the decisions to come in the latter decades of the 20th century.

Additionally, as the U.S. government faced pushback from conservationists, some industrialists sought the natural resources of other less regulated countries. To maintain the massive expectations of manufacturing and production, the United States needed to secure vast amounts of natural resources including but not limited to iron ore, coal, lumber, and oil reserves.

The long-term implications of resource security can be seen in the World Wars and every period that follows, highlighting the incalculable value of such resources during the period of the Gilded Age, as well as the contemporary period. For the first time during this period, Americans realized the economic potential of steel and oil refining.

The United States went to great lengths to cultivate the relationships and economic partnerships with countries where these commodities were not readily available, ushering in the century of American hegemony.

One might also argue such policies were successful, as, under President Taft (1857-1930; 1909-1913), a similar strategy was employed using dollar diplomacy.

Iron and steel company in Johnstown, Pennsylvania

IMAGE CREDITS

Period 1 – Political History

Thanksgiving before the image of the Virgin, Lossing, Benson J. *Our Country.* New York: Johnson and Bailey, 1895.

The landing of Admiral Columbus, Spencer, J. A. *History of the United States.* New York: Johnson, Fry, and Company, 1858.

Spanish explorers are raising the memorial cross, Lossing, Benson J. *Our Country.* New York: Johnson and Bailey, 1895.

Cultivation of tobacco at Jamestown, Scott, David B. *A School History of the United States.* New York: Harper & Brothers, 1883.

Settlers in North Carolina, Lossing, Benson J. *Harper's Encyclopedia of United States History.* New York: Harper and Brothers Publishers, 1912.

The arrival of the Indian allies at the French camp, Stephens, Alex H. *A Comprehensive and Popular History of the United States.* Chattanooga: Hickman and Fowler, 1882.

Boston Tea Party, throwing tea overboard, Stephens, Alex H. *A Comprehensive and Popular History of the United States.* Chattanooga: Hickman and Fowler, 1882.

Reading the Stamp Act, Markham, Richard. *Colonial Days: Being Stories and Ballads for Young Patriots.* New York: Dodd, Mead, & Company, 1881.

Portrait of Mercy Otis Warren, Copley, John Singleton. *Portrait of Mercy Otis Warren.* 1763. Oil on Canvas. Museum of Fine Arts, Boston. Wikimedia Commons.

General George Washington, Ellis, Edward S. *The History of Our Country: From the Discovery of America to the Present Time.* Cincinnati: The Jones Brothers Publishing Company, 1910.

Period 1 – Economic History

Pueblo girl winnowing beans, Lummis, Charles F. "The Land of Poco Tiempo." *Scribners.* Dec. 1891: 760-771.

Pueblo cart, Beadle, J.H. *Western Wilds, and the Men Who Redeem Them.* Washington, D.C.: Clark E. Ridpath, 1917.

Algonquin Indian, Hutchinson, H. N. ed. *The Living Races of Mankind.* London: Hutchinson & Co., ca 1910.

Iroquois dwellings, Lossing, Benson J. *Our Country.* New York: Johnson and Bailey, 1895.

Colonial slave market in the 17th century, Lossing, Benson J. *Harper's Encyclopedia of United States History.* New York: Harper and Brothers Publishers, 1912.

Typical Cayuse and his mount, Humfreville, J. Lee. Twenty Years Among Our Savage Indians. Hartford: The Hartford Publishing Company, 1897.

Christopher Columbus, Baldwin, James. *Baldwin Reader: Fourth and Fifth Years Combined.* New York: American Book Company, 1897.

Introduction of slavery, Ellis, Edward S. *The Youth's History of the United States.* New York: The Cassell Publishing Company, 1887.

Spaniards gambling, Lossing, Benson J. *Our Country.* New York: Johnson and Bailey, 1895.

Caravel with oars, De Oliveira, Brás. *Caravel with Oars.* 1894. *The History and Development of Caravels, Graduate Thesis.* By G. R. Schwarz. Texas A&M U, 2008. N. page. Print. Wikimedia Commons.

Portuguese galleons and carracks, João De Castro, D. *Portuguese Galleons, and Naus (Carracks) Routemap of the Red Sea Roteiro Do Mar Roxo 1540 Galleon Nau (Carrack).* 1540. Universidade De Coimbra, Portugal. *Wikimedia Commons.* Media Wiki, 3 Nov. 2013.

Spanish Armada, Lossing, Benson J. *Our Country.* New York: Johnson and Bailey, 1895.

Henry Hudson, Drake, Francis. *Indian History for Young Folks.* New York: Harper and Brothers, 1912.

Depiction of a tobacco wharf in colonial America, Depiction of a Tobacco Wharf in Colonial America. Digital image. *The Mariner's Museum and Park.* The Mariner's Museum. Wikimedia Commons.

Exploring northern Georgia, Stephens, Alex H. *A Comprehensive and Popular History of the United States.* Chattanooga: Hickman and Fowler, 1882.

Quaker woman preaching in New Amsterdam, Bryant, William Cullen, and Sydney Howard Gay. *A Popular History of the United States.* New York: Charles Scribners' Sons, 1881.

Savannah, from a print of 1741, Bryant, William Cullen, and Sydney Howard Gay. *A Popular History of the United States.* New York: Charles Scribners' Sons, 1881.

Scene on a plantation, Lossing, Benson J. *Harper's Encyclopedia of United States History.* New York: Harper and Brothers Publishers, 1912.

Carolina rice field, Bryant, William Cullen, and Sydney Howard Gay. *A Popular History of the United States.* New York: Charles Scribners' Sons, 1881.

Trading with Indians, Drake, Francis. *Indian History for Young Folks.* New York: Harper and Brothers, 1912.

Sugar cane, Richardson, Abby Sage. *The History of Our Country.* Boston: Houghton, Mifflin, and Company, 1883.

Period 1 – Social History

Spanish explorers: Cortés, Coligni, de Soto, and Verazzani, Lossing, Benson J. *Our Country.* New York: Johnson and Bailey, 1895.

Meeting of Cortés and Montezuma, Buel, J. W. *Around the World with Great Voyages.* Philadelphia: The Columbia Syndicate, 1892.

Heroic defence of Cuzco, Adams, Davenport W. H. *The Land of the Incas and the City of the Sun.* Boston: Dana Estes and Company, ca 1885.

Dutch selling slaves to the Virginia planters, Mace, William H. *A School History of the United States.* Chicago: Rand, McNally, and Company, 1904.

Domestic slave trade, Bryant, William Cullen, and Sydney Howard Gay. *A Popular History of the United States.* New York: Charles Scribners' Sons, 1881.

Slave auction, Ellis, Edward S. *The Youth's History of the United States.* New York: The Cassell Publishing Company, 1887.

King Philip, or Metacomet—Wampanoag chief, Wood, Norman B. *The Lives of Famous Indian Chiefs.* Aurora: American Indian Historical Publishing Company, 1906.

French Métis, Sellier, Charles-Auguste. *Metis Francais. La Nouvelle-France.* By Eugene Guenin. Paris: Hachette, 1900. 415. Print. Wikimedia Commons.

Puritan, Lossing, Benson J. *Our Country.* New York: Johnson and Bailey, 1895.

Period 1 – Intellectual & Cultural History

Spaniards are destroying Mexican idols, Lossing, Benson J. *Our Country.* New York: Johnson and Bailey, 1895.

Sugar plantation, Bryant, William Cullen, and Sydney Howard Gay. *A Popular History of the United States.* New York: Charles Scribners' Sons, 1881.

Roger Williams is building his house, Bryant, William Cullen, and Sydney Howard Gay. *A Popular History of the United States.* New York: Charles Scribners' Sons, 1881.

William Penn, Stephens, Alex H. A Comprehensive and Popular History of the United States. Chattanooga: Hickman and Fowler, 1882.

Portrait of John Locke, Kneller, Godfrey, Sir. *Portrait of John Locke.* 1697. Oil on Canvas. State Hermitage Museum, St. Petersburg, Russia. Wikimedia Commons.

Interior of Christ Church, Boston, Pratt, Mara L. *American's Story for America's Children: The Early Colonies.* Boston: D.C. Heath & Company, 1901.

Period 1 – Foreign Policy

Queen Isabella of Castille (left) and King Ferdinand V of Aragon (right), Ellis, Edward S., and Charles F. Horne. *The Story of the Greatest Nations*. New York: Francis Niglutsch, 1906.

Indians at a Hudson Bay Company trading post, Indians trade furs at a Hudson's Bay Company trading post in the 1800s. Digital image. *Hulton Archive*. Getty Images. Wikimedia Commons.

The Dutch trading with the Indians, Ellis, Edward S., and Charles F. Horne. *The Story of the Greatest Nations*. New York: Francis Niglutsch, 1906.

The first shot in the French and Indian War, Morris, Charles. *Pictorial History of the United States.* Philadelphia: John Winston Company, 1907.

Sir William Johnson in treaty with the Mohawks, Wood, Norman B. The Lives of Famous Indian Chiefs. Aurora: American Indian Historical Publishing Company, 1906.

Pontiac's attack on Fort Detroit, Drake, Francis. *Indian History for Young Folks.* New York: Harper and Brothers, 1912.

Thomas Jefferson (left), Jefferson: McMaster, John Bach. *A School History of the United States.* New York: American Book Company, 1897.

Alexander Hamilton (right), Hamilton: Richardson, Abby Sage. *The History of Our Country.* Boston: Houghton, Mifflin, and Company, 1883.

Period 2 – Political History

Illustration of an execution, Revolution Square, France, Pierre-Antoine Demachy. *Place de la Révolution Exécution Capitale*. Gallicia. Wikimedia Commons.

The Convention at Philadelphia, 1787, Juengling, Frederick, and Alfred Kappes. *The Convention at Philadelphia, 1787.* 19th Century. Engraving. *Teaching American History*. Ashland University. Wikimedia Commons.

James Madison, Bryant, William Cullen, and Sydney Howard Gay. *A Popular History of the United States.* New York: Charles Scribners' Sons, 1881.

The Bill of Rights 175th anniversary was celebrated on July 1, 1966, with a 5-cent stamp, Bureau of Printing and Engraving, U.S. Post Office [public domain]. Wikimedia Commons.

James Madison Bill of Rights $5 commemorative gold coin, United States Mint image [public domain]. Wikimedia Commons.

Paxton Boys' massacre of the Indians at Lancaster, Paxton Massacre, 1841. *Wikimedia Commons*. Media Wiki.

Surveying the Northwest Territory, Bagley, William, and Charles Beard. *The History of the American People.* Sacramento: California State Printing Department, 1920.

James Monroe's southern plantation, Lossing, Benson J. *Harper's Encyclopedia of United States History*. New York: Harper and Brothers Publishers, 1912.

Drafting the Declaration of Independence, Pratt, Mara L. *American's Story for America's Children: The Early Colonies.* Boston: D.C. Heath & Company, 1901.

Postage with an image of the Founding Fathers drafting the Articles of Confederation, U.S. Post Office. U.S. Postage Featuring the Articles of Confederation. Digital image. Wikimedia Commons.

John Jay, Lossing, Benson J. *Our Country.* New York: Johnson and Bailey, 1895.

Thomas Cooper, Thomas Cooper. Digital image. The University of Pennsylvania Library. Wikimedia Commons.

Harriet Tubman, the Moses to her people, Siebert, Wilbur H. *The Underground Railroad from Slavery to Freedom.* New York: The MacMillan Company, 1898.

War of 1812, Battle of New Orleans, Goodrich, S. G. *A Pictorial History of the United States.* Philadelphia: E. H. Butler and Company, 1883.

Mexican-American War, the battle of Palo Alto, Frost, John. *Pictorial History of the United States.* Connecticut: Case, Tiffany, and Company, 1846.

President James Monroe, Spencer, J. *A. History of the United States.* New York: Johnson, Fry, and Co., 1858.

Meriwether Lewis and William Clark, Henderson, Carrie. *The Lewis and Clark Expedition*. Chicago: McClug, 1904.

Map of the general route followed by Lewis and Clark, Henderson, Carrie. *The Lewis and Clark Expedition*. Chicago: McClug, 1904.

Missouri Compromise, 1820, Bagley, William, and Charles Beard. *The History of the American People*. Sacramento: California State Printing Department, 1920.

Seminole War: an attack upon Fort King by the Indian forces under Osceola, Barnes, A. S. *A Brief History of the United States.* New York: American Book Company, 1885.

Gathering cotton in the field of a plantation, Montgomery, D. H. *The Beginner's American History*. Boston: Ginn and Company, 1902.

David Wilmot, Carl Schurz, *Life of Henry Clay*, Boston: Houghton, Mifflin & Co., 1899, Vol. 2, facing p. 286. Wikimedia Commons.

Map Route of the Trail of Tears, the forced relocation march of Native Americans in the 1830s, "Trail of Tears." *National Park Service*. U.S. Department of the Interior. Wikimedia Commons.

Eyewitness's depiction of the Sand Creek Massacre, Howling Wolf. *At the Sand Creek Massacre*. Digital image. *Allen Memorial Art Museum*. Oberlin College and Conservatory. Wikimedia Commons.

John C. Calhoun, Goodrich, S. G. *A Pictorial History of the US*. Philadelphia: E. H. Butler and Company, 1883.

Bleeding Kansas: slavery debate in Congress, Ellis, Edward S., and Charles F. Horne. *The Story of the Greatest Nations.* New York: Francis Niglutsch, 1906.

President Abraham Lincoln, Northrop, Henry Davenport. *American History for Young Folks: The Story of Our Great Country*. 1898.

Battle of Fort Sumter during the Civil War, Ellis, Edward S. *The Youth's History of the United States*. New York: The Cassell Publishing Company, 1887.

General Robert E. Lee, Meredith, Roy. *The Face of Robert E. Lee: in Life and in Legend.* New York: Charles Scribners' Sons, 1947, p. 25. Wikimedia Commons.

First Battle of Bull Run, stand of the Union troops at the Henry House, Ellis, Edward S. *The Youth's History of the United States.* New York: The Cassell Publishing Company, 1887.

President Andrew Johnson, Lillian C. Buttre, *American Portrait Gallery.* New York: J. C. Buttre, 1877.

Portrait of Lincoln surrounded by Civil War scenes, Ellis, Edward S. *The Youth's History of the United States.* New York: The Cassell Publishing Company, 1887.

East and West are shaking hands at the laying of the last rail of the Union Pacific Railroad, Russell, Andrew J. *East and West Shaking Hands at Laying Last Rail.* 1869. Yale Collection of Western Americana, Beinecke Rare Book and Manuscript Library, New Haven. *Beinecke Digital Collections*. Wikimedia Commons.

Period 2 – Economic History

Eli Whitney watching the cotton gin, Hubert, Philip G. *Men of Achievement: Inventors.* New York: Charles Scribner's Sons, 1893.

Benjamin Franklin, Butterworth, Hezekia, ed. *Young Folks History of America.* Boston: Estes and Lauriate, 1881.

Transporting cotton, One Hundred Years' Progress of the United States. Hartford, CT: L. Stebbins, 1871.

Samuel Morse is making the telegraph, Montgomery, D. H. *The Beginner's American History.* Boston: Ginn and Company, 1902.

Samuel Slater, Samuel Slater, Industrialist. 1881. *The Biographical Cyclopedia of Representative Men of Rhode Island.* National Biographical. Print. Wikimedia Commons.

Lowell women at the loom, Prints Division, New York Public Library, 1211 Ave. of the Americas, New York, NY 10036. In "The Life History of the United States," Time-Life Books, Vol. 3, 1974, p. 51.

Picking cotton, One Hundred Years' Progress of the United States. Hartford, CT: L. Stebbins, 1871.

Southern industry, Bryant, William Cullen, and Sydney Howard Gay. *A Popular History of the United States*. New York: Charles Scribners' Sons, 1881.

Mr. and Mrs. Goodhue Livingston and Mrs. Vanderbilt. 1890. *The First 400: Mrs. Astor's New York in the Gilded Age.* Rizzoli, 2000. Print. Wikimedia Commons.

John D. Rockefeller, Rockefeller, John D. *Random Reminiscences of Men and Events*. New York: Doubleday, Page, 1909. *Project Gutenberg*. Wikimedia Commons.

Knights of Labor pentagram, "History: Knights of Labor." *Takver's Initiatives*. Wikimedia Commons.

Period 2 – Social History

Profile of Adam Smith, Cadell, and Davies. *Portrait of Adam Smith.* 1811. Vanderblue Collection.*Wikimedia Commons.* Media Wiki.

Shays' Rebellion, portraits of Daniel Shays and Job Shattuck, leaders of the Massachusetts Regulators. 1787. Cover of Bickerstaff's Boston Almanac. National Portrait Gallery, Smithsonian Institution, Washington, DC. Wikimedia Commons.

Mission Indians of Southern California, The World: Its Cities and People. London: Cassell & Company, Ltd., ca 1880.

Engraving of George Washington, Cerachhi, Giuseppe. *Engraving of George Washington.* 1856. Stipple and line engraving. New York Public Library, New York. By Henry Bryan Hall. Wikimedia Commons.

Abigail Adams, Stuart, Gilbert. *Abigail Adams.* 1815. National Gallery of Art, Washington, DC. *Abigail Adams and Her Times*: D. Appleton, 1917. Print. Wikimedia Commons.

Susan B. Anthony, Johnston, Francis Benjamin. "Miss Susan B. Anthony." *The World's Work: A History of Our Time.* Vol. 11. New York: Doubleday, Page, 1906. p.7362. *Internet Archive.* Wikimedia Commons.

Frederick Douglass, Harper's New Monthly Magazine. Volume 50. New York: Harper and Brothers, 1875.

Harriet Beecher Stowe, Harris, Amanda B. *American Authors for Young Folks.* Boston: D. Lothrop and Co., 1887.

Emigrants to the West, Bryant, William Cullen, and Sydney Howard Gay. *A Popular History of the United States.* New York: Charles Scribners' Sons, 1881.

U.S. political poster for the Know-Nothing Party, Fillmore and Donelson 1856. Digital image. Wikimedia Commons.

Smith's first vision, Stenhouse, T. B. H. *The Rocky Mountains Saints.* New York: D. Appleton and Company, 1873.

Gold washing in California, Bright, Marshall H. *True Stories of American History for Our Young People.* 1898.

Nat Turner and his confederates in conference, Victor, Orville J. *History of American Conspiracies.* New York: James D. Torrey, 1863.

Adoption of the Thirteenth Amendment, "Adoption of the Thirteenth Amendment." *Harper's Weekly* 18 Feb. 1865: *The Institute of Museum and Library Services.* Wikimedia Commons.

Western Expansion: street in Abilene, Buel, J. W. *Heroes of the Plains.* St. Louis, MO: Historical Publishing Co, 1881.

U.S. postage stamp honoring the Grange movement, United States. Post Office. *Stamp, National Grange.* 1967. Print. Wikimedia Commons.

Certificate of the first homestead, according to the Homestead Act, "The Homestead Act of 1862." *National Archives and Records Administration.* National Archives and Records Administration. Wikimedia Commons.

Period 2 – Intellectual & Cultural History

Charles Finney, Charles Grandison Finney. Digital image. Wikimedia Commons.

Horace Mann, Mace, William H. *A School History of the United States.* Chicago: Rand, McNally, and Co., 1904.

Frances Wright, John Chester Buttre, after J. Gorbitz. Wikimedia Commons.

Nathaniel Hawthorne, Matthews, Brander. *An Introduction to the Study of American Literature.* New York: American Book Company, 1896.

John James Audubon, Sarah K. Bolton, *Famous Men of Science.* New York: Thomas Y. Crowell & Co., 1889. Wikimedia Commons.

Passenger pigeon by John James Audubon, John James Audubon. Wikimedia Commons.

Ralph Waldo Emerson (left), Rowse, Sam W. Ralph Waldo Emerson. Harvard Square Library. Green Bird Media, 2007. Wikimedia Commons.

Henry David Thoreau (right), Lossing, Benson J. Harper's Encyclopedia of United States History. New York: Harper and Brothers Publishers, 1912.

John O'Sullivan, Rafael De La Cova, Antonio, Dr. "John L. O'Sullivan." *Latin American Studies.* Dr. Antonio Rafael De La Cova, 15 Dec. 1997. Wikimedia Commons.

Thomas Edison, Reich, Jacques. *Appleton's Cyclopaedia of American Biography.* Ed. James Grant Wilson and John Fiske. Vol. 2. New York: D. Appleton, 1887. Print. Wikimedia Commons.

Mark Twain, "Mark Twain." *Appletons' Journal* (1874). Wikimedia Commons.

Period 2 – Foreign Policy

The Battle of Fallen Timbers, Ellis, Edward S., and Charles F. Horne. *The Story of the Greatest Nations.* New York: Francis Niglutsch, 1906.

Commodore Oliver Hazard Perry, Bryant, William Cullen, and Sydney Howard Gay. *A Popular History of the United States*. New York: Charles Scribners' Sons, 1881.

Iron and steel company in Johnstown, Pennsylvania, Lossing, Benson John. *The American Centenary: A History of the Progress of the Republic of the United States during the First One Hundred Years of Its Existence.* Philadelphia: Porter & Coates, 1876. Print. Wikimedia Commons.

Made in United States
Orlando, FL
10 May 2022